GABBA GABBA HEY
AN ANTHOLOGY OF FICTION INSPIRED BY THE MUSIC OF THE RAMONES

This edition first published 2021 by Fahrenheit Press.

ISBN: 978-1-914475-04-7

10 9 8 7 6 5 4 3 2 1

www.Fahrenheit-Press.com

Do You Remember Rock -N- Roll Radio © David Noonan 2021. It's Not My Place © Philip Charter 2021. I Wanna Be Well © Christopher Bond 2021. Somebody Put Something in My Drink © CW Blackwell 2021. I Wanna Live © Clark Boyd 2021. Pinhead © Kelly Robinson 2021. Suzy Is A Headbanger © Derek Farrell 2021. Cretin Hop © Mike Burr 2021. Rockaway Beach © Lex Vranick 2021. The KKK Took My Baby Away © Kevin David Anderson 2021. The Crusher © Shaun Avery 2021. 7/11 © Amanda Crum 2021. I Wanna Be Your Boyfriend © Vinnie Hansen 2021. S.L.U.G. © Thomas Pluck 2021. Danny Says © Hannah O'Doom 2021. My Brain Is Hanging Upside Down (Bonzo Goes to Bitburg) © Bret Nelson 2021. Baby I Love You © Tina Jackson 2021. Chainsaw © Gregory Nicoll 2021. Here Today, Gone Tomorrow © James Ryan 2021. Merry Christmas (I Don't Want to Fight Tonight) © Joshua L. James 2021. Sheena Is a Punk Rocker © Wendy Davis 2021. I Don't Wanna Go Down To The Basement © Christina Delia 2021. Main Man © Joseph S. Walker 2021. Too Tough To Die © Jon Park 2021

The right of the contributors to be identified as the authors of this work has been asserted by them in accordance with the Copyright, Designs and Patents Act 1988.

Original cover artwork "Hey Ho Let's Go" © Chris McVeigh 2021.

All rights reserved. No part of this publication may be reproduced, stored in a retrieval system, or transmitted in any form, or by any means, electronic, mechanical, photocopying, recording or otherwise, without permission in writing from the publisher.

F 4 E

GABBA GABBA HEY

An anthology of fiction inspired by the music of The Ramones

Fahrenheit Press

*"GABBA GABBA HEY,
ONE OF US,
ONE OF US,
WE ACCEPT YOU,
ONE OF US…"*

Introduction
Preface
1. Do You Remember Rock -N- Roll Radio by David Noonan
2. It's Not My Place by Philip Charter
3. I Wanna Be Well by Christopher Bond
4. Somebody Put Something In My Drink by CW Blackwell
5. I Wanna Live by Clark Boyd
6. Pinhead by Kelly Robinson
7. Suzy Is A Headbanger by Derek Farrell
8. Cretin Hop by Mike Burr
9. Rockaway Beach by Lex Vranick
10. The KKK Took My Baby Away by Kevin David Anderson
11. The Crusher by Shaun Avery
12. 7/11 by Amanda Crum
13. I Wanna Be Your Boyfriend by Vinnie Hansen
14. S.L.U.G. by Thomas Pluck
15. Danny Says by Hannah O'Doom
16. My Brain Is Hanging Upside Down (Bonzo Goes to Bitburg) by Bret Nelson
17. Baby I Love You by Tina Jackson
18. Chainsaw by Gregory Nicoll
19. Here Today, Gone Tomorrow by James Ryan
20. Merry Christmas (I Don't Want To Fight Tonight) by Joshua L. James
21. Sheena Is A Punk Rocker by Wendy Davis
22. I Don't Wanna Go Down To The Basement by Christina Delia
23. Main Man by Joseph S. Walker
24. Too Tough To Die by Jon Park

Contributors
Acknowledgements

INTRODUCTION

It would have been around 1982/3 when Ramones stomped their way into my bedroom and almost 40 years later their music still makes me feel pretty much the same way it did then.

There was nothing sophisticated about Ramones and there was definitely nothing sophisticated about teenage me - a working class kid from Glasgow just beginning to feel out my own musical territory - but when I heard the opening bars of *Do You Remember Rock-N-Roll Radio* it felt like I'd just been handed an invitation to join my tribe.

There was no internet then, we couldn't just rewind the live-stream or Shazam a tune we didn't know. The music papers were our internet - in the UK that pretty much meant *The Sounds* or *The NME* occasionally John Peel, Janice Long or Annie Nightingale would point the way from their radio shows but more often than not it would involve a trip to the record store and a sometimes hilarious, sometimes mortifying, performance of half-humming/ half-singing whatever part of the melody you could remember to the guy behind the counter.

On this occasion I outdid myself - "It's kinda like the Bay City Rollers but faster and in American - it's got loads of clapping and they shout *'Let's go!!'* a lot…" - pretty sure Mick behind the counter made me shout *'Lets go!!!'* more times than strictly necessary before he had a bit of a rummage and came back with *End Of The Century* - which had been released a year or so before. "Sounds like it's these boys you're after - Ramones - from New York City. Punks." "Punks?" I said as I looked at the cover suspiciously - they looked more like Beachboys than punks - no leather, no safety pins, no sneering… the cover was a bit of a let-down if I'm honest.

If he liked you (or thought it might result in a sale) Mick would play you a tune or two from a record. He put it on and the very first track was indeed the one I'd heard on the radio - he had a gift did Mick - better than Google any day. I didn't need to hear the rest - gave him my couple of quid and hightailed it home to listen.

And that was pretty much it. My fate was sealed - like so many others *Ramones* were my gateway drug to Iggy, Patti, The New York Dolls - that whole New York scene - even if I was almost 10 years too late. Sprinkle a little David Bowie over all that and this was point zero for me - this was the root of the musicians & artists & lifestyle that would stay with me from then until now.

The first time I saw Ramones live was a year or so later at The Barrowland Ballroom in Glasgow - turns out there were a thousand or so kids hiding in Glaswegian bedrooms who felt the same way about Ramones as I did. By then I fancied myself a seasoned gig goer but I'd never seen anything like Ramones. The speed, the energy, the sheer joy. The Barrowlands had been an actual ballroom back in the day and is one of the very few venues in the UK that has a sprung wooden floor - this means when the crowd start jumping at the front the waves ripple through the floor and pretty soon the crowd at the back are bouncing up and down – whether they want to or not - if The Ramones had looked up (they didn't) they'd have seen a 1000 sweaty Glaswegians grinning madly, rising up and down, being tossed around like boats in a rock-n-roll storm.

A year or so later I'd left Glasgow and had made my way to London with a dream in my heart and £10 in my pocket - so the next time I saw Ramones was in The Brixton Academy within a few weeks of arriving there.

After the gig there were hundreds of kids like me with dyed hair and leather jackets. I wanted to know where they hung out 'cause I wanted to hang out there too. The answer of course was Camden Town in North London which became my spiritual home for many years, and so Ramones set me off on another path that night.

I can't even count the times I've seen Ramones live in venues all around the world over the years – what I do know is the excitement was always the same and I'm pretty sure that every gig was shorter than the one before

- it definitely felt like the band played faster and faster and with even more urgency as the years went on.

For me Ramones represent an honesty in music that I've always held onto - they just got on and did it - fast, passionate, and above all else real. In my experience that honesty, that realness is reflected in the people who love the music of Ramones. Every Ramone's fan, no matter what their circumstances is in some way an outsider and when one outsider meets another the outcome is more often acceptance rather than aggro.

The fact that the worldwide Ramones community is even bigger and more vibrant today than it was 40 years ago is testament to that and it's also upheld by the number and quality and type of submissions we received for this anthology.

When the concept for *Gabba Gabba Hey* first developed, we had no idea what would happen, the fact that we were deluged in stories from writers and Ramones fans from all over the world cemented just how important the music and the band are to people and how much their influence is still felt.

The stories contained within *Gabba Gabba Hey* stretch across a whole bunch of genres from horror to crime to music – some of the writers met members of the band, some went to every gig they could, some still wear the t-shirts, and others just worshipped quietly from their bedrooms but still remember the feeling they had when they heard the music for the very first time - the one thing all of them have in common is their love of Ramones.

Gabba Gabba Hey was meant to be an anthology of fiction stories but so many people sent in their reminiscences of gigs they'd been to, memories they have of the band and the music that in homage to those heartfelt stories the very first story in this 'fiction anthology' *Do You Remember Rock-N-Roll Radio* isn't fiction at all. It's an account of the night the author David Noonan (*aka DT Graves of The Cryptkeeper Five*) played drums onstage with Joey himself. It's a great story, told brilliantly and we think it kicks everything off perfectly plus it means we've broken our own rules straight out of the gate and publishing doesn't get more punk than that, right?

Chris McVeigh, Fahrenheit Press, May 2021

PREFACE

2020 was nothing like any other time period I've experienced. I've gone through some damn hard times, lost my mom way too early, had bad breakups, divorced, seen friends die from overdoses, and have been confined to a wheelchair because I was temporarily paralyzed. But that doesn't compare to the year that we've just had. A year where nothing was safe, no one was immune - an endless Twilight Zone marathon on constant rerun. And a year where live music completely shut down with no end in sight.

Okay, now there is a vaccine and all, but we can't take back 2020 where eating in a restaurant was dangerous. Now that is fucked up!

I complain about kids running around believing they are invincible, doing whatever they please as if they are entitled, but I know I am not. I've been around long enough to come to terms with my demise. I've surpassed the expiration date where I died before getting old. I am old, but I still feel like that young punk who loved to hang out in places like Oki Dog, the Whisky, and Starwood in Hollywood, looking for fun.

Nothing scared me back then. Running around the dirty streets of Hollywood was our playground of choice. Parties on skid row and downtown L.A. didn't feel unsafe, or at least I never feared for my life. We danced on graves, swung on swings before the sun came up, and listened to bands in run-down halls.

If we stayed up all night, we'd sleep in the daytime. We didn't have to worry about infecting anyone without even touching them. We might have complained about our parents or society and the government, but we weren't hazardous to others.

Now we are. We could be responsible for killing without any weapons. Our bodies are our weapons, and we are asked to do the right thing and stop going out unless what we do is essential.

I'd like to think if COVID was happening when I was young, I would have been responsible or caring enough to protect my older or immune-compromised family members, but I can't say 100% that I would.

We lived on the edge, and that's the way we liked it.

We didn't care so much about the future because there was no future as far as we were concerned. Now we are stuck with nothing to do and nowhere to go.

Brenda Perlin, Los Angeles, May 2021

Brenda Perlin is best known for her Punk Rocker anthology series, set in the music scene of the late seventies to the early eighties. It was an explosive era when the punk sound took Hollywood for a long DIY ride. She is currently working on another volume of personalized experiences she and others lived through. You can follow her on Twitter @LAPunkRocker and on Instagram @LosAngelesPunkRocker

DO YOU REMEMBER ROCK-N-ROLL RADIO?
BY
DAVID NOONAN

My arms are locking up.

It happens sometimes when I'm drumming. I'm always working to stay loose enough to let my wrists do most of the work, but often it's just because I'm trying to force people to pay attention, force them to be *Blinded by the Light* as The Boss had sung. Slamming into those skins, beating the damn things like they owed me money. This time is no different.

It's hot onstage. Fun fact for all you kids out there, it's always fucking hot onstage; less a matter of "if" and more a matter of "how much" – stage lights, multiple bodies crammed onto the stage, the crowd itself jammed like so many sardines into the club. The same club that usually turns off the air conditioning because people who are hot want to quench their thirst more. It was the end of the set and I had been doing aerobics like Jillian Michaels on the kit for the better part of an hour.

Our lead singer, Johnny, turns around and mouths at me, "Rock and Roll!" I know what he's calling for. It had started to become a staple in our set and often was our encore. As the previous song's final notes begin to fade, the screech of feedback erupts from one of the speakers and I take a quick roll call. You see, if you're calling an audible during a live performance, you better be damn sure that all your bandmates know what's about to happen. I look to my left and see that Johnny is already talking to Jimmy, the guitar player, so I look to my right and mouth it to the bass player, Mikey. A quick succession of nods to each other and I lay into my sloshed hi-hats, yelling the count out like some Celtic warrior about to charge the enemy, harnessing all the chaotic energy swirling around the venue, focusing and forming it into the most recognizable and powerful four words in all of rock and roll:

"One, Two, Three, Four!"

The staccato, almost militaristic, hits of The Ramones' *Do You Remember Rock -N- Roll Radio?* begin and the crowd knows it immediately... there are not many people who wouldn't know that rhythm. A hundred pairs of hands reach into the sky and begin clapping along with the band, becoming almost bellicose in its intensity. Johnny's voice hits the microphone hard with the first lines, starting a groundswell of multiple voices as the crowd takes ownership of the clarion call:

"Rock 'n, Rock -N- Roll Radio, Let's Go!"

I've lived through multiple times when rock and roll, America's greatest export, has been on its deathbed, gasping for air, and waiting for somebody to come along and slam a thousand volts into its slowing, dying heart. There is a cyclical nature to all things - an ebb and flow - and rock and roll as an expression, as an art form, is no different. And just like a fire, it needs constant fuel before the embers cease to burn. Right before I was born, Jon Landau had stated, "I saw rock and roll's future, and its name is Bruce Springsteen." Well before my tenth birthday, Eddie Van Halen almost single-handedly saved rock and roll guitar from extinction. The glam metal explosion of the '80s was primed for the paradigm shift that a new upstart channel named MTV was about to create.

Then came the shotgun blast to everything people thought they knew about rock and roll with the onslaught of the grunge and punk revival movements out of Seattle and California in the early '90s, heralded by the four and a half-minute revolution of "Smells Like Teen Spirit." I was never a huge Nirvana fan, but I respected them for what they did for music, what they helped to shape. Following this was a litany of acts that are now legends: Green Day, Pearl Jam, Soundgarden, Alice in Chains.

It was in this fire that The Cryptkeeper Five (CK5), my band, was forged. Five outcast, misunderstood kids from Jersey with a whole truckload of anger and attitude and the absolute need to prove everything to ourselves and the world. But it wasn't Nirvana or Green Day that we listened to late at night lying in bed, with the covers pulled up over our heads.

No.

Our fire wasn't being nourished by the quick, intense flame of this new kindling. Not at all. Our fire was kept burning by one particularly giant log. A log that had slowly and steadily nourished that eternal flame of rock and roll for over two decades. Our fuel was four outcast, misunderstood kids from Forest Hills, Queens.

Our fuel was The Ramones.

I was pulling double duty on the drums, playing for The CK5 and also filling in for a band we knew out of South Carolina called The Independents. In lieu of payment, I had arranged that my services would cover the cost of them booking us for our first-ever East Coast tour. It didn't hurt that they also happened to be managed by Joey Ramone.

I was playing a show with The Independents at a bar in the Alphabet City section of New York called Manitoba's. Manitoba's was owned by *Handsome Dick* Manitoba, the former lead singer of The Dictators, a punk band that made some waves in the early days of New York's punk scene. My bandmates, Johnny and Jimmy, had come along to hang out, have some drinks, and experience another in a long line of old, small, cramped, dusty, beat-up, weirdly smelling New York rock and roll clubs. The kind that wouldn't be nearly as legendary and amazing if they were big, well-lit, and scented appropriately. There is an authenticity that comes with the infirmities of an aging venue.

But the one thing that will make any bar in New York very real, very quickly, is when Joey Ramone himself - the living legend, the Father of Punk Rock, the voice to my soundtrack of New York City itself - sits in the back of the club, nestled deeply into his long leather parka in a dark, shadowy corner, quietly watching some of his proteges at work.

One thing that most people who haven't been on stage (or the floor, in this case) don't know is that you can't see much deeper than the first three or four rows of people. The lights get in your eyes and the shadows play tricks on you. We were finishing up our set and it seemed as if the crowd had grown substantially while we were playing. That's not unheard of, especially in New York – it really is the "city that never sleeps" - people start their night life at any hour they feel like. But it did strike me as strange, considering that we were the headlining act. Word had obviously gotten around town quickly about our guest star.

Walking forward from the back of the club, all six feet and six inches of lean, gangly frame topped off with his signature mop-top and dark glasses: Joey. Fucking. Ramone. The guitar player for the band leans over to me and says, "Joey's gonna do a couple songs with us, cool?"

Cool? Cool doesn't even begin to describe it.

Did we have Upbeat, Shindig, or Ed Sullivan growing up? Nope. That was shit my parents probably watched. And while I knew who Alan Freed had been, he wasn't really on my radar at that moment. But when rock and roll had "needed a change," when the call had gone out that it was going to be "just part of the past," this man and his four bandmates had ceaselessly pushed forward - mile after endless mile, decade after decade - spreading the word and sounding the call. A modern-day Sisyphus pushing that rock endlessly up the mountain, only to see it fall again and again.

And I was about to lay down the backbeat for him.

Surreal is a word that gets bandied about a lot. Counting this rag-tag band in to play four songs that I heard for the first time blasting from my brother's girlfriend's car stereo when I was twelve years old was a real gift. Laying down the backbeat for the man who sang those songs – delivered in his trademark bleating, hiccupping, crooning vocals - if that isn't surreal, I would defy anyone to explain to me what would be.

Four songs.

Four songs were the soundtrack to an experience that has not been rivaled in my life. That doesn't mean that I haven't had equally amazing experiences and ones that have even surpassed it. But there are points in our existence where the experience, the memory, stands singular. It claims its individuality and, while it agrees to share space with others, will not give up its rightful and earned place in our mind and in our heart.

Countless people have asked over the years why The CK5 kept a name so associated with a kitschy horror rock act. There are a lot of good answers: it's original, it's catchy, it's become a brand unto itself. I mean, if you spend twenty plus years promoting yourself, it's not the best business decision to just throw it away and start again. But one of the most dearly held reasons, and one that Johnny, Jimmy, and I shared, came earlier that same night.

Having met Joey Ramone several days prior to the show, at a rehearsal with the band at a studio in New York, I felt comfortable introducing Johnny to him. Truth be told, Joey Ramone was easily in the top five most down-to-earth, quiet people I had ever met. It was like the fame and notoriety were nothing more than a piece of clothing that he could put on and take off as easily as you or I could shrug out of our coat. But introducing Johnny would be like introducing St. Paul to Jesus; to say that Joey Ramone was Johnny's hero would be an understatement.

Johnny, respectfully yet demurely, shook his hand and introduced himself. Joey kindly mumbled something in return. Joey Ramone seemed to mumble most things unless a microphone was placed in front of him. He was as quietly awkward as most of us are throughout our formative years, yet it seemed as if Joey never fully grew out of it. Having met many artists in my life, I can say that this seems to be almost a prerequisite. If you want to see the world differently than everyone else, you're damn well going to feel that difference deep down in the core of your being.

Because of the connections between our bands, The Independents had already forwarded a copy of our latest record to Joey to listen to, so when Johnny introduced himself, Joey gave us the reason that we kept the name, the reason that nestled itself deep down in our guts.

"Oh, yeah, yeah… The Cryptkeeper Five. That's a great name."

That's a great name. How could we ever even attempt to forget that? That's like having an audience with the fucking Pope and then becoming a Protestant.

The atmosphere changed. It's a feeling that you'll get sometimes when you're in the flow. Everything – the music, the sounds, the crowd – changes, becomes easier, sweeter. Call it what you will - being in the zone, being present, mindfulness - it's something special that happens when you let go into the music. Chris Robinson of the Black Crowes described it as grabbing just a couple of notes, or a whole measure, of "The Song," the primordial song that all music came from. I always liked that. Describe it how you will, we were feeling it. We were in it. One hundred plus human beings were all sharing the exact same moment. It's what I always envisioned that Springsteen meant when he sang to, "Show a little faith, there's magic in the night."

We were nearing the end of the song. Nearing the end of the call out to whoever would listen that the embers were still red-hot, but that we needed to REMEMBER! We had to remember that child-like feeling of listening to the radio for hours on end just to hear that one song that made you feel okay. That made you feel special and part of something. To remember that feeling of "lying in bed, with the covers pulled up over your head. Radio playing so no one can see." I know that this sounds wildly melodramatic, but this is how we looked at what we were doing. This is how we talked about music. This wasn't a job. It wasn't a career. It was a calling - a priesthood. And just like Cinderella had gotten to play dress-up one night and dance with the Prince, a scared, angry kid from the Jersey sticks, with his head in the clouds, and stars in his eyes, got to dance with his hero one night.

The music was pounding out of the speakers, reaching a crescendo when Johnny slid off the neck of his guitar, grabbed the microphone in both hands, and gave the crowd something they could remember. He had been playing around with the last verse of the song, like most songwriters will do. Don't get us wrong, we love Jerry Lee and John Lennon, but we were trying to pass a different torch to the masses. We were trying to give back to that giant log that burned and burned and burned until there was nothing left:

Do you remember Forest Hills, Queens?
Tommy, Johnny, Joey and Dee Dee?
It's the end, the end of the Seventies.
It's the end, the end of the century.

[November 17th 1978, The Music Box, Omaha, Nevada, USA]

IT'S NOT MY PLACE
BY
PHILIP CHARTER

Guitars so distorted I couldn't pick the notes they were playing, but they were the right ones. Fifty bodies packed tight to the stage soaked up the rumble of bass. Cymbals smashed like breaking ice but the one aircon unit didn't have a chance against the heat. As I tended bar I noticed that each furious track ended just before the three-minute mark. Feet shuffled between songs, and I listened to everything the singer screamed or said or didn't say.

Later, when the band finished and the drinkers left my bar, I sat in the back office and listened to records on my turntable until sunrise. At that time of day, I liked jazz. You didn't have to try and make sense of it. I played along to a few tracks on Pop's old guitar before sleep. It helped me find my equilibrium. Everything then nothing. Cacophony then silence. That was how it went every night at Ortega's Bar, apart from Sundays, when I took the day to check on Mom in Queens.

I woke to the familiar hum of traffic coming from the Williamsburg Bridge. It gave me a sense of place, which I'd not had since I lost my Pop at sixteen and moved out. That was thirty years back. Those years I'd bounced around and dreamed of running a venue, but now I did, the only way to pay the bands a real wage was to sleep at work to avoid skyrocketing rents.

The place was a few blocks from the river but the sound of the bridge carried all the way to the back office. When I got my eyes open and hauled myself upright on the settee, I saw Mona tossing a beige coat on the bar. She inspected it for a name tag then pulled on a pair of cleaning gloves.

'Thought I told you to come in later,' I said. My head throbbed even though I didn't drink much the night before.
'It's already ten-thirty, boss.' She smiled and turned on the speaker system.
'No, don't you—'
Mona cranked up the volume and *It's Too Late* by The Dolls blasted out of the stereo. Her idea of a joke.

The music blared and I covered my ears until she took pity on me and turned it down. I pulled on The Ramones shirt next to me and returned Pop's Gibson 335 to its case. 'Who owns the jacket?' I shouted. 'Sure ain't yours?'

'Do I look like a cosmopolitan-drinking Midtown lawyer?' she called back. Then Mona began scrubbing away the traces of the night before, erasing yesterday like it never happened.

'Going for coffee,' I said on my way out.

It's a wonder I wasn't more out of shape — forty-eight years old with tar-filled lungs and *getting some air* was the only exercise I ever did. The sky was heavy, but I still did the loop up to the East River and back. I stretched my legs down Fifth and onto Roebling towards the coffee shop. As I waited in line, it occurred to me that New York scenes always appeared as album covers — street signs, shopfronts, groups of people, all frozen for a second in black and white.

Brooklyn now belonged to the twentysomethings with beanie hats and big headphones. Blindfolds for the ears, that's what the old man would have called them. The rhythm of these new conversations was the one type of street music that didn't make sense to me. It was like two tracks playing at once with streams of discordant words fighting for space. So many words with so little said.

That evening, I met the owner of the long beige coat. She walked in with a briefcase and a tote bag, like she couldn't keep her work and personal life in just one. I gave her the trenchcoat and she inspected it for damage. It didn't suit her red hair, but it probably cost more than all the top shelf bottles combined. This woman was not a regular at Ortega's. In fact, I'd never seen her there before. My regulars were younger hardcore music freaks who liked to write on the walls but didn't mind paying six bucks a beer. A seven-inch single peeked out of the tote bag. I imagined a vintage turntable in her meticulous apartment with its white walls and Scandinavian furniture. Maybe she had to listen to records before she could get to sleep.

When she tried the coat on, I half expected her to pull out a dictaphone and start asking questions about licensing laws. Instead, she ordered a drink.

'Tequila, lime and soda, please.' I reached for the bottle of añejo and she shook her head. 'Nothing fancy, just give me the regular stuff.'

'Alrighty,' I said, switching bottles. There was a moment of quiet. 'Enjoy the show last night, ma'am?' I pointed to the flyer for the gig: The Dirty Jockeys.

'Ain't no ma'am,' she said, ticking me off with a pointed finger. 'I'm Kristy, and I'm into new-wave punk, actually. Don't let the work clothes fool ya.'

Her accent was pure Brooklyn, abrasive but assured. She looked corporate but her 'no-nonsense' attitude brought some light into my dark little bar. Most of the other girls in Ortega's wore nihilistic expressions and a lot of black.

As I fixed the drink, I checked my own appearance in the bar mirror — stone-washed jeans, a half-grown beard, and my old man's silver chain resting over my t-shirt. Normally, I had no time for socializing. I spent my mornings trawling the listings, booking bands, and checking the trendsetting blogs. Afternoons I was shut in the office, my head in paperwork. In the evenings, I served drinks and agreed with whatever opinions people offered. All on repeat.

'Anyway, I'm Daniel. Welcome to Ortega's.' I held out my arms, showing off my underground kingdom. It wasn't a welcoming place — an empty stage, wooden stools and thousands of band stickers peeling off the black walls — but it was the music that mattered.

She looked around. 'You're Daniel Ortega? Like the president of Nicaragua?'

'Err, yeah. Not many people here make the connection. I'm just the president of this place.'

She sipped her drink. 'Can't believe I never came here before last night. It's . . . nice.'

What did she mean by nice? It was a dive bar, an escape. That was the whole point. 'Well, I never hit the big time with my own music, so I opened this place to give the other guys a chance.' I tried to laugh but it sounded weak. Suddenly, I felt the craving for a cigarette.

She scanned the posters above the stage, perhaps imagining all the concerts over the years.

'Now then,' I said, 'pick a song.' I pointed to the laptop behind the bar with the playlist. 'Show what ya' got.'

She thought awhile. 'What about something by Lost Acapulco?'

I smiled a little easier. Mexican surf? 'You sure got me profiled.' My father once told me the story of how he auditioned for Dick Dale's band, but he took a job in Queens instead, trading semi-stardom for a place in the barrio. I found the track and queued it up. 'Not sure this one could be described as a classic, but here we go.'

'Does it have to be a classic? Ain't it enough to just like something anymore?'

That made me laugh.

We listened to the twanging guitars and the shallow snare and I thought back to all the bands I'd played in before I saved enough for a deposit on the bar. While Kristy drank her drink, I told her about the shitty venues I'd played and how I wished there was an Ortega's back then. Turned out she played too. Drums. I should've guessed.

The band arrived and the place began to fill up. Soon, the clatter of glasses and distorted guitars interrupted our conversation, and Kristy picked up her jacket and walked out the door, back to whatever she'd been running from the night before.

That night before sleep, I didn't listen to jazz records, or play the guitar. I played that surf track and thought about how my Pop taught me how to play tremolo style. Hours and hours of repetition of Dick Dale riffs. It almost drove my mother out onto the street.

The next couple of months I got tired of booking bands with 'new sounds' that weren't any different, and tired of new customers who said the same things as always. Ortega's felt less like my place even though I slept there, and New York felt less like my city even though I never left.

The notes of the city were unfamiliar, and the traffic on the bridge sounded less soothing when I woke each morning. It became more like the hum of static I couldn't turn down. The far off clang of construction work on the factories turning themselves into hip apartments was noise, not music. City voices irritated me so much I started wearing headphones on my walks.

Mona and the rest of the staff thought whisky shots and guitar riffs made them belong, but the bar was trapped in the cycle of finding 'the next big thing' in rock music. Bands I gave a start to went on to sell out bigger shows, but I was still at Ortega's. Kristy hadn't returned since that day, and I even thought about booking Lost Acapulco to see if it would bring her back to the bar.

On the day of our annual staff party, I closed the bar and set out to get some air. On the corner of Broadway and Bedford, opposite the fifty-foot mural of a disinterested girl, I passed a street performer I'd never seen there before. The deep concentration on the guy's face made me stop and look. I recognized the expression from when I used to play; back when I thought I was going toward something. When I took off my headphones, I was transported back to the old New York and the raw energy of my teenage years.

The kid was African-American, about eighteen, and sat on a beat-up Marshall amp playing a black Les Paul. His Converse boots rested on a kick-drum cymbal combo. He had no sign selling CDs or asking for money, the bumps and scratches on his guitar did all the talking. He was tearing through a medley of 70s classics — Dictators, Heartbreakers, The Void — and adding his own licks in too. A dozen people gathered around but the young guitarist played hunched over, eyes fixed on the guitar neck, his hair covering his eyes. He wasn't an imitator, he was living that music. I lit a cigarette and let the sound wash over me.

When I looked up, the street was back to its sharp blends of anti-color. The cars aged, pristine shopfronts turned to broken ones, and brick walls became canvasses for graffiti tags. I was transported back to nights walking through Queens after playing guitar for six hours straight in Rocco's lockup. My fingers were swollen and sore, but that didn't stop me flipping off passing police cars.

After he finished, I spoke with him. 'Thanks for making me feel like I belong here again, kid.' I dropped a ten and a card for Ortega's into his guitar case. 'Give me a call if you ever want an opening slot.'

He cleared the street dust from his eyes. 'Awesome. Thanks, man.'

That music gave me the jolt I needed to revisit some old haunts. My walk took me the two miles across the East River into Lower Manhattan. I knew of The Mudd Club from the bootleg recordings in Mom's attic but I'd never been because it closed in '83. Eventually, I found the memorial sign on the wall. When I looked around, I saw all the ugly imperfections of that area had been worked out like the whole place had been remastered. Further down on Leonard Street, chauffeur-driven cars had replaced the empty bottles and merchandise sellers that used to clutter the street. Venues like those had given me a connection to my father, but the sounds of those places were getting harder to remember.

That evening the party was at a much newer place: The Knitting Factory. At least the tunes would be classics. It was supposed to be a thank you to Mona and others for their hard work at Ortega's, but really it was my excuse to get away from that place.

We did the usual, shooting tequila and pulling stupid faces to the camera and the night went long. I remember the band playing an Undertones song, getting me out of the booth to dance. As I made my way to the dancefloor, I felt a hand on my shoulder.

'Hey there, Mr. President.'

She looked thinner, with a little more makeup than before. No beige trenchcoat.

'Kristy.' I leaned in and kissed her cheek. 'You been blowing off my bar for this place?'

'No, this is my first night out for . . . well, not many of my friends are into this music.' I admired her passion. Even though no one around her understood her music, she needed to hear it anyway.

The band built up to the chorus of *Teenage Kicks*. 'We're the only ones old enough to know this one,' I shouted over the music. Then I held two fingers to my mouth with an imaginary cigarette between them. Smoke?

She nodded and exhaled as if she'd already taken a drag.

We went outside and smoked and talked. Well, she talked and I listened. She'd lost her mother and was worried about her job. That explained her absence from the bar.

I lit another cigarette and offered the lighter. Instead of taking it, she pinched the cigarette out of my mouth and took a drag. 'I only smoke three a day now,' she said with a smile. 'Doesn't count if it's yours.'

We listened to the muffled music coming from inside and watched our cigarette smoke rise up like the steam from the manhole covers.

'It's not like many people like us still do this stuff.' She pointed at her oversized black t-shirt and handbag combo. 'Fortysomethings going to rock bars . . .'

I shrugged. 'Guess it's another habit I can't kick.'

As we shared a smoke, she reached down and took my hand in hers. I felt like a middle-schooler again. We stood there and listened to the far-off conversations, the drowned out music and traffic moving along the wet Brooklyn street. We observed the time passing, not through watching, but by listening.

'Been feeling out of place of late,' I finally said. 'The changes around here never bothered me before, but recently...'

'I know, right? Don't recognize things like before.' A laugh escaped, but I detected the hint of a sob behind it. She gazed at the night sky, then took a final drag on my cigarette and killed it. '. . . You know I came back to the bar. Couple of times, actually. Sundays.'

'That's my day off,' I said. 'I see my Mom Sundays.' I remembered about her Mom too late.

'Oh, I guessed you had kids or something.'

Kids? As if I had a cozy house in the 'burbs and came into town to run my rock bar. 'I can't even keep an apartment, let alone a family.'

She laughed an easy laugh.

The door opened and a younger group came out to smoke their vape pens. The sounds of another song I didn't recognize leaked into the street. I had clean forgotten about the staff party.

'Got an idea,' she said. Her face brightened like she was going to suggest breaking into the principal's office and my mind raced through the possibilities of where the evening might take us. 'Let's go somewhere old,' she said. 'Somewhere we can hear what we're saying to each other.'

I laughed and gripped her arm. 'Sure thing.' It didn't matter if we ended up in an empty bar or an all-night diner, I wanted to make up for all the time I'd been looking for new sounds instead of 'things I liked'. 'As long as they've got a jukebox and tequila, I'm in.' I zipped my jacket and we went off into the night.

It was spring and I was at Mom's for breakfast. Nothing much got moving that early on a Sunday, and I liked the quiet.

'Daniel . . . Danielito! Your chilaquiles are getting cold.' She shuffled over to the trash to scrape in her half-finished plate. Mom used to have a healthy appetite and the kitchen used to be less of a health hazard.

I looked up. 'Right. Thank you, Ma.' My fork clicked against the plate as I loaded it.

'What's up with you?' she asked. 'You're so distracted.'

In truth, running the bar was becoming a distraction from what I wanted — to listen to people that I cared about and things that made me feel that equilibrium. 'Nothing, Ma. Just enjoying the silence is all.'

She tucked her gray hair behind her ear so she could hear better. 'Your Papi used to say when the city's quiet, it's not lacking anything. Silence is a note, too.'

I took another mouthful of the breakfast on the plate in front of me and let her thought sink in. 'I like that.'

La Nueva 93.1 droned on in the background and I glanced around the ground floor duplex. The sun-bleached curtains in the kitchen were the same pair from when I was a kid. My folks didn't have much when they moved here from Mexico, and my father was gone before they'd had the opportunity to modernize the place. I guess my Mom didn't like change either.

'You're so much like him.'

I looked up. 'Because of the music?'

'No,' she said, 'because you can't stay still. Always chasing the next thing.'

I put down my fork on the table. 'Yeah, you're right.'

Mom's eyes glazed over. 'He sure could play,' she said. 'Yes, he had a wonderful ear, but sometimes he couldn't hear what was right in front of him.'

Like Kristy and me, I thought. We didn't realize what we were running from, till we told each other. I drained my cup of coffee and kissed Mom on the cheek. 'It's always nice to see you.' It seemed selfish to cut my visit short, but I wanted to spend my day off with Kristy.

'Wait. There's something I want you to have,' she said. While she went to collect it, I stacked the dishes. I heard her going through the piles of his junk she still kept in the living room. What a mess it would be once she couldn't live on her own anymore — nurses, medication and assisted living bills.

She came back into the room empty handed.

'I thought you were—'

'Shhh,' she said.

Then I heard the first bars of a track I hadn't heard in a very long time coming from the living room. I turned off the faucet to tune in better and buried the lump in my throat. It was my old man's limited edition record, the jazz one she didn't like to wear out. Why was she playing it now? I listened as his archtop guitar drifted in and out of the mix, with the singer's vocals drifting over the top. Mom went and turned up the volume on her turntable. We listened together in the kitchen to the crackles and pops as the needle dug into the grooves of the only copy left, slowly erasing the recording each time it was played. I put my arm around her shoulder and we looked out of the window, remembering summer evenings spent outside, dancing and hollering. That was before I turned into a teenager who said 'screw you' to everything.

My father played his jaunty solo, tapping away at the notes and bringing some style back into the room. Those memories never came in black and white. In two minutes and forty-six seconds, *New York Swing* was over and the sound died. For a few seconds after, we listened to the note of silence.

'I want you to have it.' She said. 'Put the record in the bar. Frame it above the stage so he can hear some new music.'

Now that was an idea. I could build a display case for his guitar and print a photo. 'Gracias, Mamá.'

That was all that needed to be said. I didn't need to tell her I was finally seeing someone great, or that I was thinking about stepping back from running the bar. I didn't need to tell her that nowhere in this city felt like mine anymore, but that when the right track played and you were with the right person, it still sounded like home.

Mom sat quiet at the kitchen table and I went to get the record. The stylus lifted up, and the vinyl span on the turntable. Forty-five revolutions per minute. Around and around. I pressed stop.

[May 26th 1977, Friars at The Vale Hall, Aylesbury, England, UK]

I WANNA BE WELL
BY
CHRISTOPHER BOND

Any other night, Benji, Judy, Casper, and T-Top wouldn't have been caught dead in this part of town. It was filled with abandoned buildings and broken streetlights. Makeshift camps of stretched tarps and cardboard boxes littered the sidewalks. There was nothing but trouble over here when the sun went down. The kids knew it, but so did the cops. Which made being over here, doing what they planned on doing, even riskier.

"Hey T, hurry the fuck up," Benji hissed, calling back over his shoulder to T-Top, who was just now scrambling through the hole they'd cut in the chain-link fence. T-Top, or just T when the others felt like it, held his breath and wriggled through the last bit, grimacing as one of the severed barbs poked through his shirt and into his belly.

"I'm coming, Benji, Jesus. Gimme a minute," he said, trying his best to keep his voice down. They couldn't afford to get caught, not tonight. Benji and Casper were already on probation for petty theft, trying to run out of the 7/11 with a six-pack, instead running right into a plain-clothes cop standing on the sidewalk. Judy had been busted a month back for driving without a license, and for the little bit of weed they'd found in her jacket when they searched her. T-Top didn't have a record, not yet, but it'd only be a matter of time, according to his parents. If he kept hanging around with the same losers.

The other three were crouched down, waiting in the shadows beside a rust-flaked bulldozer. Behind them, the skeleton of the condemned building loomed against the dark sky, its outside walls already knocked down, leaving just the outline of the rooms and corridors naked to the elements. The soon-to-be-vacant lot was lit up like a prison yard with orange-tinted security lights the demolition crew had set up to ward off trespassers and would-be thieves. Vandals. In other words, them. T-Top rushed up to crouch beside them, his chest heaving, one hand absently rubbing at the hole in his shirt.

Benji noticed. "Hey, you alright?"

T shrugged it off. "Fine."

"You're bleeding, you asshole," Casper chimed in, a smile hidden between the words. He'd dyed his hair black tonight for the occasion, but hints of green and red stuck out where he'd missed a few spots. "Haven't even stormed the beaches yet and you've already caught shrapnel."

T acted offended. "Well whaddya want me to do, jerk-off? You guys only cut a hole big enough for a freaking chihuahua... I had to suck my gut in so far I'll be shitting rat turds for the rest of the week."

Benji and Casper doubled over, hands over their mouths to hold back their laughter, and T-Top joined in. Judy, always the most responsible one, the most determined, held it together the best. She put a single finger to her lips, trying to quiet them, tears leaking from the corners of her eyes. "Shut up, you guys," she managed, when the worst of it had passed. "We gotta keep it down. Just cause we ain't seen the guard, it don't mean he ain't here tonight." She'd been close to busting out, too, but her face was all business now. It reminded them of why they were there in the first place. The laughter died away. The boys looked at the ground, the unfinished building, the night sky, anywhere but at Judy.

"Sorry," Benji mumbled. "Just the nerves."

"Yeah, sorry, Judy," Casper said.

Judy nodded. She was a foot shorter than any of them but fierce as a wildcat. She was the boss of this little trip, no questions asked. "S'alright, let's just keep it together. We got work to do, and we ain't got a lot of time to do it in." She glanced down at the cracked screen of her phone. "Three hours to sunup. You guys ready?"

Footsteps scraped inside the stairwell behind them, and T-Top froze, his eyes wide. Casper froze, too, his finger still on the trigger of the spray can he held down at his side. The footsteps stopped, and they could hear heavy breathing. A flashlight clicked on, its beam sweeping across the ceiling of the room next to them.

Fuck, T thought. That ain't Judy or Benji. He glanced nervously around, out over the edge of the open fourth-story floor and to the sky that was already beginning to change from deep purple to a dark blue. They were running out of time. I gotta do something. He handed his own spray can to Casper. Casper looked at it like it was a live grenade, mouthed What the fuck? But T just shook his head, held a finger up. When the flashlight swept away from them, T leaned over until he was almost kissing Casper's ear. "Finish it for me... for her, I mean." Casper nodded.

T-Top ran out from their cover, ran away from Casper, deeper inside the empty building. He was quick on his feet for someone so big, almost coordinated. He only tripped once.

It was enough, though.

He had just picked himself up when the flashlight's beam fell on his face, blinding him. A large, meaty hand gripped his shoulder.

"Got you, you punk," a gruff voice said. "What the hell do you think you're doing up here?"

"Hey, get off me! This shirt cost me ten bucks, asshole."

"I don't give a fuck if you had to sell a kidney for it," the security guard said. He pulled at T's shirt, ripping it a little, and then he pushed the boy ahead of him toward the staircase. T stumbled, almost fell again. The guard was right behind him. "Move it, fatass, I got shit to do today, and it doesn't involve babysitting you. And what are you doing up here, anyway?"

T scoffed, pulled himself to his feet. "Minding my own fucking business, how 'bout you?"

"Smartass, huh?" the guard said. He smacked the back of T-Top's head hard enough that his back teeth clicked together.

"Screw you, man! I didn't do nothin."

The guard grunted, raised his hand again. "Move it, fatboy, unless you want another one." T-Top turned, headed back to the stairwell. He walked with his head down, his long hair covering his face so the guard wouldn't see his smile, wouldn't want to hit him again. "That's it, get those rolls bouncing. How'd you even squeeze into those tight ass jeans anyway? The guys in jail are going to love you." The guard laughed to himself.

T stopped walking, knowing it was a bad idea but unable to stop himself. He half turned to look at the guard. The man was forty-something, overweight, the buckle of his uniform struggling to hold his pants up around his prodigious belly. High school must have been hell; no wonder he was getting off on this power trip.

T grinned. "You like that, huh?"

The guard narrowed his piggy eyes, raised his hand. "Like what?"

"Fantasizing about the guys in jail. What they'll do to me. I hate to ruin your cream-dreams, man, but I'm sure it ain't like those movies you watch when your momma's not home."

"Fuck you, you little bastard," the guard said. He slapped the back of T-Top's head, hard, hard enough to bowl him over. T fell against the concrete, felt his nose crack. Blood spurted out onto the dusty floor. The guard stood over him. "You make poor decisions, don't you, kid?"

"So did your parents, you lameass rent-a-cop." It wasn't the fat kid on the ground, it was another voice, calling from somewhere back in the work zone of empty rooms. The guard turned, sweeping his flashlight wildly back and forth.

"Who's there?" he called in a voice that was meant to convey authority. "The cops are already on their way, so don't try to be clever."

A new voice, a girl's voice, came from the opposite direction. "You wouldn't know clever if it hit you in your receding hairline, asshole." The guard turned back, but there was nobody there either. An empty spray can flew out of the darkness, nailed him in the back of the head. It rattled to the floor and bounced away.

"Hey!" the guard screamed. Laughter floated from down an empty corridor off to the left. "See, that was clever, and you didn't even realize it!" The boy's voice again. How many of them were there? The guard's face flushed red. He wished he'd actually called the cops. He was spinning now, trying to light all of the shadows at once with the single flashlight.

"Th-that's assault, you pricks... and I'll be pressing charges! You just wait. You'll be locked up for a month. You better hope it's your first offense, too, or you can say goodbye to all of your chickenshit friends!"

Another can spun out from a blind spot, this one not as empty. It hit the hand holding the flashlight, and the light fell to the concrete. The lens shattered, and the light winked off. "Shit," the guard muttered. Why weren't they allowed to carry real guns? How the hell was he supposed to guard anything with a goddam Maglite? He balled his fists up, walked into the next room.

"Hey, momma's boy," the girl called out. "You don't happen to drive a shitty Dodge Caravan, do you? Puke green? One with all flat tires and a busted windshield?"

"Aww, fuck," the guard said. He ran back to where the fat kid had been, but the landing was empty now. "Motherfuck." He leaned out and looked over the open edge of the floor and down to the road, to where he'd parked his van just outside of the chain-link fence, and his heart sank. A kid was standing there, not the fat kid, but another one, one with black hair. He had what looked like a knife in his hand. With the other, he waved up to the guard. "Oh fuck, oh fuck, oh fuck," the guard said, and rushed back to the stairwell, hands holding up the sides of his belt.

They met back up three blocks away, under a bridge that held up part of the city's tram line. Casper was the last to make it. He looked ragged, not beaten up, just as if he'd pushed himself too hard, but he was still smiling. Judy offered him a smoke, and he took it gratefully.

"That was close," he said between puffs. "I felt bad for the guy, really... only popped one of his tires. Glad I did, or he might have got me."

"Fucker had it coming," Benji said. "Christ, he woulda beat the hell out of T if we weren't there."

"I could've taken him," T-Top said. "I was just waiting for the right time."

Benji and Casper burst out in laughter, but Judy didn't laugh. She walked up to T-Top, reached around him as far as her little arms could reach. "You did great, T. You saved us."

"Yeah, that was rad, T," Benji said. "Didn't know you had it in you."

"Jumped on the grenade for us, big man," Casper said. "Sheena woulda been proud."

"Good," T said, trying to hide his flushed face. "At least I didn't ruin my favorite shirt for nothing."

Early mornings in the hospital were the nicest times of the day, Sheena thought. That's when the world was the quietest, before the noise of traffic on the freeway reached her window, before a stampede of doctors and nurses and visitors rushed past in the hallway outside her room. Before the doubts and the fears and the insults in her head really wound up and started chattering, before they got so loud she couldn't think. She sat up and pulled the sheet down to her waist, glanced out the window at the new sun. She allowed herself a fragile smile. Her gaze drifted down to the bandage that ran from wrist to elbow, and the smile faltered. She peeled back the edges of the medical tape, slowly, meticulously, and inspected her handiwork.

She'd done it the right way this time, the way you do it when you're serious and not just looking for attention, not that she had ever been looking for attention before. But this was the way when you don't want to wake up and see the pain you've caused, feel the pain that's been eating at you for days and months and years. The cuts were jagged, deep, ugly. Stitches and sutures were holding her forearm together now, closing the wounds, the skin around them already scarred with a dozen tiny cuts from the times before. She'd committed this time. Down the road, not across the tracks. It was a small miracle that she was still alive.

Sheena pressed the bandage back in place and held her hand there for a moment. The nurse would be in soon to check the wound for infection and give her her morning meds, for the pain and for the crazy, something to help her sleep while she healed up. But was she healing where it really hurt? On the inside? Was she getting any better there? It was impossible to tell. There weren't stitches holding that together, just her. Her family hadn't even come to visit. And where were her friends? Where was Judy? Where were Casper and Benji and T-Top? Sheena's face grew hot, and tears stung the corners of her eyes. Stupid she thought. I scared them off. Nobody wants to be around the crazy girl. She wiped at her nose with the sleeve of her gown. Casper's mom had killed herself when he was eight, and he'd been the one to find Sheena this time, lying in a pool of her own blood, nearly dead. No wonder he didn't want to visit her at the hospital. And the others, well, they were just looking out for themselves, weren't they? Isn't that what life had taught them to do? Maybe they thought it was contagious, the depression and the anxiety and her penchant for self-destruction. Maybe they thought they would catch it. Or, maybe they thought she was already a lost cause, a goner. It would probably hurt less when she left them for good if they didn't come around.

She hung her legs over the edge of the bed and sighed. Outside her window, the sounds of the city waking up and coming to life stirred something in her, memories of a time when the mornings felt pregnant with hope and bursting with opportunity, when she couldn't wait to get up and get out of the house, couldn't wait to do something. Those memories belonged to a different person now, a different life. A different her.

No, she thought, shaking her head. Those are MY memories. I want that again.

But was it possible?

She thought it was.

The city was waking up, and she was waking up, too, in a lot of ways. Sheena looked down at her legs. They were pale, skinny things, weak from the blood loss and from the days spent lying in the hospital bed and pigging out on daytime tv. She was tired of laying around, of feeling sorry for herself. The muted sunlight called to her. She shuffled toward the window, placing her hands against the sill to steady herself.

She gasped, brought a hand up to her mouth. Her eyes were wide and dancing, reflecting the golden sun. The gasp changed, turned to a laugh, her first real laugh in weeks. The soreness was gone, the weakness forgotten. Her heart swelled. She touched the glass as if to make sure it was all real, to make sure she wasn't dreaming anymore.

Across the street, an old apartment building was in the process of being demolished to make way for another parking garage or a strip mall, whatever vital thing the city deemed necessary for progress. The outside walls had already been knocked down, the building sliced open in cross-section, laying bare the hallways that ran the length of each floor. Someone had been busy overnight. Two of the hallways near the top, formerly gray and dull and crumbling, had had a makeover. Giant, two-toned letters covered two of the hallways that faced the hospital in floor-to-ceiling neon pinks and electric greens, bigger than any billboard, brighter than any flashing sign on the Vegas strip.

Sheena stared at the building, not noticing the tears that streamed freely down her cheeks. She ran her fingers across the glass of the window, tracing each gigantic letter:

SHEENA IS A PUNK ROCKER

Yeah, I guess I am, she thought. She laughed again. It felt so good, she couldn't stop. The morning had come, and she was still alive. Despite herself, despite everything.

A nurse walked in, a couple of pills and a glass of water in her hands. She nearly dropped them; it was the first time she'd seen the patient out of bed by herself. And the girl was crying, her shoulders trembling.

"Do you need help?" the nurse asked. "Are you alright, dear?"

Sheena turned, smiling though her cheeks were wet.

"I'm fine, thanks. Or, I will be."

[July 8th 1988, Hollywood Palladium, Los Angeles, California, USA]

SOMEBODY PUT SOMETHING IN MY DRINK
BY
CW BLACKWELL

Usually when I knocked a guy off-balance, I'd throw a merciful slug to the gut and sweep his legs to finish the fight. If there were a code, which there wasn't, it would be: fight to win, but keep the trauma surgeons out of it. Problem was, the rich fucks that went to Ritger's backyard fights wanted more than a win. They'd been winning their whole lives, after all. Winning at business, winning at life.

They wanted a thrill.

They lived and died by the sucker bets—the broken noses (3:1 ODDS), loss of consciousness (5:1 ODDS). Bites, rib fractures, eye gouges. And even though Ritger expressly forbade it, fatalities (20:1 ODDS) had a place on the secret menu, if you knew how to ask.

The kid I was about to take down looked fresh out of county lockup, like he'd exchanged his gram-a-day meth habit with more rec-yard workouts than a CrossFit junky could stomach. He had that hungry look in his eyes: broke, desperate, something to prove—at least that's how he looked before the uppercut. Now he could barely find me in the ring, eyes slippery and blinking. Capillaries shot to hell.

He threw a bad punch and I dodged, buried an elbow in his kidney.

He curled on the ground like a spider.

What was the payout on pissing blood for two days?

"Sit down, Cruz," said Ritger. He'd brought me into the house after the fight and poured two scotches from the liquor cabinet, handed me one. "Try not to get any blood on the chair."

I sat where he told me, some ancient-looking French thing that looked as if it were looted from a museum. Maybe it had been. I had no idea what he wanted to talk about, but I figured any minute he'd hand me the prize money in a manilla envelope. I thanked him for the drink, glanced around the ornate office. Shiny awards on the shelves, photos of exotic locations.

"Nice office," I said. I didn't know what else to say.

"You don't have to compliment the decor," he said, taking a sip. He pulled open the drapes and held them so I could see into the backyard. "Tell me what you see."

I looked. "People."

"You're a man of few words, aren't you? A simple man? Sure, they're people. Rich people. Influential people."

"Well, I figured that." I drank. It was the best scotch I'd ever had.

Of course it was.

He closed the curtain and went to his desk, slid open the top drawer. He set down the drink and now he had something else in his hands: a sealed jar. When he handed it to me I almost let it slip to the floor. Inside was an eyeball floating in some kind of preservative. The iris had grayed somewhat, but I could tell it had once been somebody's baby blue.

"A few years ago, I placed a side-bet on an eye gouge," Ritger said. "This was down in Ventura during the Great Recession. Lots of great fighters back then. Guys just like you, Cruz. Guys that needed cash and were willing to fight for it. This little peeper earned me half-a-mil, just like that."

I turned the jar and the thing floated lazily in the glass.

It seemed to be tracking me.

"Not exactly something you could keep on the mantle," I said.

"Why not? I'm proud of that thing. It brought me closer with a community that has helped grow my wealth to unimaginable heights. Who doesn't love seeing a 'B' next to their name in the newspaper? It all started with that little eyeball."

"So, you're telling me to play to the sucker bets?"

Ritger took the jar out of my hands, placed it back in the drawer and shut it. "If you're going to keep winning, I'll need more side-action from you. It keeps people talking, makes them feel good."

"I'm not taking anyone's eye out."

"That was just an example, Cruz. But would it hurt you to bite off an earlobe? Tyson did it. Dislocate a finger, maybe?"

I shook my head. "Used to be breaking someone's nose was enough."

"What can I say? The world's developed a higher tolerance for violence." He spun open a safe and handed me the envelope I'd been expecting. It felt heavier than last time, maybe two grand heavier. "That's three in a row for you, pal. You've earned a three-win bonus."

I stood up, tucked the envelope under my arm.

"Now, head down to the road for a ride back to town," he said. He chomped his teeth in the air, made a little click click sound. "See you next month, killer. Remember what we talked about."

Winning fights was the easy part.

Getting the money into the bank was trickier.

I owned a little auto shop on the westside, just a two-bay joint with a loft and a kitchenette. My customers liked me, and I stayed busy for the most part. I padded the till with as much fight money as I could. Sometimes I'd use the cash to fix up old cars and flip them. But as much as I'd been fighting, I couldn't wash it fast enough and it started to build up in my closet. I had this anxious thought that I was just one audit and a search warrant away from getting jammed up in federal prison.

You can fight ex-cons all day, but you can't beat the IRS.

"Another bar fight?" said Jaclyn Diaz, a regular customer with a candy-apple red Karmann Ghia. She liked to notice things about me, and she always had a wink buried somewhere in her words. "One of these days, they'll haul you in, you know. You can't pick fights with the barflies forever."

"I don't pick fights, Jackie"

"Can't imagine anyone starting a fight with a burly guy like you."

"Guess I just have one of those faces," I said. "Punchable."

"Hardly. It's a good-looking face, Cruz. Don't mess it up."

Normally, I'd be even more evasive. The less attention I gave to my side-hustle the better. But Jaclyn was a broker who specialized in international listings, and I had my eye on a couple of bungalows down in Costa Rica, on the Pacific side. I'd even made a trip down there just to check out the view from the front porch. I could hardly think about anything else. I had enough for the property, but I wanted a bigger nest-egg to make it last.

I wasn't buying a round-trip ticket, after all.

"Got any new listings?" I asked.

"A few." She flicked her phone and showed me some photos. Little adobe bungalows right on the sand. Little slices of paradise. "They're building a new cantina and an eco-park in Punta Arenas. You better move fast before the expats get wind of it, if they haven't already. Look, this one even has a Tiki bar with a built-in margarita machine."

"That's a lot of tune-ups and brake jobs. I'm still saving."

She winked—a real wink this time. "If you weren't such a night owl, maybe you'd get more done."

"Fair enough. Maybe I'll lay low for a while."

"Sure you will, tough guy."

I didn't lay low. Not even close.

I won a fight in Salinas against a spooky-eyed combat vet who briefly took me to the ground. Some are better grapplers than others, and I managed to flip him and put him to sleep in a minute or two. An easy five grand. I fought a parolee in the Oakland Hills who'd clearly been told to work the side bets. I kept feeling his hot breath in my ear, teeth clicking. He managed to put a thumb in my eye before I shook him off and palmed his nose sideways. Seven grand.

When the driver picked me up for Ritger's elaborate summer solstice party, I had my heart set on twenty grand or more. He always had the biggest purses by far. Maybe it'd even be enough to hit my goal. I'd sell the shop, flip the rest of the spec cars. If the money didn't last a lifetime, it might get me close enough. With any luck, I'd be sipping rum and cokes on the beach come wintertime.

Ritger's place sat atop a clearing in the redwoods, somewhere east of the reservoir. Fighters were under strict instructions to wear a blindfold once the driver turned off the highway. But it wouldn't be hard to find if you followed the conspicuously fresh blacktop amongst all the shoddy mountain roads. I figured the point was to avoid seeing the driver punch the gate code at any one of the three gates that led to the estate.

Ritger came down from the main house to greet me, which was something he hadn't done before. "You're in for a real treat, Cruz," he said, fake teeth gleaming in the evening sun. "It's a good crowd tonight. Maybe the best."

"Who's the other fighter?" I'd just taken off the blindfold and my eyes were still adjusting. I shielded the sun, noted all the high-end cars in the driveway. I watched an old man step out of a black and chrome Bentley with a college-aged escort in a skin-tight cocktail dress. If a good crowd was a rich crowd, then it looked good indeed.

"Some pineywoods Texas kid," said Ritger. "Looks like he can hold his own."

"Is he here yet?"

"Already in the ring." He guided me up the driveway and around to the back of the house where the other fighter waited, then he squeezed my shoulder, said: "I've got something I want to do before the fight, just a little spiel for the politicians in the crowd. Just play along."

Putting up with Ritger's antics was always half the work.

The party guests gathered, dressed in semi-formal evening attire. They watched me like a zoo exhibit, rich men and high-class hookers alike, gawking and pointing as I took off my shirt and warmed up with a little footwork. It wasn't so much of a ring as a large sandpit lined with oil torches. The Texan sized me up, too. He beat his palm with his fist. He had a tough-guy, king-of-the-prison-yard stance that might have worked for him in other venues, but not here. To me, he was just another nose about to be broken.

Ritger gave his speech, making lazy metaphors about bare knuckle fighting and the business of Silicon Valley entrepreneurship. Then he did something I didn't expect. A waiter came around with two shot glasses on a tray and offered them to the Texan and me. I waved it off, but Ritger insisted, hoisting his own glass into the air.

"To the fighters!" He shouted with the flair of a Roman general. "When we go further than the mere satisfaction of our ambitions, we surpass even our greatest hopes for power and riches."

He drank. The crowd drank.

The Texan puffed out his chest and drank.

I took the glass, smelled the rim: astringent.

I shot it down my throat.

It was theater, after all.

The first indication that something was wrong came about two-minutes into the fight, after we'd each landed a few superficial blows. I circled the Texan, drawing him in, walking him back. Trying to get him nice and tired for the big assault. But then he stopped, placed his hands atop his head and screamed at the sky. A sound of pure rage, veins standing taut along his neck. He sounded like the goddamned Incredible Hulk all of a sudden.

Then, I felt it too.

Heart racing, teeth grinding.

I tried to shake it off, but every muscle surged and flexed, blood pounding in my ears. The crowd vanished, Ritger vanished. I forgot all about the prize money, the beach bungalow, the rum and cokes. It all fell away and something else took its place. Something potent and all-consuming.

Bloodlust.

The scene played out as if by film reel. A celluloid frame of gnashing teeth—blood spatter in the next. The sound of bones cracking. Unending, ear-piercing screams. I thought I'd fallen into some unknown precinct of Hell. I even saw flashes of fire, felt the heat on my face.

Then: a jolt of electricity.

And another.

For a moment all was still. But the film reel started again, the images coming faster now. The blood fell away, the sandpit vanished. Only the redwood forest now. Ferns whipping my ankles, berry vines tearing my thighs. I'd never run faster, never longer. I could have reached the Oregon border if I hadn't lost my footing, tumbled down a root-studded embankment where I careened onto the banks of a shallow stream.

I woke many times in the night to the sounds of frogs and night bugs.

Consciousness came and went.

Sometime in the daylight—maybe the next day, maybe longer—I got to my feet and took stock of my injuries. I didn't know what the hell had happened. Two fingers on my left hand were badly dislocated, pinkish bones breaking through the palm. I thought it could have been the fall, but then a memory came: the Texan had snapped them like kindling.

But that was before—

"Goddamn," I said, my voice just a frail croak.

—that was before I'd torn him to pieces.

But there were others, I was sure of it. A blond man, maybe a security guard. A skinny kid with a handheld taser. I'd attacked them all.

I pulled myself up the embankment one-handedly, inch by inch, using the roots as footholds. When I reached the top, I hobbled along a deer trail back the way I'd come. Sure, I wanted answers. I wanted to know exactly what they'd put in my fucking drink. But I mostly focused on Ritger and how much this was going to cost him.

I found the estate an hour later and trudged across the back lawn toward the main house. When I came around the corner, I surprised a young security guard with a cop-style mustache. He panicked when he saw me and fumbled for his radio. I took it from him and laid it across the bridge of his nose and he folded like a cheap suit.

I didn't expect to find Ritger in his office, but I got lucky.

I don't think I'd seen anyone so terrified.

"What the hell did you do to me, Ritger?"

"Cruz. Thank god you're okay. We were looking for you." But he'd slipped his hand into his desk drawer—I kicked it closed again. Bones cracking. He screamed like a child, and I showed him my mangled left hand.

"Quiet down. Can't be any worse than this."

He pleaded for his life. He really thought I was going to kill him. To be fair, I hadn't made up my mind. "I can give you whatever you want," he said.

"I don't want much. I'm a simple man, remember? Tell me what was in that goddamned drink."

"Okay. Look. It's a synthetic hormone, and it was just for show. Just to liven things up a bit. But I didn't think…"

"A what?"

"Well, the hormone is only part of it. Also, methamphetamine and PCP. It amplifies the fight or flight instincts. You did both."

"How many did I kill?"

He didn't say anything at first, just watched me. Shaking.

"Besides the Texan?" He swallowed. "Two others."

"Jesus. What did you do with the bodies?"

"I handled it, Cruz. I-I know people. It won't get out, promise."

I took him by the throat and threw him to the ground. Inside the desk drawer, I found the nine-millimeter he'd been reaching for and I jammed it behind his ear.

"Unlock the safe," I said. "But don't you dare reach inside."

Ritger did what I said, the dial softly clicking as the numbers spun. The safe cracked open and he peered up at me. "Now what?"

"Stand up."

He stood slowly, showing his trembling palms.

"What am I going to find in the safe?" I said.

"Money. A couple of handguns."

"What else?"

He dropped his shoulders and sighed. "Just kill me. Please."

I opened the safe with my toe. Stacks of manilla envelopes inside.

"Is that all cash?"

"Just kill me," he repeated.

I didn't kill Ritger.

Sure, I ruined his fake teeth. But I knew whatever I took from that safe made screwing with me too risky—and I was about to find out exactly what that was. I found the keys to his Porsche 911 and drove it to a chop-shop way up Bear Creek Road where I dumped it for ten grand, a prepaid flip phone, and a Honda with a clean record. When you've been wrenching your whole life you know how to find these places. I'd loaded all the envelopes into a duffle and found a spot in the redwoods to park and go through everything. Much of it was cash, maybe two-hundred grand. I found another nine-mil and a couple loaded magazines. A handful of gemstones and fake IDs.

But one of the envelopes contained legal paperwork—tax filings, sworn affidavits. Things of the catch and kill variety. Things that might ruin a man's life if they got loose. Some of the affidavits even had lurid photographs attached that would make national news even in this desensitized and apathetic society.

I spun the car around, gunned the Honda down the mountain. I could still feel the roofie smoldering behind my eyeballs. I knew a fight doctor in the East Bay that would look at my hand. No doubt he'd fix me up just right. The bones would mend, but I wasn't sure I'd ever get that fight out of my head. I worried the mental projector would start up again and flash those memories inside my skull for the rest of my life. Maybe that monster inside me would even reprise his role, thirsty for carnage.

Then again, maybe a truckload of rum and cokes would keep him quiet.

I thumbed the flip phone, called around till I found Jaclyn.

She answered with that little wink in her voice.

"Jackie," I said. "Start the paperwork."

"Oh wow," she sounded elated. "Which property?"

"I want the one with the Tiki bar and the margarita machine."

[April 11th 1980, Santa Cruz Civic Auditorium, Santa Cruz, California, USA]

I WANNA LIVE
BY
CLARK BOYD

I cling to the dream as long as I can.

Dad's serving them up across the plate, and I'm knocking them back out, one after another, into left-center. I never use aluminum, not even when I sleep. In my hands is one of Dad's black ash specials, crafted on his old foot-pedal lathe. He got the wood from the trees that grow around our cabin in New Hampshire. Just the feel of that handle in my hands, and the repeated sound of wood meeting hide. Even in the dream, it gives me a sense of power.

Then the chainsaw wakes me. Fully.

I smell burning wood too, but my fire went out long ago.

My eyes find the rack inside the front door. That's where I keep "The Three Stooges." Moe, Larry, and Curly. Moe's a full-size ax. Larry and Curly are hatchets. Under Dad's watchful eye, I crafted their handles on his lathe. There's one extra space. We swore that one day we'd finish the set, but then decided Shemp's a dick.

This war's been a dick, too.

"Lyndie," Dad assured me, "arcane knowledge always becomes useful again."

At 15, who was I to argue? I loved watching him work a piece of wood on that lathe. The gentle sound as he peeled away the layers with his chisels, moving meticulously toward a shape buried deep in his head. The smell of the shavings and his bourbon.

Six years he's been gone.

I watched it happen from the basement window of our house in Framingham. He stuck me down there when the factions surrounded us. Both sides wanted our provisions, our trees, anything to feed their war. My father never took sides. Instead, he stood on the porch and yelled at everyone to leave us alone. Then someone shot him. It doesn't matter who. After that, it was gunfire for two straight days, followed by chainsaws. When I came out of the basement, everything around me had been reduced to stumps. Including Dad.

For months after that, all I heard were engines and weapons rending the entire fabric of life around me. I longed for quiet. I started dreaming of the trees around the cabin, and of hitting line drives into the outfield with Dad. Thwack. Thwack. Thwack. In the end, it wasn't so much the fighting that drove me up here. It was just getting away from the noise.

Loud sounds still give me debilitating panic attacks. But luckily, this area's been quiet. Most of the fighting is still "concentrated" around Boston. Concentrated. Jesus, that's a joke. Two sides split into four, and then four into eight. What will they call this war when it becomes a 16-sided free-for-all? How about 32? 64? Not civil, that's for sure.

Those engines really wrecked my calm this morning.

Someone's closing in on the cabin. I can't even light my own fire to take the edge off, because it might alert them. And I'm not ready.

I sit quietly and chew on a Slim Jim.

Resources are what these Fuel Monkeys crave. But once they see me, they'll want other things too. The cabin. The lathe. The axes.

My body. First to fuck, then to eat.

Dad always taught me to study the position of the fielders when I stepped into the box. That means a recon mission. I've got to know what I'm up against.

They're eating lunch, but it's not rabbit or deer.

I smell a sick sweetness wafting up from their spit. The fat sizzles as the juices fall into the flames. From my perch in a nearby tree, I use the binoculars to get a closer look. It's a haunch, all right. Human. Probably a POW they brought along on this little excursion to serve as a food source. Panning right, I see a body bag hanging from the branches of a nearby tree. They've put the rest up there so the bears can't get at it. These guys are hungry and vicious, but not brain dead.

I count three of them. Camo head to toe. Long brown beards flecked with white.

I grew up in what my Dad, a moderate in an immoderate world, politely called "uncertain" times. I always thought that seemed generous. And now, as I use the binoculars to look at the jumble of homemade "brigade" patches on their camo vests, I can't tell what these three men support or despise.

It doesn't matter. They probably don't even know themselves. Or care.

Meanwhile, the rest of us either swim in their uncertainty or we drown.

Here's what they do know: Power and guns, gasoline and oil, the unrefined mechanics of killing and taking. On the ground, I see their weapons and a few gallons of gas. And next to the fuel cans, the chainsaw. They've also got an old truck for hauling their booty back to whatever "garrison" they imagine they belong to.

Close up, I won't be able to stand the sound of their machines. The din will drive me insane. I will curl up in a ball on the ground and start screaming.

I'll end up like Dad.

As the men drink their homemade liquor by the fire, I decide I've got one shot at this. I have to lure them to the cabin and do a hell of a lot more than just yell at them.

Smoke signals. That'll work.

If I'm lucky, I'll get an hour or two before they see my fire.

Sure enough, an hour and a half after I light the wood, I hear their truck coming up the dirt track toward the cabin. They've got the beast running on watered-down gas. The F-150 farts and backfires its way along the rutted road, belching smoke. The noise gets the bile rising in my throat. I want to lay down and cry.

One look at the Stooges, though, is enough to keep me on my feet for now.

The men stop near the porch. The light is fading, but I haven't sparked any candles or lamps. For now, let them wonder if anyone's home.

I peek out the window, watching as they slither out of the truck. They're tipsy, but still soldiers. Their heads are on swivels, and their hands hover near their weapons. One watches my front door while the other two talk behind him.

"Hello! Anybody home?" It's a flat, Midwestern accent.

I stay silent.

"You can come on out," another one yells. "We see the fire."

The third unzips his pants and begins to urinate on my porch steps. The other two do the same and soon all three are laughing. Let them bask in self-satisfaction for a minute.

Then one of them spies my present.

When I got back to the cabin earlier, I took Moe and started on one of the oldest black ashes near the cabin. I stripped away some bark and took out a juicy notch near the base. A visual appetizer for the Fuel Monkeys. See, I started your work for you!

I see them pointing at my handiwork. Then they look up at the canopy of ashes swaying, greedy looks in their eyes.

That's when I step out onto the porch, unarmed and head lowered.

When they hear me, they raise their guns. The sound of all their chambering and cocking makes me wince. Between the three of them, I count two handguns and a shotgun, all of which are now pointed at my head. One of the men, corn-liquor stupid, tries to drop to one knee but ends up on his ass instead.

"Well, look at this," says the one with the longest beard.

"Fellas," I say. "Can I ask you to get off my property? Please?"

"Your property? How do you figure that? This is war, little girl, and we have the guns. Which means we take the property. Whatever we want, really."

He points to the truck bed, which is filled with a cord of wood and some tools they've gathered, at gunpoint, along the way. The body bag rests on top of the haul.

"How many people did you have to kill?" I ask.

"None of your business, bitch. But five. We're eating on one right now."

Cannibalism is a popular scare tactic these days. Or so they think. I let his veiled threat hang in the air for a moment, then raise one corner of my mouth in a smirk. I run my tongue over my lips.

I can feel their eyes on me now.

They're tipsy, full of John Doe Stew, and at least one of them, the beard with the shotgun, is giving me "the eye." And once one gets the idea... Well, suffice to say it won't end well. For them, I mean.

"Here's how this'll work," says Shotgun. "Peckerwood Phil's going to use the last of the daylight to buzz your, I mean our, ash trees. Blitz will do recon and see if we might want to set up shop here. And I'm going to come inside and keep an eye on you. Smells like you got your own fire going."

He smiles, thinking I'm too young and naive to get the sex joke.

"No need," I say. "I don't even own a gun."

"Then we'll just get cozy."

He motions toward the door with the barrel of the gun.

I step through the door and duck right.

My hand finds Curly. I've practiced a lot on an old log out back, but I still flip the hatchet once, just to remember the weight and get my grip like I want it. Then I swing it as hard as I can as Monkey #1 steps through the door behind me.

"How old…"

That's as far as he gets before the blunt end of the hatchet hits him full in the chest. He drops to the floor and tries to raise the gun. I flip the hatchet and hit him again, this time with the honed blade. It slices easily through his camo vest and buries itself halfway into his shoulder. As I pull it back out, his gun falls to the floor and a small geyser of blood erupts from the spot where his arm was once fully attached to his shoulder.

"Old enough to mess you up," I say.

"The fuck?"

I bring Curly down above the bridge of his nose, and then leave the hatchet there. He's still wobbling on his knees. I watch him try to focus, one last earthly time, on the handle in front of his nose. He's going cross-eyed with the effort.

"My name is the Lorax," I whisper in his ear. "I speak for the trees."

Then I kick him in the head and he topples to the floor.

Solid single. Right up the middle. That's what Dad would've said.

I grab Larry and Moe from the rack, step over Shotgun, and head for the door.

The kill's been quick and clean, so the other two have no idea what's coming. When I step out onto the porch, Blitz is taking another leak. He looks at my blood-spattered face.

"Holy shit," he says, fumbling to put away his little prick.

Before he can zip up, I've launched the hatchet across the 10 feet that separate us. Larry lodges with a sickening thud in his abdomen. Blitz manages to scream once as I move toward him. He staggers back and hits the railing. Now he's trapped. Dick out. Bladder empty. Entrails a scrambled mess.

I plant Moe right in his thick, red neck.

The head doesn't come off as I'd hoped, but oh well. The triple's the hardest part of the cycle. Let's call this one a long double in the gap.

Peckerwood Phil, who's been busy gassing up the chainsaw, hears his buddy scream. He turns around and scans the porch, where he's greeted by the dead-fish stare of his half-decapitated comrade. As I glare at Phil, I put my foot on Blitz's knee for leverage and reclaim Moe. Time to dance with Monkey #3.

Here's where I reckon I'll get shot. Or worse.

But I get lucky.

Phil panics, forgetting he's got a handgun strapped to his thigh. Instead, he reaches down and fires up the chainsaw. When it comes to life, the sound makes me want to go fetal. My knees buckle, and I stifle a cry. Sweet suffering Christ, the noise. I place the head of the ax on the porch and lean on the handle for support.

Phil sees his opening and runs at me with the chainsaw. His finger's on the trigger, gunning the engine as he sprints toward the porch steps. He's screaming like it's an attack on a well-fortified enemy camp, instead of on one thin, 21-year-old brunette armed with an ax.

Still, the noise paralyzes me.

I tried, Dad. I tried.

Another strong breeze moves through the ash trees. For a moment, it breaks the machine's spell. The fear-fog clears. I remember what I know how to do, and do well.

Take batting practice.

I move to the far end of the porch and crouch low in my stance. Phil's coming fast, but I still have time for the ritual. I quickly tap Moe's head on the ground twice and then waggle the ax head in small loops above my head.

The count's full. I know I'll only get one more pitch.

Phil has the chainsaw at chest level, so I'm going to have to swing at something low. Maybe even out of the strike zone. When he's five feet away, I step forward and whip the head of the ax towards a spot I've been eyeing since this dipshit started his berserker run. Just above his left kneecap. I swing hard but foul it off. Moe's blade knicks the side of Phil's knee. It's enough to hurt him, but not bring him down.

The glancing blow knocks the ax from my hands.

Phil's already regrouping. So, I do the unthinkable. Before he can fully recover, I grab his arm and try to shake the chainsaw from his hands. I scratch and bite. I grab his beard and yank. I put my knee in his groin. Finally, the machine drops to the porch. The blade stops whirring, but the engine's still running.

And then I pick it up.

It's heavier than I imagined. I wrap my finger around the trigger and tentatively press it. I feel a surge of power run up my arms. To my surprise, the sound doesn't faze me.

By now, Phil's come to his senses and is reaching for his gun.

Grimacing, I get the chain moving again and step to Phil's side as he turns, pistol drawn. I raise the saw and block his hand as it comes up and around. The gun barks and I feel a burning sensation. Then the chainsaw bites into his forearm, bucking its way through the ulna, and then the radius. Within seconds, I'm done. Phil's disembodied hand lies on the porch, its twitching fingers still wrapped around the smoking gun. He scrambles, trying to retrieve the weapon with his other hand. Tragi-comedy at its finest.

I snort with laughter. Phil looks at me with hate in his eyes.

"All we wanted was fuel!"

We both watch as blood pumps from his ragged stump.

"You didn't say the magic word."

I gun the chainsaw engine.

"Please, I'll give you anything you want."

"Too late, Peckerwood."

I put the blade against Phil's chest and pull the trigger, spraying blood and bone across the porch. As he screams, I lean into it, forcing the chainsaw through his chest cavity until the tip comes out his back. I finally let go of the damned machine, and it sputters to a halt. My world goes blissfully quiet again. Then I realize Phil's bullet has grazed my shoulder and I'm bleeding. Just a little, though.

It's a bloop single that's rolled underneath an outfielder's glove and all the way to the wall. No error, though. Call it a triple.

"Nice one, Lynn," I hear Dad say.

I have no use for politics, but I do think the moment's right to choose a side.

Mine.

After I patch myself up, I park the F-150 at the entrance to my property. I prop the bodies upright against the vehicle, making sure visitors can see the hatchets and the chainsaw. Let the bastards come looking for their comrades. Or let their enemies come and try to start something. Hell, tell the bears to wander over and eat their fill. Let any and all see what this woman is prepared to do to them if they fuck with her or her trees.

I'm not afraid anymore. Not of their machines, not of their vacuous noise. I'm an army of one with my own insignia—the silhouette of a young woman with one finger raised to her lips. Shhh…bitches.

Tomorrow morning, I'll finish taking down that black ash.

Then, I'll fire up my feet and work the lathe until I've got two new hatchet handles to replace the ones sticking out of Shotgun and Blitz. I'll rummage around and find two new ax heads. Dad always kept extras in the shed.

Shemp's still a dick. Sorry, pal, no ax for you.

For now, I've got Moe for protection. And the guns. Of course I kept them. I may be a touch unstable, but I'm not stupid. I go back inside my cabin and put a few more logs on the fire. I sit down and start eating another Slim Jim.

Damn, it feels good to hit for the cycle.

[March 6th 1977, Olympic Hotel, Seattle, Washington, USA]

PINHEAD
BY
KELLY ROBINSON

Sometimes I think about stuff that happened to me a long time ago, and it doesn't seem real. I know it was, because I was there and all, but it's like I was a different person. I don't recognize that guy, you know? I'm so far away from it that it feels like I'm remembering someone else's memory.

A lot of those kinds of things happened when I worked at the record store, I guess it was '79, '80. Me and my friend Kenny worked nights, and when it was slow, Mike Neff would come hang around the store waiting for us to close so we could go watch some bands and drink some beer. We always called Mike Neff by his full name, always, and I don't know why. Sometimes he brought Turtle along. Turtle was really Lester Barnes, Jr., and his dad was a congressman or some shit. He got his name because he was slow as fuck. I don't mean he didn't move very fast—well, he didn't do that either—but he was about the stupidest thing on legs. You'd think he was some kind of burnout, the way he talked, but he didn't do any more drugs than any of the rest of us did back in those days. We didn't mind him being around, because at least he always had his own money, so he wasn't always trying to bum off of us, which is a lot more than I could say for Mike Neff.

Most nights began the exact same way, but you know how it is when you're young, and everybody else around you is young, and you're all drunk and a little crazy and just, I don't know, yearning for something. You start out drinking a beer at a punk show and the next thing you know you're all throwing furniture off of a roof somewhere, or setting fire to the downtown Christmas tree, or swimming naked in the pool of an apartment where none of you even live. Or sometimes you watched other people do the insane shit, and you just came along for the ride, because what else was there to do? Like when a guy called Boneyard stapled his dick to a board on a dare and had to go to the emergency room. There was blood all the hell over the place. He tried to claim later it was some kind of performance art, but we never stopped laughing at him, not even years later. I mean, I laughed too, but it was also pretty fucked up. That's what it was like then. If you had stopped to think about any of it, you'd be like the guy in the Talking Heads song asking, "Well … how did I get here?"

The whole thing with the pinhead started like that, when we were at the record store one night. Wednesdays were always pretty dead. Kenny had set up this old black-and-white TV behind the counter, and we used to turn it on to watch Dr. Specter's weekly show. Dr. Specter was this old guy who introduced the horror films on channel 2. They had an even older guy who hosted the westerns on Sunday afternoon. He was about a thousand years old, and probably remembered the actual wild west. Mike started calling him Roy Codgers, so of course that stuck.

Dr. Specter was dedicated, I'll give him that, but I think they gave him about a dollar and change to decorate his set. There was one of those jointed cardboard skeletons on the wall like people put on their door for Halloween, and a sign he'd probably made himself. Sometimes his "assistant" would be on, too, and she was obviously his wife or something. Maybe even his mother, a dumpy woman in some kind of muumuu. She was all hunched over and it was hard to tell if that was some kind of character thing or just how she really walked. I know it sounds pathetic, but I really loved that shit.

Mike Neff would make dumbass cracks through the whole movie if we didn't shut him up, and Turtle was always on some pointless jag like "Why is air?" I'd make them shut up for something like *Island of Lost Souls*, but I'd let it slide for some of that lame 1950s sci-fi jazz like *The Killer Shrews*. (Kenny played drums for a spectacularly awful band called Killer Shrews for a while. Man, I forgot about the Shrews. They sucked even worse than the movie.)

This particular night, the movie was *Freaks*, this old MGM horror deal from 1932. I had always wanted to see it, so I was making it really clear to Turtle and Mike Neff and even Kenny that if they weren't going to zip it, there'd be knuckle sandwiches all around. It's a crazy flick, if you haven't seen it, and it has actual circus performers in it, midgets and whatnot. One guy is pretty much just a torso and he crawls around like a worm. We were all blown away by this one scene where the freak show people are all around this dinner table with the pretty blonde, and they start chanting, "Gobble, gobble, we accept you, we accept you, one of us." We all knew right away where we'd heard that before. Well, except for Turtle. Kenny explained to him that it must have been the inspiration for that Ramones song, except Joey sounds more like he's saying "gabba gabba."

"What's the name of that song?" Turtle asked.

"Pinhead," said Kenny.

"It says "Pinhead" right there in the lyrics, doofus," I said. "They must have got the whole idea from the movie, with the pinheads and all."

"What's a pinhead, anyway?" Turtle asked.

"People with tiny skulls. It's some kind of deformity." I pointed out the girls in the dresses on the screen. "They had their heads shaved with those little ponytails on top to show off their weird head shape."

"Who shaved their heads?" Turtle asked.

"How the hell do I know? Maybe they went to the Pinhead Barber Shop," I said. He asked the dumbest questions.

"Dude, I know a guy who has a pinhead," said Mike Neff.

"No shit?" Turtle believed anything.

"Yeah, right," said Kenny. "Does he go to the Pinhead Barber Shop?"

"Probably works at the 7-11," I scoffed. Mike Neff was always pulling some kind of shit or telling some tale, and I remembered when he tried to claim some chick who worked there had been part of the Manson family.

"I don't mean he has a pinhead," he said. "I mean he owns one."

"What does that even mean, he owns one?" I was incredulous, but that's typical with any of his stories.

"I'm not shitting you. He's like the keeper or something. And it's not a him, it's a girl. He shows her to people for five bucks."

"What the hell, man?" I didn't believe him, but it seemed like a pretty fucked up thing, even for Mike Neff. I believed him even less when he said he heard about it from Boneyard. He kept insisting, though. In fact, over the course of the next several months, whenever there was nothing to do, or when we'd hear that song, or watch Dr. Specter, he'd bring it all up again.

"Hey, we should go see that pinhead," he'd say, and we'd joke like we were going to do it, but we never made any real plans. We didn't really believe it, anyway.

One time, though, we ended up with fuck-all to do on a Friday night. We tried to go see a band at The Sewer, but apparently so did everybody else, and since the club was so small, they weren't letting anybody else in because of fire laws or something. (Kenny used to joke that Joey Ramone wouldn't be able to lie down in there.) You couldn't go in unless somebody else came out, and there were like forty people waiting around outside, so we just said screw it. We were walking around trying to think of something to do when Mike Neff got all excited and said this is it, this is the night we're going to see the pinhead.

"God, no, I'm not going on some Mike Neff goose chase tonight," I said, and Kenny was on my side. Turtle didn't give a shit. He was like, "Whatever, man."

Mike Neff kept insisting, because we were so close to the place where the guy supposedly lived. "What have we got to lose?"

"Five bucks is what," I said. "If there's even a guy to take it."

"Oh, there's a guy," he said.

"How do you know where he lives? You said you haven't even been there?"

"Boneyard pointed it out to me when we walked past it one day. He said, 'That's where the pinhead lives,' and he told me about the guys who went to see it. It's right around the block. Come on!"

I stopped walking. "Boneyard didn't even see it? He just knew some guys? God, this isn't even second hand, it's like fourth or fifth hand. What the fuck?"

Then Kenny was all calmly like, "Let's just check it out." I was surprised, since Kenny was sort of the voice of reason I was always trying to be, except nobody listened to me. Maybe since Kenny spoke less, he always seemed more like the authority. So I figured okay, you know what, if nothing else, we can mock Mike Neff for the rest of forever for believing something so stupid.

The place was at the basement level of an old brick apartment building, so we had to go down some sketchy steps to get to it. I already didn't like the looks of it. Mike Neff rang the buzzer, which was hanging off the wall at the end of a bunch of bare wires and looked like it was just waiting to electrocute somebody. The rest of us hung back on the stairs, waiting to see if he was going to fry or something.

An old man eventually came to the door, and no shit, he was the oldest man I had ever seen. He was like Dr. Specter and Roy Codgers' ages combined. He didn't say anything. Mike Neff said, "We're here to see … uh, the pinhead?"

He looked us over and just said, "Twenty dollars."

We handed our fives over and followed the man through the door into a dim room that wasn't much bigger than The Sewer and smelled far worse, which is saying a lot, because The Sewer was a perpetual funk of urine, beer, and vomit. The place was packed floor to ceiling with junk. I wish I could have seen it all better, but there were no windows since it was basement level, and there was just one crummy lamp—a table lamp, but it was on the floor. You had to focus hard just to pick out anything in the piles, but there was a lot of old carnival stuff, and I mean really old. A ventriloquist doll that had a banjo and looked like it was wearing blackface. A dessicated feejee mermaid. Magic act cabinets and such. There were some big wooden boards with freak show oddities painted on them, saying things like "*The Penguin Boy—Alive!*" and "*Jo-Jo the Ostrich Man.*"

Everything was all covered in a layer of dust, and there was all kinds of garbage everywhere—literal garbage, like opened bean cans and barfy-looking Kleenex—but some of the stuff was so cool, I didn't even care. I spotted a poster for the Lon Chaney film *The Unknown* that was probably worth a fortune. I thought I might ask him about selling it, but then I was momentarily distracted by all the framed pictures hanging next to it. I wish cell phones had been invented then so I could have at least had some light to see them in more detail, but from what I could see, it was a wall of freaks: dozens and dozens of photographs of carnival sideshow performers. I don't even remember all of them, but it wasn't just your usual assortment of midgets and ladies covered in tattoos, but some real strange shit: people with awful deformities, conjoined twins with their tops off, a guy with a half-eaten rat in his mouth. I remember one picture was an armless guy smoking a cigarette with his foot, and it was signed, "*All the best, from Paul.*" I couldn't help imagining him signing the picture with his foot. It might actually have been worth the five bucks just to see some of this old stuff. It was like a grimy, putrid museum.

I didn't have long to look at it, though, because the old man barked, "Well let's go see what you came here for."

He led us into a second room that was even darker.

"Wiring in here is all fucked up," he said. "Can't plug in more than one thing at a time." He made us wait there while he unplugged the lamp in the front room, leaving us in complete darkness for a few minutes, huddled together, wondering what the hell we were even going to see. If you'd asked me to bet at that moment, I would have put my money on some kind of mannequin that he'd try to pass off as a taxidermied pinhead or something, some kind of carny con. But then we heard a sound: like a grunting, from the center of the room.

He came back and plugged in some kind of old rusty spotlight, illuminating a big cage.

"Ladies and gentlemen," he said all dramatically, which made Kenny snort. "Feast your eyes on the Incredible Wotzit."

Inside the cage was a pinhead, all right. An actual living person, like the ones from the movie, only far older. The little shaved topknot was gray, and her face was lined and haggard. The flowered sack of a dress was worn and stained. She held it out and curtsied, and did a bit of a dance that was the saddest thing I've ever seen. It made me sick to my stomach.

We were mostly dumbstruck, but Turtle was busting a gut laughing the whole time, and then he actually started chanting, "We accept you, we accept you, one of us."

"Shut up, Turtle. God." The whole thing made my skin crawl.

"Is there some reason you have to have her in a cage?" I had to ask.

"Oh, Pinny likes it in there," the old man said. "When the show first folded, I took her home to stay with me. Had a house back then, and she had a room with her own bed and everything. Cried every night for weeks. Then one night I found her in the garage, curled up in the old show cage. She missed it. Look—it's not even locked."

He opened a door on the side and left it ajar. Pinny just continued that shuffling dance, grinning like a maniac and holding out the edges of that dirty dress.

"What was that you called her?" Kenny asked. "The Incredible ..."

"Wotzit," he said. "I tried out a lot of names back in the traveling days. Whatever would lure in the paying customers. The guy I bought her from in '32 had her on display as The Monkey Girl. I tried her out as The Last of the Aztecs, which I thought had a nice mystique to it, and for a while there, she was just Pinny the Pinhead. Then I came up with the Wotzit. What is it? Let them figure it out," he cackled at this last part.

"Me and Pinny made a decent living back then. Could have made more. People used to love her so much, they would throw coins at her through the bars. This numbskull tossed 'em back!" Pinny made a chattering noise as if in response.

"We made up for it, though, didn't we, Pinny?" he went on. "Back in the day, plenty of people were willing to pay extra after hours to spend a little more time with her."

"Oh my God," muttered Kenny, as it dawned on him.

"That's nice that they wanted to spend time with her," Turtle said.

"They didn't pay extra to play Chutes and Ladders," I said. "Christ, Turtle."

"Of course, we were both a lot younger, then, but those were the days," he said. "The whole gang was still alive. Jolly Irene, Joe Kramer. He was the man with the rubber neck. His head would always be turned around backwards while you were talking to him. You always knew when he was mad at you, because it was the only time he'd turn it righways, so he could stare you down."

Despite how sordid it all seemed, I would have liked to have heard more of the carnival stories, and I was about to ask him about the armless man, and if he signed the picture with his foot, but right at that moment, Pinny lifted up her dress and pissed right through the bars of the cage. Kenny and I were the closest, but we all got splashed.

"Whooooooooa," said Turtle, "She's pissing on us," as if we somehow hadn't noticed.

"What the hell, man?" I started backing out of the room, light or no light, and Kenny was right behind me, trying to feel his way out. "Fuck this, I'm out of here."

The other guys were shuffling out behind me best as they could, with the front room and the path to the door in total darkness.

"The pinhead is a dude!" said Mike Neff.

The old man was following us, laughing. "Ever notice you never saw a boy pinhead? They're all girls. It's part of the show. We put 'em in dresses because it was easier to change their diapers."

I think he was trying to get the lamp plugged in to help us get out of there, but we somehow stumbled out into the street before he could even get it turned on.

It was nighttime, but it still seemed bright outside compared to the darkness inside that apartment. We walked awhile before we even said anything, not even sure where we were going, just wanting to put some distance between us and that place. Turtle said something about wanting to go get a beer, and maybe that's what everybody else did. I never asked them if they ended up going somewhere in their piss-stained jackets. I just wanted to go home and take a shower.

Now, I'm the only one of us who still lives around here. Every once in a while, I pass that building, which is all boarded up now, and I wonder what happened to those two. I guess they're long dead, along with Dr. Specter and Roy Codgers. I really wonder what became of the stuff, too. I can't believe I didn't ask about that Lon Chaney poster. It probably ended up in a dumpster somewhere.

I hardly ever go anywhere anymore, maybe to a party once a year, if we have a sitter, and then the wife and I go to the kind of party where people have drinks, and dinner sitting around a table, and maybe play some dumb game after. It's never the kind of party where somebody gets their dick out, much less staple it to a piece of plywood. Sometimes I see my old friends if they come to town for Christmas, except for Mike Neff, who had a heart attack about a year ago. We end up having a quick drink out somewhere after all the family stuff. Turtle—well, Lester, these days—actually has kids now, and is on the school board, if you can believe it. We talk a lot about those days, about shows we went to, about some of the crazy things we did, but not once, not one single time, have we ever talked about the pinhead.

[March 20th 1994, Bomb Factory, Dallas, Texas, USA]

SUZY IS A HEADBANGER
BY
DEREK FARRELL

The mook had no idea what hit him.

He was short and at least fifty pounds overweight, his eyes spaced so far apart he could have stood in Union Square and checked out the Empire State Building and the World Trade Center without moving his head.

You might think that would have made it easy for him to spot predators coming at him the way a gecko in the wild can.

But you'd be wrong there. He didn't spot me for a predator till it was too late. I slammed my right hand into the point where his fat neck met his shoulder, the skin glistening with greasy sweat, and he went out faster (and a lot less noisier) than Gary Gilmore.

The taller, younger, dude with a glistening pompadour and a Spanish name tattooed across his naked chest ripped his gaze away from my tits while simultaneously letting loose a noise that was silenced before it formed words.

What can I say? A .38 pointing at the 'N' in 'Juanita' will do that to a boy.

"Hi," I tossed the empty pizza box and smiled, showing all the teeth in my head.

My mom worked three jobs to pay for the orthodontist, so I like to make a point of showing them off. Plus, like she always used to say to me: 'Suzy: You're plain. Now, plain is better than ugly, just like luncheon meat is better than cat food; but neither of 'em is steak. So, if you aint never gonna be pretty you can at least have a pretty smile. Who knows? You might catch a man yet.'

I'd already caught this man, though the way his eyes darted to the .45 sitting just beyond his reach I figured he'd mistaken my smile for weakness.

"I wouldn't," I said, nodding to a chair on the other side of the room and indicating with a flick of the wrist that he should park his ass in it.

I moved sideways so I could still see the mook while I had a short word with Raoul Esteban.

"I've got a message from a friend," I said and before I got any further Esteban – glowering now at having taken orders from a mere woman – snarled.

"I don't got no friends."

"I didn't say he was a friend of yours, Raoul. The gentleman in question is a personal friend of mine. And of Marco Romano."

He still glowered, but under the glower something paled.

"Yeah," I smiled again, nodded. "I figured that'd ring a bell."

"You're gonna die for this," he sneered.

I shrugged. "So listen, Raoul. Yeah," I smiled as the light came on behind his eyes, "I know your name. And it's because my friend and I know your name that I'm here. Y'see, Mr. Romano knows who you are, and he knows that your uncle is Enrico Perez."

He stretched his head first to the left then the right, clicking vertebrae each time as though trying to telegraph to me that the fact he was sitting in a chair while I pointed a gun at him was of less concern to him than the tension knots he'd developed during a long day of being a hardass gangster.

"Now Mr. Romano and Mr. Perez have an agreement. The wholesale provision of certain substances to the street retailers in this neighborhood is the sole concern of Mr. Romano, Mr. Perez having agreed to keep his snub little nose out of this in return for Mr. Romano's agreeing to keep away from everything north of 170th.

"We know that Mr. Perez has no idea that his own flesh and blood has decided to breach that covenant and open shop in direct competition with Mr. Romano."

"Shows what you know," he snapped, and I waited.

"We know," I said when nothing more was forthcoming. "And I've been sent here today because I do certain work for Mr. Romano."

"I'll bet you do." He grabbed his crotch. "You wanna maybe do some of that certain work on me?"

I gave him the hundred-watt smile again. "I'm a headbanger, Raoul. You know what that is? When people upset Mr. Romano or his friends, they vanish. Mostly. Bits of them might pop up in the East River now and again, and their last known addresses may show signs of violence, but mostly people like you and," I jerked my head at the now-moaning mook, "are never seen again."

I made sure he saw me slip the safety catch off, saw him realize he could have rushed me at any time up till now, watched as he blushed with shame at the fact his naivety had been exposed, then went on.

"But I'm here 'cos Mr. Romano doesn't want you vanished. See, if you vanished Mr. R would likely have a problem with tu amado tío. One that he doesn't want to have. So here I am. Like a school teacher with a naughty schoolboy. Banging some sense into your head."

"Fuck you, bitch," he said.

On the opposite side of the room the mook groaned, pushed himself to a seated position and – realization dawning – made a growling noise. He looked as though he was about to stand up.

"Pack your bags, Raoul." I wasn't smiling now. "Pack 'em and get the fuck out of Midtown."

"Or what?" he demanded.

I flicked the gun away from him for a second, and the mook's head exploded like an overripe melon, a surprisingly dark eruption of gore spattering on the wall behind him. In the aftermath, the only sound was the noisy AC unit still chugging away.

"He wasn't related to Perez," I said, the gun back on the kid before he had even come to his senses.

"Pack. Get the fuck out. And don't come back."

I was lying, of course. I didn't know Marco Romano. I mean anyone who reads The Post with any consistency knows Romano, and I'd actually seen him in the flesh. Been introduced to him. But I doubt he'd have any recollection of me.

And I'm not a headbanger. Sitting behind the wheel of my Pinto I chuckled at that one, my eyes never leaving the doorway that I expected Raoul Esteban to come out of sooner or later.

There was always a chance I'd miscalculated: That he might go out the window and down the fire escape; but I was fairly sure that he'd have some bulk to transport and so the front door would make more sense than the risk he'd take dragging it down the fire escape.

I'm good at calculating risk. Averages. Possibilities and maximum losses. It's what I do. Which – as I've already said – is not head banging. I'm trained as an actuary. Actually working as a book keeper at McLaren and Westwood, which is where I had been introduced to one Marco Romano, whose private finances (the ones the IRS never gets to see) are handled personally by Mr. Westwood.

My Boss.

Who is the sort of cheap lazy sonofabitch who can focus on only one layer of a cake at a time. And since Mr. Romano's primary concern is in making sure that neither the IRS nor the cops ever see his actual income statements, that's what Westwood focuses on: Hiding the cash.

It was me who noticed an odd statistical anomaly in the numbers. Me who noticed that while sales of Mr. Romano's product had been dropping every month for the past six or seven months the street price (and don't ask how I knew this) was constant.

Now you don't need to spend as many nights as I once did at CCNY to know how supply and demand works.

If the same number of consumers want a product where supply has dropped by fifteen per cent in the past three months then the consumers should be paying more. But they weren't, which meant the supply was constant.

Which meant someone was undercutting Romano.

It didn't take me long to find out who. Just like it wouldn't take Romano long – once he or his lazy-ass bagman figured out the numbers didn't add up – to work his way back to Raoul Esteban who, as the thought ran across my mind, walked through the doorway from the building I'd not long left.

He stood on the stoop, hefted the holdall in his hand and tried to look calm and collected. But his every twitchy move telegraphed panic as he jogged down the street a little to where a tan-colored sedan sat, engine running.

Esteban yanked the passenger door open, flung himself into the seat, the bag cradled to his chest like a baby, and the car pulled away, tires shrieking.

Then stopped.

It was 6pm in Midtown.

I could have followed them on foot and still overtaken them.

Instead, I waited a couple of minutes, then started up the Pinto, pulled out into traffic three or four cars behind the sedan and crawled along behind them.

My mother had this thing about cockroaches.

She was a New Yorker; of course she had a fucking thing about cockroaches. If it wasn't the roaches it was the bedbugs, the risk of Dominicans moving the sixty blocks from Spanish Harlem to Hell's Kitchen and taking up residence in her apartment building just to fuck with her, or the fact she had raised a daughter who was six-two by the time she was fifteen and, worse, plain.

These were the things that kept her awake at night.

But mostly, it was the roaches.

And it was my mother who taught me how to handle a roach infestation.

"When you switch on the light, Suzy, the little motherfuckers'll run. Let 'em. You go running around stamping on the ones you can see all you'll end up with is a mess and a nest somewhere that the sonsabitches will still be crawling out of a month later.

"Instead, you switch on the light and you watch 'em. You see where they go. You track 'em to the nest and you can take out the whole fuckin' lot of em in one go."

Wise words.

I'd been watching Raoul Esteban for a few weeks, so I had some idea of how much he and his gang of amateurs had been pulling in.

I also knew they had a central point where they stored the cash. But I hadn't been able to find it yet.

Hence the performance on W49th.

Nothing, I'd figured, would send the roaches back to their nest quicker than making it clear to Esteban that the jig was up.

He'd either head there to circle the wagons or to close down operations, grab the money and head for the hills. Either way, he'd lead me straight there just as soon as this goddamned traffic started moving again.

The sedan headed uptown and eventually turned east, making its way on to the Queensboro bridge and, as we wound our way through the deserted landscape of Hunters Point, the roads emptied out.

Eventually, just as I was considering dropping the tail, they turned right and into the parking lot of what looked to be a derelict factory.

I drove on, turned right at the next block, then pulled up.

And waited.

My mom died a couple years ago, but she lived long enough to see Ronald Reagan capture the White House.

"That fuckin' cowboy," she'd croaked, her voice actually sounding like a bottle of Jameson and forty smokes a day. "A fuckin' B-movie actor. We're doomed, Suzy. Doomed."

Before she died, there'd been a few boyfriends but only one who was even faintly consistent.

Eddie Mullen.

Known, to all who knew of him, as Ed the Exterminator.

I often wondered what – beyond the roaches – my mother and this small dapper man could have had in common. But maybe the roaches were enough. Either way, Ed the Exterminator was in and out of our lives for a decade, and at the funeral he held my hand longer than anyone else, stared into my eyes and told me that if I ever needed anything – anything – I had his number.

So, once I'd decided on my plan, I'd called him.

And discovered he was in Bellevue, his whole body shattered by the toxic fumes and poisons he'd been surrounded with his whole career.

When I'd seen this shrunken thing in the chair, the brilliantined hair now grey and lifeless, the once so-smooth and bright face now dull and mottled with tufts of grey stubble where an orderly had only half-heartedly shaved him, I'd dropped any thoughts of asking him what I'd been intending to ask.

He'd chuckled at my horror. "Looks like the roaches'll still be around long after both me and your mom have gone. I guess it'll be up to you to do something about them now."

And as he spoke those words, something sparked, and I'd told him. Told him how my plans for a better life had ended up with me working for McLaren and Westwood. Told him what they did and who they did it for. And told him what I'd discovered, and what my plan was.

He was silent for a long time afterwards, then he reached a palsied hand out and held mine lightly this time.

"You know she worried about you," he said, his eyes watering a little. "You stand out. She was afraid you'd get hurt."

Ed smiled a little, nodded. "But I think you'll be just fine."

The overalls were too short in the legs and too tight around the crotch, and the baseball cap – pulled low to hide as much of my face as possible – was a little too tight. I knew if it stayed on too long I'd have a headache.

But then, I figured, Raoul Esteban and his pals would have a lot worse.

I scoped out the factory as well as I could: it had previously housed the Huntsville Coat and Galoshes company, and from what I could see Esteban and his gang were the only inhabitants now. They were either squatting or had persuaded the owner to look away as they turned the place into their clearing house.

The central heating and air con units were in the basement and it took seconds and a decent bolt cutter to get me into that space.

I let the door close gently behind me and stood, my eyes adjusting to the darkness. My body was bathed in sweat as the hot humid air wrapped around me like a living thing, pulling me deeper into the core of the building.

Deeper towards the heart of the air conditioning system – a behemoth that looked like a Frankenstein's monster of various bits of machinery added to as the technology developed. I was glad to hear it whining furiously, though unsurprised. It was July. Who in their right mind, if they had an aircon unit, wouldn't have it turned to max right now?

From above me I could hear muffled voices. It was impossible to tell from this distance what they were saying; hard, even, to be sure whether their tones were angry or panicked. I liked to imagine panicked, and the sound of various feet moving back and forth across the floor above my head supported my hope.

God bless the New York public libraries: I still have my card. It had come in handy because although Ed had been able to explain, firstly, how to turn what he had in his basement workshop into what I needed, and then how to use that to achieve my desired result, I'd needed to see some diagrams so I could be sure of finding the right part of the system.

It took me five minutes to find the condenser unit and another five to slot the cardboard discs into the workings. I figured it would take ten, maybe fifteen minutes for the results to kick in so I packed up my tools and made my way back to the Pinto, stripping out of the overalls and dumping them and the toolbox back in the trunk.

Then I drove the car back to the former home of the Huntsville Coat and Galoshes company, the aircon blasting air so cold my teeth were chattering by the time I pulled in to the parking lot.

I turned off the engine, and with one eye on the clock I waited.

The first thing they might note would be the scent. I couldn't figure out a way to stop that, but I figured most of them would be so busy figuring out how to respond to what they'd been told was Romano's ultimatum that a change in the way the air smelled would be last on their list of things to give a shit about.

But then their eyes would start to itch.

They'd cough, looking at each other in surprise as their own coughing was echoed by their colleagues.

I figured the panic would really set in when the itching became a burning, the almond scent in the air turned into a metallic taste in their mouths before their tongues started swelling like fat glistening slugs, filling their mouths and swelling so far down their throats that the sheer bulk of tongue began to block their airways.

I wound down the window.

The lot was silent, the whole area deserted, the stillness almost oppressive. Somewhere in the east, the sun was going down, the sky slowly turning a dusty pink behind a curtain of smog.

I turned on the radio. One of the old rock stations so many had abandoned as we raced into the eighties and out of the twentieth century. They were playing a song by The Ramones, a set of repurposed Bo Diddley rhythms and Eddie Cochran guitar riffs thrashed out as Joey sang about his girl. And for a minute I was back in the railroad apartment in Hell's Kitchen, hearing the scratch of my mom's key in the door lock and scrambling to turn the volume down on the radio so she wouldn't shout at me for being a fuckin' noise nuisance.

I figured, by now, the hysteria, if it hadn't infected them all, would at least be kicking off in some of the smarter members of the gang as the vomiting and convulsions started. And it was at that moment that I heard the gunfire and one of the windows on the top floor exploded outwards, a man – fat like the mook and topless like Raoul had been when I'd arrived at the Midtown apartment – hung out of the window gasping for air, his eyes bulging, seemingly unaware of the jagged broken glass lacerating his chest and shoulders.

His eyes darted around desperately as though he was looking for something.

Who knows? Rescue? Responsibility? Maybe God.

Whatever; they met mine briefly before darting onwards as he was dragged backwards into the building, another frantic face taking his place and trying desperately to consume what I guess passed for fresh air, though we were in Long island, so…

I began to hear the sounds of chaos – screams, shouts, shots, the ratatatatat of an Uzi.

A fuckin' Uzi.

I turned up the radio, The Ramones' snarling love song filling my head.

And – as I had been doing my whole life – I waited.

But not, this time, for long.

I'd been eyeing the gas mask on the passenger seat and hoping I wouldn't have to actually go into the building when the front door burst open and Raoul Esteban, his pompadour disheveled and his movements jerky, staggered out, dragging a bulky suitcase behind him.

A moment later another man, this one wearing a polo shirt and chinos, fell through the door and I saw his mouth move as though he were saying or shouting something to Esteban.

As Esteban turned and fired the submachine gun at him, I realized I recognized polo-shirt guy.

Lew Westwood.

Which explained why nobody had brought Romano's attention to the sales discrepancies.

Esteban kept firing the gun, bullets pouring into the prone figure until the magazine was emptied, at which point he flung the weapon at Westwood's head and dragged the suitcase over to the sedan.

I opened the Pinto's door and stepped out.

The sedan was locked, and Raoul had clearly not had the foresight to dig the keys out of the pocket of whichever corpse had driven him to the factory, so he was both gasping furiously and snatching desperately at the door handle when he saw my reflection in the driver's side window.

He turned, his eyes filled with blood, mouth gaping, face bloated and blotchy, and made gasping scratching noises that I assumed were not meant to be complimentary.

I gave him my dazzling smile again, lifted my right arm so he could see the .38 and at the same time ducked down and put a hand over his, easily pushing his grip away from the handle of the suitcase.

"Lemme help you with that," I said, and he released it, his hand moving towards his side.

Which was when I shot him.

I take no credit for the red hole that appeared and bloomed in the dead center of Esteban's forehead. Ray Charles could have hit the guy at this range and still got him right between the eyes.

Raoul's mouth was still gaping as his knees sagged and he fell forward. I stepped back so he collapsed face down on the asphalt, and then I stepped forward again and put another two bullets in the back of his head.

Oh, there was no need for those. There was no need for any of it, to be honest: He was dead before he even came out of the building. A lungful of Hydrogen Cyanide will do that to you. Ed kept a stock for some of the more intransigent critters he had to deal with, though it had taken some work to condense the product sufficiently to make something strong enough to kill a factory full of adult males.

The bullet between the eyes had just been something I always wanted to do, and the two follow-ons were designed to make sure that when Perez was told of the attack, of the deaths of so many of the sons of his own mob, he'd see the extra two taps for what they were: A giant Fuck You from Marco Ramone.

And in the war that followed, Ramone, Perez, and whoever the fuck else got sucked into the carnage would spend so long destroying each other that I'd be safe. I was hoping that whichever one ended up finally wiping out the other one would just always assume that the money had burned somewhere along the line.

Because these giants of criminal enterprise would surely never allow themselves to imagine that a third party, some nonentity, could have wiped out the next generation and started a war that would see them, in turn, devastate each other.

I dragged the suitcase over to the Pinto, heaved it into the trunk, and I drove.

Away from the filth, away from the smell of bitter almonds and greed.

Away from the land where the roaches had learned to walk on two legs, where nothing but their survival counted to them, and within two days I was in another country, one where a B-Movie Cowboy wasn't president.

My mother was right: we were doomed.

I'd tried to clean up, but just like my mom I knew that even when you traced them back to – and destroyed – the nest, there would always be more cockroaches in the morning.

[October 27th 1977, CBGB & OMFUG, New York, New York, USA]

CRETIN HOP
BY
MIKE BURR

"Hey! Wait a minute!"

I put my head down, try to walk a little faster without seeming alarmed.

"Hey! Honey! Slow down! We just want to ask you a question!"

The big hand on my shoulder stops my forward progress. I shrug it off and turn around, taking care not to be too aggressive.

"So, uh, we were wondering what a good-looking young lady like you is doing out by herself at this time of night?"

Four of them. Out of one of the straight bars after a long day of work. They're blowing off steam. They have thick muscles under flannel and denim. This is probably going to hurt.

I set my jaw and flip the hair away from my face.

"What!?! Aw shit, this is a dude!"

They start laughing and pointing at the one they call Jimmy. He's turning red; maybe he really thought that I was a woman. For a spilt second I wonder how that would have gone, what these guys would have done to some poor secretary or shop girl getting off work late. How would their fun be different?

I can't think about that for long, because it's me thankfully, regrettably, on the street with them. I begin to nod and smile, trying to render myself utterly harmless. I stop short of laughing, definitely not wanting to antagonize Jimmy. I slowly modify my raised hand into a short wave, nod, and try to be on my way.

I breathe through my nose and put one foot in front of the other, slowly, resisting the urge to run. Predators are encouraged by a chase. Maybe I'm overreacting; it was a simple mistake, and the four of them will have a story to laugh about tomorrow. I probably shouldn't be so quick to judge.

"Hey."

I stop again and turn around, backing away in quarter inches. I try to look friendly.

"Where are you going?"

It's Jimmy, and he's still red, but the other three aren't laughing anymore.

"Nowhere, really? Just out."

"You sure it's not a costume party?"

Jimmy's laughing now, a sharp donkey bray. His buddies are standing there, looking bored. He turns on them and they immediately start laughing again, forced.

"Is that a wig?"

Jimmy reaches out and pulls at a piece of my hair. I step out of it and he lets go, the lock trailing from his fingers for an instant before falling limply back against my head.

"Shit. That's real!"

Jimmy turns to his buddies and they look at each other as if they have just discovered the lost continent of Atlantis.

"How long does it take to grow your hair that long?"

He makes a point of looking interested, which sets the hair standing up on the back of my neck. He doesn't care about the answer to the question. He is a cat playing with a mouse. I try to see past them, in a vain hope that someone will come by. Jimmy and his buddies aren't the type to beat the snot out of somebody with witnesses. There isn't even a bum sleeping in a doorway.

"I don't know. A while I guess."

"Like, a year? Two years?"

"Sure."

"Well which is it?"

"What?"

"Is one year or two years?"

"I just don't really know. Sorry."

The word tastes like vomit in my mouth. I'm not sorry. I have to be sorry. And I don't know when I started growing my hair. I remember when my mom's boyfriend made a joke about taking me to his barber and then bloodied my lip when I said no thanks. There was the time when Coach Hicks told me to line up with the girls in gym class. The guy at my job who wanted to talk to the manager because he didn't want to pay such a dirty kids for his burger. I could have told Jimmy roughly when any of these things happened or just made up a date. I could have said anything. The answer was just a part of the charade.

"About the same time you started wearing your mom panties?"

"Huh?"

"You heard me. You one of those freak boys? You headed down to the pier?"

Jimmy's not laughing at all now, and his buddies look nervous. This has happened before. His fist makes quick contact with my chin before I can answer or run. It doesn't hurt so much as overwhelm me. I lose my bearings and try to find my feet. Jimmy hits me again and I taste blood. My knees go weak. I try to go forward so I can break my fall with my hands, but I run into Jimmy and he pushes me backwards.

"Tough guy, eh?"

I barely register what those words mean when there is an explosion of color in front of my eyes. I am on the ground, heaving, the concrete scratching my cheek.

"Come on, man. We better go."

A new voice. One of his buddies is trying to get Jimmy to leave.

"Yeah, man. I think he's learned his lesson. Let's go by the house and grab another beer."

I can see Jimmy's feet. He is wearing heavy boots.

"Okay. Yeah."

Three of them start up a conversation, begin to walk away. They're relaxed, having defused the situation.

Jimmy doesn't move. His boot swings back in a slow arc, giving me an instant to brace for what's to come. I finish curling into a ball just as he makes contact with my midsection. My lungs are empty. I try to fill them and cough and spit. I open my eyes and brace for another, but Jimmy has started walking away. He's worried that he's going to lose his group.

"Hey queer, you want some cake?"

I am beyond response. Jimmy raises his middle finger and spits in my direction.

"Fuck you! Queers don't get no cake!"

Jimmy lets out a war whoop and takes off down the street after his buddies. They stop and light cigarettes before turning the corner. They'll go home, maybe to their families, and probably never think about me again. I'm just a little bit of fun after a hard day's work.

They know I'm not going to the cops. What do I tell them? I've been assaulted by every other guy in this neighborhood. I'd probably catch another beating for taking them away from whatever it is cops actually do to make money.

I cough again. Spit out a little blood, but breathing is relatively painless, and running my tongue around my mouth reveals that all my teeth are in place and intact. I get to my hands and knees and then stand. A wave starts behind my eyes and comes to rest in my stomach. I swallow hard and take a deep, painless breath. I put a foot forward for a tentative step and then another. I check for my wallet and brush the dirt out of my hair; put my hands in my pockets and hunch over. I don't want to attract any more attention.

After a couple of blocks, the bum finally comes wandering out of the alley. He's on a stinker and probably a thousand years old. Not a threat.

"Hey. You got your ass kicked."

"Yeah."

"Usually it's me, but tonight they got you. You got knocked right the shit out. Thanks, brother. These old bones are grateful."

He starts laughing so hard that he's shaking, like a pervert Santa Claus. I nod to him, and he shadowboxes a little bit, miming my defeat. I give him a thumbs up. The scene is absurd enough that I crack a smile. There is a dull ache in my jaw and the gnawing feeling of helpless failure, but I'm alive, and I can at least take a small victory in giving this bum a night off. I keep going, hating myself for needing to look over my shoulder.

I hear it from down the block and my pace quickens to the rhythm. Soon I see a few of the heads out front blowing plumes of smoke into the air, fuck the police style, and grubby kids trying to cadge a few dollars for beer or a ticket inside. The dopers size me up and return to their skinny joints. The kids, seeing fresh meat, move in immediately.

"Hey man you got any cigs?"

"Let me have a dollar."

"Come on come on come on. I'm just trying to get inside."

"You're rich. You know it. Share the wealth!"

"Cool jacket! You got to have some money. Let me hold a dollar."

I produce a few crumpled bills and press them into the closest hands. There are some words of thanks and a couple of makeshift Buddhist blessings. The rest of the group, seeing that I have completed the ritual, drifts off to find greener pastures.

Adam's at the door. He's wearing aviators with yellow lenses so he can spot the frat boys' fakes and send them away, shrugging his massive shoulders. He's got his action jeans on in case they don't take too kindly to it. He doesn't smile when he sees me- part of the job is the persona- but he cracks upon seeing the results of my earlier adventure.

"Buddy, what happened?"

"Some red asses got a hold of me. You should see the bite marks on their ankles."

I shadowbox for a couple of seconds. It seemed to work for the bum. Adam's bottom lip pooches out.

"Nope. You need a hug."

Adam envelops me in his sweaty, tree trunk arms. My face is buried in his beard. I am embarrassed at once, and more so when a couple of guys start waving their IDs around.

"Give me a second! My friend's had a bad time tonight."

He holds me at arm's length, appraises me like a parent.

"I fucking hate it that people are like that."

"It happens."

Adam nods with understanding.

"How about it's on us tonight, then?"

Forgetting my jaw, I mime jaw-dropping surprise. The pain pulses and I immediately stop.

"Thanks man. I appreciate it."

"Now get out of here before I change my mind."

He turns toward the impatient guys, scrutinizing each millimeter of their licenses. I descend the narrow steps and head through the short tunnel into the room. The band hasn't started yet; the sound guy is spinning *Heroin* at a teeth-rattling volume. It's early. The crowd is sparse. People are drinking from plastic cups and leaning in close to have conversations. I head to one of the mirrors advertising beer and try to catch a glimpse of myself. Boots look better when they're scuffed up; I've presented better. I smile at my reflection, and finding myself less than Frankenstein, I head to the bar.

I duck the first bartender I see and wait for Jessica. I always kind of wait for Jessica. She comes around the corner, gets a look at me and reacts in mock horror.

"Oh honey, was the bus that hit you okay?"

"Headed to the bus graveyard."

"Is that like the elephant graveyard?"

"Worse."

"Is it at the bottom of the river?"

"With all the bodies."

"Spooky!"

I hand her a bill and she gives me a foamy beer. She doesn't ask if I need change. I know she has kids and hates leaving them to work here, and that tips are sometimes few and far between. She seems like she would be cool to her kids and it's just a couple of bucks.

I post up in the corner, nod to a couple fellow travelers, sip the beer and feel the carbonation hit my split lip.

The lights go down. I drain my beer and launch the cup towards the stage, where it meets and lands with twenty others.

The lights come up and the first chord cuts through the crowd. We head for the stage as the singer tells us to fuck right off and that we're all posers. That's the last we hear from him. The mix is off, all bass, and no one's paying that much attention anyway. The music is just the background for the action on the floor. It's wheels within wheels. Bodies slide past each other then hook and collide, spinning off in different directions to reconfigure. There is a rush to the front and the singer tries to make like Iggy Pop, Jesus jumping into the crowd. It's Tuesday. There's simply not enough mass to hold him. Skinny arms make a valiant effort, but the wave falls back on itself, and everyone goes flying.

I'm outside the collapse. One of the outliers barrels toward me. Without thinking, but more thinking of stupid fucking Jimmy, I push the dude harder than I should away from me. It feels wrong, but there's no explaining that at this point.

He finds his feet and squares up.

"Hey! Fuck you!"

"I know! Fuck me!"

He looks confused.

"What are you? Aggro? Fuck! You!"

"No! And right! Fuck me!"

A circle forms around us.

"Do you wanna fight, fucko?"

"No! Fuck! I want to dance!"

"What?!"

"I said I want to fucking dance!"

The tension dissipates even before he breaks into a broken-toothed grin.

"Fuck! Yeah!

He is on top of me in two seconds. The circle closes in, people thinking an ass kicking might still happen. I don't even have the time to square up. His hands grip the sides of my head.

"That! Is Beautiful!"

He kisses me full on the lips and then pushes me as hard he can into the ring of onlookers, now into it for a different reason. They catch me before I hit the floor and launch me back into him. We meet shoulder to shoulder and go flailing. The circle does not release us, but tosses us back until we are sweaty and exhausted. I put up my hands and the dude pulls me into my second sweaty hug of the night. He gets close to my ear.

"I'm sorry, man. I should watched where I was going."

"No man, it was me. And I've had a shitty day."

"You and me both, brother."

He raises a middle finger to the singer, who has just wished us good luck on our marriage.

"Hey man. Stay cool."

He raises a fist as the band jumps into another song. In a moment, he's lost in the tangle of bodies.

I pop my jaw and follow him in.

No matter what happens, there's no stopping.

[November 27th 1989, Eissporthalle, Berlin, Germany]

ROCKAWAY BEACH
BY
LEX VRANICK

Rockaway Beach, NY, July 22, 1978 - 7:49pm,

A hazy orange sky melts into black like a candle snuffed out — light one minute, smoldering dark the next. The stars blink lazily into view, one by one, Christmas lights flickering on a string. Rickie shuts her eyes. The daytime heat has seeped out of the sand, leaving it cool against her skin. Down the beach, a boombox blares WLIR, close enough that Rickie can make out the melodies, far enough that the lyrics drown in the push and pull of the rolling waves.

Beside her, Felix clears his throat. Rickie feels a shadow fall over her. She opens one eye to find an offering: Felix's outstretched arm, a lit cigarette dangling from his fingers. She accepts, taking it delicately between two fingers. She sucks in, relishes the burn, the way the smoke swirls down, down, down into her lungs. She breathes out slowly, lets it escape through her nostrils.

"You good?" Felix asks.

Rickie is quiet. She takes another puff from the cigarette and blows the smoke up toward the sky. She hands the cigarette back to Felix. She does not look at him, but she can feel his gaze, the way it trails up and down her body, lingers on the sharp profile of her face.

Ahead of them, down the sloping shoreline, Trish stands with her feet in the water. Sea foam fizzles around her ankles and the soft summer breeze tosses her hair. She is stone-still, eyes closed, chin tilted toward the sky. Silver moonlight glows on her skin and in it, a glint of read on her temple. Rickie looks to her hands, where that same red, drying and flaking, clings to her fingertips.

"Rickie," Felix says, half-statement, half-question.

Rickie holds out her hand and Felix passes the cigarette back. Rickie takes a long, slow drag and lets the smoke escape in a sigh. She smiles. "I'm good."

Eight hours earlier…

The sun blazed hot in a cloudless sky. Sweat beaded at Felix's brow, gathered at the nape of his neck. His t-shirt clung uncomfortably to his skin. He pulled at the hem, fidgeting, so distracted by the heat he didn't hear the chime of the overhead bell, didn't see Rickie emerge from the gas station quick-mart until a Coca-Cola can hit him in the stomach.

"We're fucked," Rickie announced.

Felix fumbled for the can. Condensation turned the aluminum slick and slippery; he caught it one hand, it slipped — he grabbed it with the other, it slipped again. By the time Felix had it pinned between his palms, Rickie was halfway across the parking lot. Felix cracked the tab as he stepped off the curb. The heat of the asphalt burned through the soles of his Chucks. He stopped a few paces behind Rickie, lingering in the sparse shade of a dying maple tree.

Felix took a swig of soda. "How fucked?" he asked.

Rickie didn't answer. Instead, she yanked open the passenger door of her Buick, a secondhand pile of metal and gears not-so-lovingly dubbed Scraps. She dragged her backpack from its floor, zipper open, bag gaping like an open mouth. She popped open the glovebox and fed it 8-tracks, a book of matches, a half-empty carton of Camels.

She slammed the door, rounded the car and opened the driver's door. She reached beneath the seat, fished out a battered copy of *Punk* and a Stephen King paperback, the distraught face of Carrie White obscured by a yellow sticker marking the book used. Rickie took a few things from the backseat — uneaten bags of chips, granola bars, a balled-up sweatshirt. She shoved them all into her backpack and sealed it shut, shouldering it before kicking a tire for good measure.

Felix whistled. "That fucked."

Rickie exhaled — sharp, annoyed.

"Scraps is scrapped," she said.

"For real?" Felix asked.

"For now," Rickie said. She turned her pockets inside out. "I don't have jack shit to pay for repairs. We could toss in a few bucks of gas, but who knows how far it'll get before it craps out for good?" Rickie kicked the tire again.

"So…" Felix said, the 'o' dragged out.

"Hitch for now," Rickie shrugged. "Circle back in a few days, if we can scrounge up some cash. Otherwise…" she trailed off, and Felix bowed his head somberly. He made a sign of the cross over the Buick.

"Rest in peace, Scraps."

Rickie sighed, "Amen."

They walked alongside the road, passing the Coke back and forth until they'd drained the can. Felix dropped it in the grass, crushed it beneath his foot. Rickie watched the road, one hand shielding her eyes from the sun. Cars passed — family sedans, station wagons with kayaks strapped to their roofs. "That one seemed good," Felix said, pointing at the retreating taillights of a beat-up Chevy. Rickie shook her head.

"Older couple," she said. "Gave us the side-eye."

"What about that one?" he asked, jutting his chin down the road, where a tan VW bus was gliding into the left-hand lane. Rickie considered it.

"Might be full," she said.

"Might not be," countered Felix. As the bus drew closer, Felix extended his thumb. Rickie squinted against the glare of the sun, straining to see the driver. A man, she guessed. Tall enough for wisps of his unkempt hair to graze the roof. The passenger seat was empty. Felix stepped ahead of Rickie, leaning toward the road. Rickie held her thumb out, too. The driver seemed to notice, pumping the breaks and steering toward the shoulder. Rickie dropped her arm, took a step toward the road — and the bus stopped, just yards away, and reversed back onto the road.

"Oh, come on," Felix said, exasperated. The bus sputtered, smoke pluming from the exhaust as the engine rattled. The whole body shuddered, and then the bus peeled away, tires screeching. "Hey!" Felix shouted, jogging after it. He only made it a few paces before giving up, arms raised in defeat. "Asshole," he said.

Rickie, though, wasn't quite paying attention. She kept walking, quick and purposeful, her eyes on the van — the red break lights as it slowed for traffic, the back windshield, the round face inside.

"Rickie," Felix said, but Rickie kept moving. "Rick," he tried, trailing after her. He grasped her wrist but she slipped between his fingers. "Come on," he said, reaching for her again. She picked up her pace.

"Something's not right," Rickie said at the same time Felix said, "We'll get the next one." Felix paused. Rickie didn't.

"What do you mean?" he asked.

Rickie did not elaborate. She ran.

"Rickie!" Felix shouted. She was fast, clumps of dirt and loose blades of grass kicked up in her wake. Felix took off after her. Up ahead, the van weaved between lanes — right, left, right, left — until traffic bottlenecked, both lanes converging into one. Horns blared. Lights flashed — breaks on, breaks off. Felix caught up to Rickie, grabbed her wrist and held on this time. "What are you doing?" he said.

"Getting us a ride," she said. She kept moving, pulling Felix along with her. The van was stopped ahead of them, wedged between a pick-up and a Bug. As they approached, Rickie laced her fingers with Felix and squeezed his hand. "Be cool," she said. "Okay?"

"Okay?" Felix said, dumbfounded, straining to see whatever danger Rickie sensed. She dropped his hand. He lingered behind her as she crossed the grassy shoulder onto the road.

"Hey!" Rickie called. The driver looked at her without turning his head, then looked away. "Hey!" Rickie tried again. She was at the driver's door now. She knocked it, feigning timidity, and chewed her lower lip. She motioned for the driver to lower his window. "We just need a lift," she said, voice raised to be heard through the glass. "We don't need to go far."

She stood there, waiting. The creep-crawl of congested traffic inched forward. The VW's tires creaked as it moved with the flow, and Rickie walked alongside it, still signaling the driver to roll the window down. When she persisted, he did — slowly — stopping it halfway.

"I'm sorry," Rickie said, her voice pitched up and so sugary sweet it almost made Felix sick. She twirled her hair around one finger, turned her eyes down toward the ground. "It's just," she said, fluttering her lashes at the middle-aged driver, "our car broke down. And it's sweltering out here. Do you think we could hitch a ride?"

The driver had shoulder length hair, artfully messy, and a rough stubble pricked his jaw. When he looked like he was about to say no, Rickie leaned toward the window. The hiss of the VW's air conditioner kissed her face and she sighed into the artificial cold. "I promise," she said, "we really don't need to go far. You can drop us at the next gas station."

She pressed one hand to the car door. The driver sighed.

"It's open," he relented, nodding toward the door.

"Thank you," Rickie said, her relief exaggerated. She glanced at Felix, her mask slipping for the briefest of moments as she jutted her chin toward the front of the bus. Felix hesitated, but nodded, and rounded the hood to slip into the passenger seat. Rickie slid open the side door and let herself in.

"Thanks for this," Felix said when Rickie stared at him, expectant. "We appreciate it."

"Sure," the driver said. He spoke like there was gravel tumbling in his throat, hoarse and gruff. The bus was cool inside, and filled with the crackling sounds of the radio. It stuttered some funk song, the riffs cutting in and out as the VW eased along the road. It smelled faintly of weed and stale beer. The floor was littered with dented cigarette boxes, empty bottles. Rickie stepped on near-finished roll of duct tape. It stuttered some funk song, the riffs cutting in and out as the VW eased along the road.

Rickie set her backpack next to her on the middle bench. She turned, pretending that the girl in the corner of the back-most seat was a surprise.

"Hi," Rickie said. The girl looked at her with wide, dark eyes. She was young — in her teens — but not too far behind Rickie's twenty years. Her lips were chapped, her blue nail polish chipped. "I'm Rickie."

The girl opened her mouth, but the driver's voice came out. "She doesn't like strangers," he said. The girl pressed her lips together. Rickie frowned.

"She can't tell me that herself?" She spoke to the driver, but her eyes stayed on the girl. The girl's hair was oily at the roots and tangled at the ends. The girl grabbed at the ends, twirling them as Rickie had her own just moments before.

"Like I said," the driver said sternly, "she doesn't like strangers."

Rickie met Felix's eyes, then asked the driver, "Is she your daughter?"

The girl looked nothing like him, all dark eyes and hair where he was light, blond. The driver hesitated a second too long before he said, "Yes." Rickie looked to Felix again. Felix exhaled. Rickie raised a brow. Felix looked at the driver.

"I'm Felix," he offered lamely.

"Ed," the driver said.

"Ed," Felix repeated. He looked to Rickie for guidance, but she had her eyes on the rearview, watching Ed carefully.

"I can't take you far," Ed said.

"You don't like strangers either," Rickie said. Her eyes were intense in the mirror, but Ed refused to meet them. He kept his eyes sternly on the road. He shrugged.

"Not much," he said.

"Is that why you drove away from us?" Rickie said.

"Didn't even see you," Ed lied. Rickie narrowed her eyes, but Ed still refused to look. He checked the rearview only when she turned to look at the girl in the backseat. Subtly, the girl shook her head. Ed's grip on the steering wheel tightened. Felix watched Ed's knuckles turn white.

Rickie smiled at the girl. The girl shrank back.

"What's your name?" Rickie asked.

The bus lurched — a hard stop. Rickie's breath stuck in her throat as she collided with the back of the driver's seat, hard. The girl went rigid. Felix's arm hit the back of the passenger door with a loud thwack!

Rickie raised her eyes to the mirror to find Ed looking at her.

"Sorry," he said, but Rickie knew that he wasn't.

"It's fine," Rickie said evenly.

"You two might be better walking," Ed said. "With traffic, and all."

"Like I said," Rickie said, mimicking his tone, "it's hot." 95 degrees and somehow climbing, the sun high and strong, no breeze or clouds for relief. Rickie let her gaze slip to the window. Outside, heat rose off the pavement in hazy waves. "We appreciate the ride," she said.

Ed said nothing.

Rickie unzipped her backpack, reached inside. She felt Ed's eyes flick to her. "Smoke?" she asked, plucking out the Camels. She shook four cigarettes out and handed two to Felix, who poised one between his teeth and offered the second to Ed.

Ed took it. Rickie handed the third to the girl, who warily accepted. Felix produced a lighter from his pocket, lit his and Ed's cigarettes before passing the lighter back to Rickie. She lit her own, then handed it the girl. The girl turned her unlit cigarette over and over in her hands. She looked at the lighter, then shook her head.

Rickie shrugged. She unzipped a side pocket on her backpack, slipped the lighter inside but left the compartment open. "Where are you two headed?" she asked.

"Home," Ed said.

"Where's that?" Rickie asked.

"Not too far," Ed said. "I'll have to drop you somewhere."

"That's fine," said Rickie. She flicked gray ash onto the floor of the bus, crushed it into the carpet with the heel of her boot. She looked at the girl, smiling. "What's your daughter's name?" she asked Ed. She didn't turn to him, but could feel him watching her. She could feel Felix's eyes, too.

Ed was quiet for a long time. Then he said, "I don't need a stranger knowing our business."

Rickie looked past him through the front windshield. The traffic was letting up, the right lane opening again. Cars drifted past the white dotted line, exhaust fumes rising from their tailpipes as their engines rumbled back to life. Absently, without looking, Rickie slipped her hand into the open pocket of her backpack. Felix followed the movement, but snapped his gaze back toward the road when he caught Rickie's warning look.

"Turn left up here," Rickie said.

"'Excuse me?" said Ed.

"I know a place up here," Rickie said, gesturing at the turning lane with the glowing end of her cigarette. "You can drop us there."

"I'm not going out of my—"

"It's right off the turn," Rickie interrupted. She scooted forward on the bench seat until she was right at the edge, her nicotine breath on Ed's skin. She saw little bumps rise up on his neck when she exhaled a cloud of gray. "Right up here."

Ed turned. He looked at Rickie in the rearview. She stayed quiet, letting him pass one right turn and then another. "Right here," she said, nodding to the right. Ed turned again, and before he could register the alley for what it was — dark, empty — Rickie crushed the lit end of her cigarette into his neck.

"What the fu—" Ed started, gasping at the burn. In one swift motion, Rickie pulled a switchblade from her backpack and flicked it open. She pressed herself against the back of Ed's seat, wrapped her arm around him and sliced the blade against his throat.

The angle was off — the cut, shallow. Blood oozed from the open slit. "You fucking bitch," Ed choked. His hands flew off the wheel. and grabbed at Rickie's arms. Instinctively, Felix grabbed the wheel. The bus jerked from side to side. The girl in the backseat screamed, a strangled sort of sound. She ducked down, her head in her hands, hands pressed against the cushion.

Rickie pulled herself forward, forward, forward — let Ed's struggling help her, let his scrambling pin her to the back of the driver's seat. The knife poked at Ed's throat, a knick here, a cut there, until she pressed it firm against his Adam's apple.

"You fucking bastard," she said, teeth gritted, and she pointed the tip of the blade in towards his body as she dragged it clean across his neck.

His howling turned to guttural, gargling gurgles. Rickie could feel the thrumming of his pulse, could feel it slow. He coughed, choked, sputtered.

"Grab it," Rickie told Felix, her eyes on Ed's dropped Camel. Felix did. He grabbed it and snuffed it out in the ashtray so fast the embers flew up and sparked against his fingertips. Ed's foot dropped like a lead weight on the accelerator one second before Felix yanked at the emergency break. The tires squealed. The scent of burning rubber rose into the air, nauseating. The bus jerked forward, then back.

Rickie fell against the seat, her switchblade falling.

She smiled.

"What the hell," Felix said. He was gasping for breath. He stammered and stuttered And then, louder, more high pitched, "What the hell?!"

Rickie ignored him. She twisted in her seat, peered into the back of the bus. "Hey," she said softly. "Hey," she said again. The girl didn't remove her hands from her face, looking nervously at Rickie through the gaps of her fingers.

"Is—" she asked. "Is he—"

"Yeah," Rickie said.

"Oh, my God," the girl sobbed. She cried into her hands. Rickie reached toward her and when she made contact, when she squeezed the girl's shoulder, the girl leapt forward and flung her arms around Rickie's neck, crying, "Oh, my God."

They all sat there, stunned and silent. The radio crackled softly, punctuating the girl's choked sobs. "You're okay," Rickie told her, whispering against her hair. "You're okay."

"Rick," Felix said. A thousand questions built up inside him, but he couldn't get any of them out of his mouth. They all lingered in his eyes. The only thing he managed to say was, "What the hell?"

Rickie didn't answer — not just yet. As the girl's crying dissolved into hiccups, Rickie pulled away, smoothed her dark hair back. Her thumb, slick with blood, lingered at her temple as Rickie lifted the girl's gaze to her own.

"What's your name?" she asked.

"Trish," the girl stuttered.

"Where are you from, Trish?" Rickie asked.

"Bronx," Trish said.

"Anyone looking for you?" Rickie asked. Fresh tears welled in Trish's eyes as she shook her head — no, there was no one. Rickie pulled her into a tight hug, repeating, "It's okay," until Trish settled again. "Take a rest for a minute, okay?" Rickie told her. "We're gonna take care of this asshole."

She gave Felix a look that meant he was supposed to follow her, and he did. They exited the bus and Felix helped Rickie drag Ed's body out of the driver's seat. They propped him in the corner of the alley, where, after Rickie fished a wallet from the pocket of his jeans, they left him — anonymous and alone.

"What happens when someone finds him?" Felix asked.

"We'll be gone," Rickie shrugged.

She handed the wallet to Felix, who counted the money as they returned to the VW. Rickie slid into the driver's seat, Felix taking the seat beside her. Rickie fiddled with the radio knob until a familiar melody burst through the speakers: It's not far, not hard to reach.

"Dude," Felix said. He held the wallet open to her. "There's, like, five hundred bucks here. And some change."

"Looks like we can save Scraps after all," Rickie grinned. She met Trish's eye in the rearview mirror. "You have anywhere we can drop you off?" Rickie asked, and Trish shook her head.

"I was working," she said, voice trembling. "He picked me up on…I, I don't remember which corner. I— I don't have anywhere to go."

"It's okay," Rickie said, calm and even. "Neither do we."

She looked at Felix, and he nodded. "You can stick with us," he said. "If you don't mind being a little aimless."

Trish smiled. "Thank you," she said.

Rickie revved the engine. "Anywhere you'd like to go?"

Felix shrugged. Trish looked out the window, at the faint shadow Ed's body threw across the alley. She closed her eyes, breathed in deeply, opened them when she exhaled. "I'd like to go to the beach," she said.

Rickie's grin grew. "The beach it is, then," she said. She backed the van out of the alley. Felix reached toward the console, turning the volume up. We can hitch a ride to…

Rockaway Beach, NY, July 22, 1978 - 8:32pm

The water is cool against Rickie's skin. She takes slow, steady strides until she arrives at Trish's side. Trish drops her gaze, watches the lazy waves lap up and down the shoreline. Her feet sink further into the sand with each pass of the ocean's gentle touch.

Rickie bends over, dips her hands into the Atlantic. She rubs her fingertips together and watches as the blood, long-dried, flakes off and sinks into the foam.

"Thank you," Trish says. Rickie looks up. She straightens herself, touches her wet fingers to Trish's temple, rubbing gently until the blood comes off her skin, too.

"You picked a good spot," Rickie says. She glances down the beach, where a group not much older than them erupts in raucous laughter. There are beer bottles stuck in the sand around them like little flags claiming the land. A bonfire burns at their center, the warm glow making all their happy faces look dreamy in the night.

"I'll say," Felix agrees, stepping into the surf to join them. He flings his arms around each of the girls' shoulders. Rickie and Trish link arms behind his back, holding him steady between them. "So," Felix says, tipping his head up toward the star-speckled sky. "Where are we crashing tonight?"

Trish follows his gaze. A wave washes up, and then runs back down the shore. They all sink deeper into the wet sand. "Right here," Trish says. She looks to Rickie, a happy glint in her eye.

Rickie nods. "Right here."

[August 17th 1995, Phoenix Plaza Amphitheatre, Phoenix, Michigan, USA]

THE KKK TOOK MY BABY AWAY
BY
KEVIN DAVID ANDERSON

The box was unremarkable, full of ash, bits of bone, and a few teeth. A decent undertaker would've made sure the cremated remains were nothing but fine gray-powder. But even in death coloreds didn't get the same level of service as whites. Calvin wasn't sure why he hadn't disposed of his daughter's ashes. Nothing in the box reminded him of the vibrant eighteen-year-old, heading out to the bus stop on her way to Los Angeles, her childhood dream. But three years later, it was all Calvin had left. He placed a hand on the box, sliding it a little closer, as a sheriff's car pulled onto his property. Calvin poured another whisky. If they were coming to arrest him, he didn't want to go sober.

Deputy Emmett Karl stepped from the car wearing street clothes, placing a Stetson over his thinning hair. Calvin couldn't recall if he'd ever seen the much younger man out of uniform.

"Hey, Calvin."

Using Calvin's first name like they were old friends pissed him off. Disrespectful, but not uncommon in Thankful, Alabama, a town that never acknowledged losing the civil war.

"Afternoon, Deputy."

"I ain't no Deputy. Quit, yesterday. I'm on my way to drop off this car, and then I'm movin' north."

"You drive all the way here to tell me your travel plans. We've never said more than twenty words to one another in ten years."

"Yeah, that's part of why I need to raise my kids somewhere else. It shouldn't be that way between…" He pointed with a folder he carried toward a chair. "Mind if I sit?"

Calvin wanted to tell Emmett to just state his business, but there was something different in his manner. He didn't have that superior-swagger all white men with guns carry like it was their God-given-right. Emmett looked more like someone needing to confess.

If a preacher's what he's looking for, Calvin thought. I can pretend.

Emmett stepped up onto the porch, and sat, his head hung low like a ten-year-old heading into the principal's office. He looked at the box under Calvin's hand. "That Linda?"

Calvin hoped to skip over the chit-chat. "I've never seen you on this side of town. Now, Emmett, why are you here?"

Emmett removed his hat. "Got nothing but respect for you and your family. You served this country in Korea and Vietnam. Took a bullet in each I heard. Hell, your daddy was Testigi airmen for god-sakes. It just ain't right."

"What ain't right?"

"What they did…" Emmett looked at the box. "…to your Linda."

Calvin's eyes narrowed. "The man who hurt my little girl is in the ground. Shot dead by your boss."

"Just a seasonal farmhand. A Mexican come up for work. He wasn't even in Thankful when your daughter…"

Even though Emmett sat in the shade sweat bubbled on his brow. "Sheriff killed the Mexican when we found out who really killed Linda."

"What?"

"Know the station Linda tried to catch the Greyhound?"

"Yeah."

"There's an apartment complex across the street. Real shithole, lots of break-ins. The owner installed cameras. The tape from that night ain't around no more but…" Emmett reached into the folder and pulled out three eight-by-tens. "I had these stills made." He slid them across the table.

Calvin saw shame on Emmett's face but didn't give a damn. He scanned the images. All different but they told the same story. Four men dragged Linda, into a pickup truck. The pictures were black and white, but they didn't need to be in color to see that none of them were Mexican. The confederate flag bumper sticker told Calvin what kind of men they were.

"The sheriff told me to shred this." Emmett brought up the folder and set it on the table. "It's all there. Identities, witness statements, the real autopsy report. I wouldn't read that."

Calvin took the folder.

"After I found out who had done it, I was ordered to sit on it for a day or two. Next day they shot the Mexican. Case closed," Emmett said. "You'll understand why when you read that."

Calvin flipped through the pages.

"I planned to take that to the FBI, a dozen times. Even chose a secret meetin' spot like that Deepthroat Watergate guy. Never went through wit'it. I'm good at planning, but piss-poor at follow-through."

Calvin felt sick. "Why you tellin' me this now?"

"I'm leaving." Emmett stood. "Been planning for a while. Now that my wife is pregnant, it's time. Don't want to raise kids in a town that elects a Grand Wizard for mayor." Emmett looked at Calvin expectantly. Seemed to Calvin Emmett was waiting for him to say something like congratulations for being such a socially conscious white-man. If true, Emmett would have a long wait.

"Now you know." Emmett put his hat on and stepped away. "What you gonna do?"

Good thing none of Calvin's guns were within reach. "You sit on this for three years, and on your way outta town, tail tucked, you gots the nerve to ask me, 'what I goin' do?' Fuck you, Emmett."

"I deserve that." The ex-lawman took a breath, then headed to his car. He opened the door and turned back. "There's a good chance they'll all be there tonight. Some punk-ass kraut-band coming in. You know the place."

Calvin nodded. Everybody knew the fucking place.

"Good luck to you, Calvin." Emmett drove away like a man who'd just lit a fuse.

Calvin didn't need luck. All the luck that ever come his way always ran south. No, all Calvin needed, all we wanted, was in a footlocker he'd brought back from Vietnam.

If ever the KKK had a clubhouse in Thankful County, it was Corkey's. Outside of town, flanked by longleaf pines with its backend hanging over a gator-infested swamp, the roadhouse catered to all kinds of assholes, Klan, neo-Nazis, neo-Confederates, and a group of youthful white-supremacist shit-stains calling themselves skinheads. Calvin had no idea what a skinhead was but the folder Emmett dropped off said it was a busboy, skinhead named Luke, that come forward to finger the men that took Linda. The poorly-typed report Calvin stared at, sitting in his Nova, parked a quarter mile from Corkey's, didn't say what caused the kid to come forward. Maybe a Sieg-Heil here and there was okay, but kidnapping, raping, and setting a young black-woman ablaze was a bridge too far.

Emmett was right though. Once Calvin knew who really killed his daughter, he understood why they'd pinned it on a Mexican. Poor S.O.B. But oddly, it was respectful. Most black folks suffering a similar tragedy wouldn't get any answers or an investigation into their loss. They at least respected, or feared, Calvin enough to try and give him some kind of closure. Even, though it were a lie.

Calvin held the four rap sheets one last time, making sure their faces were seared into his memory. Rob Packer, oldest of the foursome, sported a ZZ-Top-beard, was an avid Holocaust denier and hosted the most popular right-wing AM radio show in all of Thankful county. Nick Ochs looked clean-cut in his mugshot, but the thirty-four-year-old, son of Thankful's mayor, was anything but. He'd beaten two rape charges and served as the local Klan's Nighthawk, a position often overseeing the enforcers or Wrecking Crew. Kevin Seefried, fifty, and Adam Johnson, thirty-six, both served time for assault but neither had any known Klan association. But it's not like they advertise membership. There's a reason they wear hoods.

Calvin stepped from his Nova and realized he'd parked too close to the swamp. Driving in with his headlights off he'd misjudged and put his back wheels in deep mud. He'd need a tow to get out. Oh, well, he thought. Likelihood I'm coming back is slim. He tossed the keys on the dash, grabbed Linda's box and his gear, then headed to Corkey's.

It was near 2 AM when the band stopped playing. Its name, Stoze Jungs, was painted on their van in large Nazi propaganda-style lettering. From Calvin's vantage point he could see a small crowd still inside, eight vehicles outside, including the Nazi-music van in the back where the band loaded their equipment. But only one vehicle concerned him. The one his daughter had taken her final ride in. And it was there.

From a crouched position behind a stump, Calvin eyed the band preparing to leave. It gave him an idea. Most likely the back entrance would be left open, and that's where he'd enter. Without any idea what the layout was, he thought it best to move quietly, stealthily, until it was time to make his presence known.

When the Stolze Jungs pulled out, Calvin stuck the box and his bag by the stump and started his approach. It'd been fifteen years since he'd worn his fatigues, and they were tight in all the wrong places. But the combat boots, the KA-BAR blade strapped to his belt, the Browning-High Power single-action handgun he'd won in a poker game from a drunk Australian officer, and the M-16 he'd hunted Charlie during two full rotations in Vietnam, all seemed to feel just right.

He moved along a rickety dock connected to the building's rear, then stepped up onto stairs leading to the deck that hung over the swamp. He held his breath moving up the steps, knowing that if anyone came out the back, they'd bump into him immediately. The element of surprise would be lost.

As luck would have it, he arrived at the back door unnoticed. He could hear the jukebox in the main room, twangy, guitar blaring. The hinges on the door squealed like a pig, but no one could hear over the music. Calvin entered a hallway, bathrooms to the right, and what looked like an office door, closed, on the left. Straight ahead was the main room. Judging by the outside it was probably a thousand square feet. Lots of places to move, lots of places to hide. He moved down the hall when he caught sight of the pictures in the hallway. Some black and white, some in color, but all telling the same horrific history. Holding riffles like they were big game hunters, Klansmen posed in group photos over dead, mutilated black bodies. Just good ol' sportmen of the south, lording over trophies of dark-skinned men, women, and children.

Calvin's blood boiled. He'd always known certain white men considered Calvin and his kin nothing more than animals. But he couldn't imagine them feeling free and safe enough to take pictures like these, frame them, and display 'em on their fucking walls.

Pondering the grotesque art gallery caused Calvin to momentarily take his eye off the ball. The office door behind him opened. Calvin spun on a heel and found himself face-to-face with Rob Packer.

The fifty-six-year-old zipped up his fly like he'd just taken a piss. His eyes narrowed. "What'cha doin' here, boy?"

Calvin didn't answer, just glowered.

Packer's eyes slowly widened, clearly recognizing Calvin, and perhaps remembering why he might come looking for him one day. Packer took a step back, and that was all the confession Calvin needed. Fast as lighting, he unsheathed the KA-BAR and without pause, thrust the well-used blade up. The knife entered Packer under the chin then cut straight up, impaling the brain. With a practiced twist and arcing withdrawal, Calvin retracted the blade making sure it did far more damage on the way out than it did on the way in.

As the body crumbled, Calvin pushed it back so it'd fall into the office. He stepped in to the sound of a scream. A young orange-haired woman peered up at him with brown eyes. On her knees and naked from the waist up, she had her hands on the hips of a bare-chested man, a swastika tattoo across his chest. The man's pants were around his ankles but for some reason, he didn't bother pulling them up before lunging at Calvin. Stumbling, hands reaching out, he started to fall. As he did, Calvin dragged the KA-BAR across his throat. Swastika-man fell to his knees, hands clutching his throat attempting to stop the fountain of crimson exiting his neck.

The woman had seen enough. She bounded up and ran. Calvin kicked the door closed and she ran headlong into it like a cartoon character. Calvin grabbed a fistful of orange hair, pulling her close. He pressed the blood-soaked blade under her chin. "Your name, girl?"

"Jenny," she managed, lips quivering. "Jenny Cudd."

"Well, Ms. Cudd, way I see it, you got two choices. On the other side of this here door, you can turn right, head on out there and warn them yahoos what's comin'."

There was a sickening plop as swastika-man fell forward and hit the floor.

"Or you could turn left, tiptoe out the backdoor. Maybe live long enough to think about some of your life choices." He lowered the knife, then opened the door, slowly. When he let go of her hair, she turned slightly to look him in the eye. She was maybe twenty, twenty-one. Same age as Linda would be.

Her eyes darted around, unsure. Calvin gestured with the knife toward the door. Jenny backed into the hallway, keeping eyes on Calvin. He had no idea which way she'd go. Could go either way. But Calvin never relished the feeling that lingered inside him after killing a woman. In-country he'd done it one too many times, and although they'd tried to kill him, it never felt right.

Jenny took a breath, then headed to the backdoor.

Making better choices already, Calvin thought.

In the corner of his eye, he saw someone stumble into the hallway. Calvin stepped back and closed the office door, hoping it was someone heading to the can. The feet shuffled closer. Calvin could tell by their irregular cadence that their owner was drunk. The shuffling stopped outside the office door.

The man in the hall pounded on the office door. "Hey, Rob. You guys 'bout done? Ya'll need to leave some Jenny for the rest of us, man."

Calvin grabbed Packer by his ZZ-Top-beard and dragged his body onto the other younger, but just as dead, man. It would look confusing to anyone walking in, one white-man on top of another, if only for a moment. But a moment is all Calvin wanted.

The man pounded on the door again, and this time began to open it. Calvin stepped behind the door. The man staggered inside, looking at the pile of limbs and white flesh on the floor. "What the fuck you homos doing?"

Calvin closed the door. The sound of it caused the man to spin around, and Nick Ochs got his first and last look at Calvin. His free hand covered Ochs' mouth and he pushed him back against a wall. Nose to nose Calvin said, "You remember my daughter, Linda?"

The man tried to scream, and that's when Calvin sunk all eight inches of the KA-BAR into his crotch. "Yeah, you remember."

Slicing upward the blade got hung up on the man's thick gator-skin-belt, but with some elbow-grease, Calvin powered through. Afterward, it was clear slicing all the way to the collarbone. Ochs' eyes rolled back, going white. He was already dead when Calvin stepped back to avoid the splash of innards now free from their confinement.

He stood in the middle of the room, surveying his work. Calvin couldn't believe his luck. Although pleased with how things had gone so far, he was getting tired of this one-at-a-time shit. He cleaned the knife on the back of Ochs' shirt and put it away. He unslung the M-16, peeked outside then moved from the office. Plodding down the hall he glanced at the gallery of nightmares on the wall. Horrific, but it fueled his rage.

Walking into the roadhouse like he owned it, Calvin fired into the jukebox, grabbing everyone's attention, and silencing Lynyrd Skynyrd. He scanned the faces of the six men in the room while aiming at the man behind the bar, a fat-man in suspenders, slowly reaching under the counter.

"You the owner of this establishment?" Calvin barked.

Fatman's eyes beamed with pride. "Been in my family three generations." His hand clearly still reaching for a weapon.

Calvin gestured toward the hallway. "So, you're responsible for the art gallery back there?"

Fatman grinned, shrugged like it was no big deal.

Calvin fired three times. One bullet went through the neck, the other two the chest, severing a suspender. The shotgun Fatman grabbed flew up above the bar briefly before disappearing along with its owner.

Calvin eyed the five men huddled by a pool table. "Well, I'll be damned." Kevin Seefried and Adam Johnson stood amongst them. *With luck like this maybe I ought to head south, get one them lottery tickets.*

One of the nameless others stepped forward with a pool cue in his hand. "You're one dead nig—"

Using the SS insignia on the man's T-shirt as a target, Calvin released another burst. The man fell back into a table sending half-drunk beer steins crashing. He had thought to mow them all down right then and there, but before SS-man hit the floor, Calvin knew his luck had run out.

The familiar ping-clunk of his riffle failing to extract accompanied by the hot-gas-smell of gunpowder residue from a corroded chamber filled his nostrils.

Fuck.

The men rushed Calvin seizing weapons on their way, pool balls, cues, Seefried grabbed an American flag and pole, a black-swastika emblazon across the red, white, and blue.

He dropped the M-16 and went for his sidearm. It had just cleared the holster when three of them tackled Calvin. They went down in a tangle of limbs, fists flying. Calvin felt the barrel of the Browning touch crotch. He fired sending a slug and a set of testicles into the floor.

Adam Johnson, now a eunuch, screamed and fell back, both hands clutching the pulpy mass between his legs. A fist clutching a nine-ball smashed into Calvin's face. He felt hands grab for the Browning. Knowing he had only seconds before it was wrenched from his grasp, Calvin flicked his thumb up, locking the slide by engaging the safety.

Two nameless men sat on Calvin's chest, one, bald, tattoos on his neck had the Browning. He turned it around and placed the barrel on Calvin's forehead. "Bye-bye, Spear-chucker!" He tried to pull the trigger. "Shit!"

He frantically turned the gun around in his hands like a teenager with a Rubiks cube. Calvin chuckled, knowing it was only a matter of time before dumbass figured out the problem. "What's wrong, cracker?"

Baldy suddenly smiled as he found the safety. He turned the gun back on Calvin. "So'long..." His head jerked violently left to the sound of a gunshot. Baldy's noggin had a gaping hole in the side. He fell forward.

A voice behind them shouted. "Get off him."

With his one free hand, Calvin pushed Baldy to the side and looked over in astonishment.

Emmett stood between them and the front door, his revolver pointing at the other man still holding Calvin to the floor. "Emmett?"

Before Emmett could respond, his body spasmed forward. Something exploded from his chest. Seefried, who had chosen not to join the melee on the floor, had snuck up behind Emmett and impaled him with the flagpole, the red white, and blue bursting through his sternum.

The man on Calvin grinned. He turned his attention away from Emmett, who had dropped to his knee's hands at his chest. He drew a fist back but, in an instant, had clearly changed his mind about throwing the punch. Calvin, having freed the Browning from Baldy's dead grasp, pointed it at the man on top of him, and with no hesitation, shot him in the face. He sat up and met the eyes of Johnson a few feet away, still screaming and whining about the state of his Johnson. To shut the man up Calvin put two in his chest.

A blur of movement raced toward the door. Seefried, after impaling a man in the back, had apparently had enough. Without aiming Calvin emptied everything the Browning had left. Seefried made it through the door, but Calvin knew at least one shot had found its mark.

Calvin stepped over to Emmett and knelt. He'd seen enough wounds to know that Emmett didn't have long. Emmett's hand came up, and Calvin took it. "You're the dumbest white-man I know."

"High praise," Emmett said.

"What about your plan? Going north, startin' a family?"

"I told you." Emmett coughed blood. "I'm good at planning, just piss-poor at follow-through..."

Calvin felt the man's hand go slack. He laid it down, then closed the dead man's eyes. "Dammit, Emmett."

A moan came from outside. Calvin got up and moved to the front door. Seefried had at least two slugs in him, one in the left knee, the other in the hip, and he moaned like a baby. Calvin looked around for something blunt to end the man's whining, and something else caught his eye. A confederate flag hung down off the roof like a banner. Calvin ripped it down, spun it, making a hideous rat's tail. He rolled the crawling man over onto his back then plopped down on his chest.

"Tell me something, Seefried." Calvin wrapped the flag around his neck like a noose. "When you set my baby on fire, was she alive?"

Seefried stopped squirming for a second, eyes going wide. He then nodded, grinning.

Calvin then straggled him, slowly, staring him in the eyes until the very end.

Before setting Corkey's ablaze, he carried Emmett's body out. He wrote a quick letter to his wife and stuck it in his shirt pocket. She and Emmett's unborn kid had the right to know what he'd done, and that he wasn't a complete asshole. At the very least he deserved a proper burial, unlike the rest of them.

For two days Calvin drove west, using the keys in Seefried's pocket. Keys to a particular pickup truck. He stuck to back roads. It was only a matter of time before they'd come for him. He didn't sign the note left with Emmett, but he'd let Jenny go, and even though she probably didn't know Calvin's name, Thankful, PD would put it together. He just hoped he had time to do one more thing.

Exhausted, Calvin parked the truck right on the pier at Santa Monica, California. He grabbed Linda's box and got out. Moving down the pier he didn't realize how much he staggered. He hadn't stopped to eat or sleep, didn't think it was worth the risk. People cleared a path, especially when they eyed his blood-splattered fatigues.

His vision got cloudy as he heard voices around him.

"That's the guy they're looking for?"

"Think he's got a gun."

"Call a cop."

Feeling faint he moved to the railing. Leaning against it he tried to catch his breath, looking out at the waves breaking below. The sun felt good on his face. This was as good a spot as any. He took the box in both hands, as two cops ran up behind him.

"Drop the weapon!" one screamed.

Calvin had no weapon to drop. Just a box. He tried to turn around, show them what he held, and that's when the first bullet struck. It hit his back with a meaty thud, followed by a second, then a third. He fell against the railing. It wasn't the first time he'd been shot, but it was the most chicken-shit. The Viet Cong had the decency to shoot him in the front.

The box fell open as Calvin hit the pier. The breeze blew ash out over the water. "You made it, Linda. You're in L.A."

[September 26th 1987, California State University, California, USA]

THE CRUSHER
BY
SHAUN AVERY

He hoped it would be another short fight – short enough that he wouldn't have time for any of the weird feelings he'd had since the last one. More than that, though, Bud just liked short things. Like that name he'd used for most of his life now, B-U-D, just three simple letters. Like that song he'd taken his wrestling name from, full Ramones version, anyway, that two-minute-and-change classic by one of the greatest rock-and-roll bands to ever gabba-gabba-hey their way across face of the world. And like his girlfriend, walking across the ring towards him now.

Alice was a midget.

That was how he'd met her, many years ago. Live midget wrestling was not quite as popular as it had once been, not when you could see the same thing, and much else besides, online, but it still had its place, and a night after body-slamming Big Jack Crack into submission, a bout that had almost broken Bud's nose again when he'd just had it set the week before, he'd been up for a little downtime and so had gone along to a midget show he had heard about from Del Teller, another fighter on the circuit. Never had it struck him to ask, though, and little did he realise until he got there, that it was female midget wrestling that he had come to see. Nor that his breath should be sucked from his body when he saw one of the wrestlers . . .but that was exactly what happened, when she came out into the ring and he noticed she was wearing a Ramones T-shirt to fight in.

He hoped she won after that, was thrilled when she did, when she tossed her opponent over her shoulder, high up into the air and out of the ring, the other woman's face cracking on the ground when finally she finished her fall. At which point the surrounding crowd went wild, ran into the "ring," which was really just a chalk square on the ground, and some of them picked the winning woman up, hoisted her on their shoulders, cheering her, chanting her name in the way these fans always did, splitting the word in two: "Al-Ice! Al-Ice!" Seeing this, Bud, who'd been standing near the back of the crowd all night, trying not to get recognised, just wanting to enjoy the fight and forget who he was for a while, had to admit it: he felt a little jealous at this – at those people touching the fighter, getting their hands on her bloody, sweaty skin. He thought about just tossing a few of them aside, but he didn't think this would do wonders for keeping hidden. Besides, he was still a little sore from the fight with Big Jack, so instead he waited until the celebrations were over, catching up with the woman as she reached her RV, parked nearby.

She had her back to him, was standing outside the place, looking in her handbag for her key. He saw her tense up when he approached, thinking, perhaps, he was a crazy fan who had followed her. So he tried to appear friendly and non-threatening as she turned around. Held up his hands to show they were empty, said, "Hi."

"Hello." Her voice was neutral as she said this, giving nothing away.

"Great fight!" he went on. Not thinking too much about what he was saying, just letting his tongue roll with it.

"Thanks." Her tone was still defensive, the woman not quite meeting his eyes.

Bud pushed ahead, anyway. "Sorry if I'm bothering you. I just –"

"Hey." Her eyes were finally on his face, and he saw recognition in them. "Don't I know you?"

"You might." He shrugged. "The name's Bud." He smiled, feeling the pride he always did whenever he said this next bit: "But some folks call me The Crusher."

"Like the song, huh?"

"Yeah!"

"Cool choice." He was happy to see her flash him a smile. "You know it's based on a real guy?"

"It is?" He'd always thought it was just another fictional character, like Jackie, or Judy, or the legendary punk rocker Sheena. "Damn. Hope he don't sue."

"I think you'll be okay." She laughed, then nodded over her shoulder towards the RV. "You want to come inside, grab a drink?"

He did, and by the time the night was over, he ended up grabbing a whole lot more than just a drink.

Bud came out of these happy memories now, found they'd made him feel kind of warm and fuzzy, the way he always got whenever he thought about Alice, whether she was there with him or not. Which she was right now, reaching him as he leant against the ropes in his corner of the ring. Grinning up at him, then glancing around the place. "Hey," she said. "Sure nice to be indoors, ain't it?"

He grinned straight back, told her, "sure is." And it was. He was used to fighting in car parks, pub loading bay areas, out in the woods, basically anywhere that was outdoors. For this bout, though, his manager Max had managed to find a down-on-his-luck gym owner, who was prepared to let them use his premises for an illicit fight in return for some of the proceeds. Which was highly illegal, of course, an unlicensed, mostly unregulated bout like this, and because of this, they'd even had to use a secret knock to get in, him and Alice. Bud had liked that.

What he was less keen on, though, was the thoughts and feelings he'd pondered earlier, the one he'd been having ever since his last match. Seeing them take that young guy away on a stretcher, he had started to wonder, to ask himself if this was all worthwhile. He even asked his manager, Max, about it in a bar recently, hoping his old friend would be able to reassure him. But Max had turned away, changed the subject, so Bud had been doubtful ever since.

Some of this must have flashed on his face, because Alice, over in the corner, said, "Hey, you all right?"

"Yeah," he said. "It's just –"

Before he could finish, though, the door swung open and the gym owner began letting the crowd in. Bud watched them enter, and despite some of the worries he'd been having, he found himself getting excited, like he always did at this point. They lined up before the ring, some of them alone, some of them in couples, all here to see a fight. Looking so excited about it, too – so how could any of it be wrong, what he did to make them feel that way?

Then Max entered, cut through the crowd, stepped between the ropes into the ring.

Bud noticed how Alice stepped away as he did this. She'd never been all that keen on Max, right from the start, though this was never a problem he'd had with her old manager, guy called Norm. He was once the one to drive her RV between fights, getting a hotel room nearby to sleep in after her fights, allowing Alice, and eventually Bud, too, some privacy – a slightly different approach to Bud himself, as he and Max travelled to bouts separately. Norm, though, had been old then, in his sixties, thinking about retiring. So in his own words,

Bud coming along when he did, to take over the role of her travelling companion, was "a gift from God." Not sure he had ever believed in such stuff, Bud still got a kick out of those words, and the money he got from selling his own RV and moving into Alice's was nice. Plus, it meant their careers could sort of run in sync with each other – him at a fight one night, her at one the next.

That was how it had gone, these past few years. But now Bud was wondering if all good things had to end, and he was trying to work out how to talk to Max about it as the man approached. His manager got in first, though, telling him, "This is going to be a big one for you, my boy."

"Yeah?" Bud did a few arm flexes to limber up a little. "Who am I up against?"

"New guy," Max said.

"Yeah?"

"Yeah."

"Where's his manager?"

"He doesn"t have one." But Max seemed to be looking everywhere but at him as he said this, and that made Bud wonder.

Alice, too, it seemed. "He's freelance?"

Max shrugged. "Sort of."

Bud was about to ask more, not satisfied by this response. But that was when the gym door swung open, and the crowd turned around. All of them gasping as one, and Bud could understand why. For he felt much the same . . . now he finally saw what his opponent would be.

This was how he saw it, too – "that," and not "he." Because the man stomping across the gym towards the ring, the awed looking crowd parting to let him through, was a giant.

Max, too, appeared impressed as he vacated the ring leaving Bud alone, as he glanced over at Alice he saw her shrug, a worried expression on her face.

Bud got that, understood her apprehension. But he could admit no fear himself, so he walked to the centre of the ring, waited as his foe entered the ring. Sized the man up when he finally did so, saw the man was jacked as well as tall – huge of chest and bicep, skin well oiled, like him wearing only shorts, socks, and shoes. Bud stared up into the man's face – something he didn't have to do with too many people – and searched for weakness, perhaps some fear of his own in the man's eyes. But there was none. Plus, it was strange. As he stood there, staring, it was almost like he was getting . . . lost inside those eyes. Bud didn't know why, but he was. There was just something about them, something sort of dazzling.

He swung his eyes towards Alice, who could only shrug once again. But then her eyes narrowed, and she nodded towards Max, on the other side of the ring. Bud tried to think about it, but he couldn't tell what she meant, what she was thinking.

Then his opponent punched him in the stomach.

Bud doubled over, coughing, and the crowd – many of them long-time fans, people who had seen him win dozens of fights, men and woman rocking Ramones T-shirts of their own in honour of him – sighed out another sea of gasps.

He nearly fell to his knees, almost bowled over by a combination of the punch and the crowd's reaction. That first especially, though. Wow, it made him think. *That felt like I've never been punched before.*

As he thought this, the guy threw another, this one going for his face. Bud caught this one, acting on instinct, throwing up an arm to block the blow, though wincing as he did so, body still rocked by the force of that first blow.

"Good . . . good move," he said, getting to his feet. "What's . . . what's your name, kid?"

The guy sneered. It didn't seem to suit his face somehow. "None of your concern." Their eyes met. "But I know what your name is. Max told me all there is to know about you."

Bud frowned. There was something in the way the guy had said this, something that hinted he and Max were familiar with each other before tonight. Backing off, he risked a glance at his manager, hoping for an answer on his face.

That was a mistake.

For his opponent then took the chance to grab Bud, slung him over his shoulder, getting ready to slam him to the ground. With a body as powerful as his behind the blow, Bud knew that would hurt. A lot. But he suddenly found it kind of hard to focus on that, was instead captured by the upside-down sight of something on the man's back. Two huge surgical scars, one on each shoulder. Red and sore-looking. As if something had been recently – very recently – removed.

Bud shook his head, blinked himself back into the moment, prepared for the pain of eating mat. But instead of slamming him, his foe instead dropped him onto his back, stood over him, saying, "No. Not yet, sinner." Locked eyes with him, and he was almost lost again. "I want this to last. Get up."

He did so, becoming slowly aware of Alice calling out his name. This was easy to pick out, as the crowd were strangely quiet, perhaps sensing, like he was, that something odd was happening here, something different. He took a second to look in her direction, saw she was frantically pointing towards Max, followed her finger to him, saw that Max had a savage grin on his face. But Bud was losing. So why would that be?

A savage smile.

Bud was losing.

Max told me all there is to know about you.

The connections were there, but he did not want to make them.

Still, though, these thoughts spurned him on, and he threw himself at his foe with increased rage, with more aggression than he had shown so far. Fought him across the ring, and though the new guy had strength, Bud had experience, and he used every trick he'd learnt across the years to even up the odds. Soon grabbed the man and lifted him and spun him round and slammed him headfirst into the mat of the ring – making the crowd roar.

He should have been thrilled, Bud knew. But all he saw was the last guy he had fought, being taken away on that stretcher to be dumped outside a hospital somewhere, and the hundreds before him. Saw all the broken bones, the bloody teeth lying on the ground. Asked himself once again if it had been worth it – asked even, in fact, if he were evil, for all he'd done – and snapped back to the present as he stepped away from the man, moved his eyes to the front of the crowd, where Max was standing, watching. He no longer had the smile on his face, had his eyes now on the fallen foe, who was groaning back there on the mat. Saw, too, his manager fiddling in his coat pocket for something, wondered if Max was reaching for his phone.

Then realised something else.

The crowd – long-time fans and new faces alike – were chanting out his name.

"Crusher! Crusher! Crusher!"

A smile of his own fell across his face, one he didn't even have to think about. Spun his head around to face

Alice, hoped she would be feeling some of this thrill of his. But she still appeared worried, and he guessed he understood that. He'd voiced some of his own concerns to her, found her a whole lot more understanding than Max had been. I don't want to give up, she had told him, still enjoying her own wrestling career. But I'll stand by you if you want to.

God, he loved her. But he loved the roar of the crowd, too – for now, at least – and as they continued to chant his name:

"Crusher! Crusher! Crusher!"

He let the moment take him, and he leapt up onto the ropes, supporting his weight between them, and yelled back to the crowd:

"I'm the Crusher! I'm the King of the Ring!"

Then heard movement behind him, and made to jump back down, to finish off his foe.

But it was too late.

The opponent was up, and as Bud turned . . .

A punch took him in the back. But it was like no other punch Bud had ever received, even more than the first one he'd received this bout. This one seemed to snap him apart, to break his whole body . . . and not just his body, but everything inside of it, too. And there was a flash of light as the blow connected, and he didn't know how that could be but it was, and his opponent saw it, too, both of them blinded for a second, and he felt himself falling back, and it was like everything was moving in slow motion as he tumbled back towards the mat, and he saw his foe standing back, an amazed look on his face, and it was like he was moving in slow motion, too. And then Alice was running across the ring towards him, and Max was on the move, too, and . . .

And then the man was speaking.

"I . . . I see now," he was saying. "I see your friend lied to me."

Bud found he could suddenly stand again, did so, then stared around in confusion, saw everyone else in the gym seemed to be frozen.

"No," the man said. "Not frozen. We're just moving on a different plane to them, that's all."

"What? What are you talking about?" Bud returned his gaze forward, stared at the man. "What are you?"

"It's hard to explain," came the reply. "I guess I'm what you'd call an angel."

"An . . . an angel?"

"That's right."

"So how'd you end up here, fighting me?"

"I was . . . captured," he said. "Some bad people I was hunting caught me, used demonic magic to erase my memory of what I was." Their eyes met. "That was when your friend bought me."

"Why? Just to fight me?"

The man – the angel – gave a grim little smile. "Not just to fight you. He was hoping I'd kill you." Then frowned. "Though I see now he has a back-up plan."

"But . . .why?"

The smile returned, more genuine this time, warmer. "You expressed some doubts to him, didn't you? I saw that when I punched you – when I hit you with that blow, I saw it all, saw your whole life. You felt guilt about your past foes, told him about this. He became worried you were going to leave him. That was when he decided to teach you a lesson, one I believe your kind know well: if I can't have you, no one else can."

"But you're an . . . you're an angel." Bud frowned, trying to make sense of all this. "Why would you ever want to kill anyone?"

"I'm an angel of vengeance," he replied, "sent here to punish sinners," Bud remembered the guy had called him this before, during the fight. "That's what I was doing when they caught me, hunting sinners. But they turned the tables on me, imprisoned me, sawed off my wings to stop me escaping. Then wiped my mind, knowing my need to hurt the guilty would remain, was a part of my soul that couldn't be erased." Pointed out into the real world, and Bud saw the people out there seemed to have moved a fraction, that Max seemed to be inching his way closer and closer to the ring, still fiddling in his pocket for that phone of his. "He persuaded me that this was you," the angel concluded. "But I saw differently, my friend."

Bud, though, could only hang his head at this. "What about the others, though?" he asked. "All those people I hurt?"

The angel shook his head. "All willing participants in the fight, Bud. You never hurt anyone that wasn't asking for it, or trying to hurt you back." He let out a laugh. "And haven't you taken one or two knocks from them in return?"

"Yeah, but . . ."

"No buts." The angel stepped forward, laid a hand on his shoulder. "You're a good man, Bud. Now prove it."

"What do you –"

But then suddenly they were back in real time. Bud was lying on the ground – but feeling no pain, in fact feeling good. Alice was standing over him, concern on her pretty face. And then finally Max was coming to join them, and he had finally stopped fiddling in his pocket – and what he pulled out was not his phone but a knife.

The angel was standing back, nodding, a smile on his face. Then suddenly he was speaking in Bud's mind: *that's his back-up plan. He plans to use that on you, then throw it to me – claim I cheated when you beat me. And you know how the crowd deals with cheats . . .*

He did. But he had no time to think about that yet. For now Max was crying, "Bastard!" and Alice let out a scream as she saw the knife, plunging down towards Bud. "No one leaves me!" he went on, rage on his face, dripping spit as he attacked. "No one!"

But Bud was prepared. Felt some power inside forcing him on, and he reached out a hand to grab Max's wrist – and with a simple flick, snapped it.

Max let out a scream of his own, dropped the knife. Where it very well could have fallen into Bud's face. But instead stopped in mid-air, hung there.

Bud looked sideways at the angel.

The angel winked.

Alice, stood there, saw this, eyes widening, and Bud thought for a second about what would come later, when he had to explain all of this to her. If he could.

For now, though, he kicked Max aside, and then he stood. His manager stood watching him, put a hand to his broken wrist, pain on the man's face. Bud ignored him for the moment, instead turned his eyes to Alice.

"Bud?" she said. "You okay?"

"Yeah." He gave her a wink, passing on the one the angel had just given him. "I'm all right, baby."

The angel, meanwhile, had grabbed the knife, was holding it up for the crowd to see. "Look what this guy did!" he was yelling. "Look what he was going to do to your winner!"

The crowd booed, turning ugly.

The angel smiled to Bud. "Your move, friend."

"No!" Max cried, seeing his once friend step towards him. "Please, no!"

But it was too late for denials, and with a roar, Bud picked Max up and threw him into the crowd, let them deal with him.

Then they walked away, all three of them, leaving the ring and heading for the exit at the other side of the gym. Where, still doubtful, Bud asked the angel, "Was that okay, what I just did?"

The angel rolled his eyes. "Angel of vengeance, remember?"

Bud nodded. "So what will you do now?"

"Find more sinners," he replied, and Bud noticed he still held the knife in his hand, seemed sort of attached to it. "Real sinners." He glanced across at Alice, who had remained silent thus far, seemingly still shocked by all of this. "Ma'am."

"What's . . . what's going on?" she asked, swinging her eyes between the pair of them.

"Ask him," Bud told her, still not sure he could explain all of this. But then he heard a strange sort of crack noise from the side, and suddenly the angel was gone.

"Shit," he said, hearing Alice gasp at this. "I'll tell you later, sweetie-pie." He hoped he would, at least, and realised with some sadness that would probably not be a short tale. "But not here," he added, as they left the gym behind, stepped out into the night.

King of the ring, baby, he thought then, looking back at the gym, at his past, one last time. That's what I am, what I've been. But maybe, he now told himself, maybe he could become king of something else one day. With Alice as his queen, the only one he'd ever want, the only one he'd ever need. So with that in mind, and hand-in-hand, they walked towards that future together.

Off to find whatever that something else would be.

[April 27th 1977, Faubourg Hall, Geneva, Switzerland]

7/11
BY
AMANDA CRUM

I met her at the 7/11.

Those were the head-spin days, nights full of rotgut and nicotine and afternoons spent sleeping behind yellowed curtains. There were three of us living in that rancid apartment, cockroaches in the sink and pillows full of forgotten dreams.

We all worked part-time shifts at the Burger King on Exeter; the Paper Hat Society, we called ourselves. Georgie walked home more than once with stray dogs at his heels, chasing the scent of meat on his cuffs. Georgie had the worst luck, man. Always getting hurt at shows, even the tame ones where the stage was just a little square of carpet. Always losing shit. Keys, money, women. He was a good kid, though, never said a bad word about anybody. When his girl broke it off with him, me and Pauly pooled our money and bought a keg, kept him partying for two days straight. He puked his guts out. Pauly said, Hey, at least you're not thinkin' about that skag while you're pukin'. And he was right. That was the thing about Pauly; he was the wildest of us and had never had a real girlfriend, just a succession of chicks who liked to party, but somehow he gave the best relationship advice.

Me, I was a loner. Girls meant drama, girls meant feelings. Even the party girls who came home with them from the club always wanted to stick around and talk afterward. I didn't want no part of it. I just wanted to play guitar. It was all I thought about whenever I had to do something else. I'd be shuffling fries into cardboard boxes and playing "*Bruise Me*" in my head, I'd write riffs behind my eyes when I laid down at night. Pauly and Georgie, they loved to play too, but it was a different kind of love. Pauly wanted attention. Georgie wanted girls. I just wanted the beat.

But that day at the 7/11, I felt something shift. It wasn't like riding the Thunderbolt at Coney Island. More like when you're listening to a good song in the car and something sounds off, but you can't place it until someone fixes the treble. Something about her made me want to stand near with my arms outstretched, a human shield. She was short, that was part of it, but I think it was because of her eyes. They were real dark. Sweet. Like my third grade teacher, Miss Ellis.

She was watching some kids play Space Invaders, so I walked over with my hands shoved in my back pockets. I was wearing my best shirt, a ripped-up Ramones tee that showed off the tattoo on my bicep, and I saw her notice it right away. She smiled a little and looked back at the game, ignored me. I was a goner.

"You got next game?" I asked.

She shook her head, glossy brown hair feathered into a halo, and laughed. "I just like to watch."

I slapped a quarter on the machine and waited my turn, ready to show her how it was done, but when I took my place at the controls I caught a whiff of her perfume and it nearly did me in. She smelled like the good part of the beach, the clean part where the sand is warm and the water is clear. I looked at her from the corner of my eye and she was smiling, not looking at the screen at all.

"What's your name?" I asked.

"Dawn."

"Dawn," I repeated, rolling it around on my tongue. It suited her. "I'm Mike."

"Hi, Mike," she said. There was a tiny silver foil star on her cheek, a celestial beauty mark. I fought away the urge to kiss it, just barely. "You got a car, Mike?"

I did, but I was already late getting it back home. Me, Pauly, and Georgie all shared that rust bucket, putting a dollar's worth of gas in at a time. Long ago, it had rolled off the assembly line in Detroit as a Chevy Nova, but years of neglect had left it nearly unrecognizable as anything other than junk.

"Yeah," I said. Fuck it. She wants me to take her somewhere, I'm not saying no.

"I've got some time to kill before I can go home," Dawn said, then leaned forward and whispered conspiratorially, "I'm supposed to be at a school thing."

Arrows slid through my heart. "You're in high school?"

Dawn laughed. "No, it's orientation for college. I didn't feel like going and I don't feel like having some big conversation about it with my parents. I'd rather drive to the beach with some loud music."

We drove.

It was coming on fall and the light was tangerine and violet on the margins, night waiting to swoop in and take over. We listened to the radio and she sang along to every song; it was the sexiest goddamn thing I ever saw. I nudged the car into a spot at the back of the beach parking lot, facing the water. The sun was disappearing in a spectacular display, probably the most romantic view I'd ever seen in real life. Or maybe it was just that I'd never looked for one before.

"Sorry about the car," I said, clicking the engine off. The backseat was littered with spare drum parts, fast food boxes, soda bottles that clinked together on the floorboard every time I made a turn. With her clean skin and scent like the air after a storm, Dawn was supremely out of place. "I share it with my roommates and they're kinda pigs."

Dawn shook her head. "You don't have to do that."

"Do what?"

"Be sorry for who you are or the things you have. I like this car. It's punk rock, like you."

I had never blushed before, but I could feel my cheeks burn a little at that. She tilted her head back, white throat a pale column in the dying light, and closed her eyes.

"Why'd you skip your orientation?" I asked, suddenly self-conscious despite her words. Too much silence had that effect on me.

She shrugged. "I just get tired of listening to people talk, you know? It's like everyone's talking at me instead of to me. Sometimes when I go home I put on my headphones and turn up the volume and just drown everything out."

I almost told her about all the times I did the same thing, but the words died on my tongue. They wouldn't sound sincere, I thought. Instead I said, "Shit, that's all they do in college. Talk. You better get used to it."

She turned her head to look at me, the corners of her mouth turned up a little. "And what makes you such an expert? Are you in school?"

"Fuck no," I said. "I'm in a band."

"I know," she said.

"Have you seen us play?"

"No. But I knew you had that look about you. I knew it when I saw your tattoo."

My hand went to my bicep automatically, but hers was already there. Our fingertips brushed and I pulled mine away, let it fall into my lap. She traced the ink lightly.

"A record album with a mohawk," she said, and I knew she wasn't making fun of me. I wanted to say something witty, but all I could think about was the feeling of her fingers on my skin. Suddenly her hand slid up my arm, across the back of my neck, into my buzzed hair. "How come you don't have one?"

I shrugged, tried to stay cool in spite of the gooseflesh walking up my back. "I don't know. Never thought I could pull it off, I guess."

"You could," she said, and I pictured myself with spikes like armor. Maybe.

"I never met a girl who liked music as much as you do," I said.

Her face was serious. "It keeps me dreaming. As long as I can listen to my songs I can imagine a way out of here."

"Is that why you're going to college? Because you want to leave?" The thought filled me with dread. I watched a couple walk up from the beach, shaking their heads like dogs to dry their hair, and wondered how many more days we'd get to swim before autumn set in. Summer seemed to get shorter every year.

"I love my family, but I have to get away from them," she said. I thought of my father and his fists, of blood on the linoleum in our tiny kitchen.

"Yeah. I know the feeling," I said.

She kissed me then, and she was warm and soft, and when she pulled away I could see the sun in her dark eyes. Like magic.

"Where the fuck have you been?"

It was a fair question. Time had sped away from me at the beach and Pauly was pissed, pacing through the apartment looking for his shoes. We had seven minutes to get to our gig at Shorty's.

"I drove out to the beach," I said, grabbing my leather jacket.

"Why the fuck would you do that? There better be gas in that fuckin' car, Mike."

"He met a girl," Georgie said suddenly from the doorway. His tone wasn't accusatory, more like awestruck. Pauly still cut a glare at me from across the room.

"Did you?"

"What do you care?"

"Girls are a death curse for bands, man," Pauly groaned.

"What are you talking about? You have a new girl here every other night."

"Yeah, for a good time. Broads like that only care about one thing. They're not concerned about how much time I spend with them, or how much money I spend on them. Girlfriends aren't for guys like us. The minute you show 'em you're interested, they'll suck you dry."

"It's not like that. You don't even know her."

"Lookit, you're right. I haven't met her yet and she's already fucked up one gig."

I'd known Pauly since we were six years old and we'd never had a fight, but I wanted to mangle his face in that moment. He seemed to know it and said nothing else, although I could sense more waiting under his skin. We stared at each other for a long time. Neither of us was willing to ruin a lifelong friendship over a girl, but that was the closest I ever came.

"Come on," I said. "Danny will be waiting."

The club was dark, loud, and smoky as usual. A band I didn't know was playing a shitty cover of a Sex Pistols song, but the crowd didn't care. It was Friday night, payday, and they were out for blood over a good time. Bodies pressed and writhed in a sea on the floor, sweat mingling with cheap beer and perfume. I spotted Danny in the corner and nodded; he was too busy breaking up a fight to yell at us for being late. The three of us made it to the dressing room--a broom closet with two hooks for hanging up clothes--and caught our breath.

"That crowd is fuckin' gnarly," Georgie said, lighting a cigarette. "Last time we played to people like that, I got my head busted open with a beer bottle."

"We're here to play punk rock, not The Carpenters," Pauly said. He shot me a look I couldn't read and jumped up and down a few times, his way of warming up.

When the music stopped we made our way to the miniscule stage. The cover band had disappeared into the throng, leaving their instruments behind. I kicked a guitar out of the way and watched as it was swallowed up by the crowd. I looked down into those raging faces, red and purple masks of fury, and saw Pauly watching me from the corner of my eye. Behind us, Georgie counted off and we fell into the music face-first.

I pictured Dawn and how she'd looked when she pulled away from our kiss. She was gentle and gentle things didn't often come my way, and I'd wanted to tell her but didn't. Some things lose their weight in the sunlight. Girlfriends aren't for guys like us, Pauly had said.

I pushed all that away. She'd do me no good up on stage. Instead, I focused on the chords and the vibration under my feet as the audience began to thrum with the music, forming thrash circles that seethed and burned with energy. I played until my fingers bled and tried to ignore the image in my mind of those dark eyes full of sunset.

[July 4th 1976, The Roundhouse, Camden, London, UK]

I WANNA BE YOUR BOYFRIEND
BY
VINNIE HANSEN

1971

Drew rode into Philip, South Dakota, on a Harley with red and gold flames shooting across the gas tank. Leather gloves gripped high handlebars and a battered canvas pack was wedged between his back and the sissy bar. He stoked fear in the hearts of parents and envy in the hearts of teenagers.

Because there were only two choices in town for coffee, soon enough Drew swaggered into the Park Inn Café, his tight jeans slightly flared at the ankles, stars running up the sides. He twirled on a stool. Shaggy black hair and brown eyes faced me. "Coffee." He studied my face for a second and added "Please."

I was seventeen, and I pleased, all right.

The ding, ding, ding of the bell signaled Mr. Rafferty's bacon and eggs waited on the pass-through—had been waiting there since the already-legendary motorcycle roared up in front of the café.

I placed a steaming white ceramic mug before Drew like an offering to a god. "Cream or sugar? Or anything?"

He flashed dimples. "Black is fine. But I might like some of that anything?"

I blushed.

Ding. Ding. Ding. Mr. Anderson thunked two more orders onto the service window counter, narrowed his eyes at me, and shook his jowls at Mr. Rafferty's plate. "Put a wiggle in it, Virginia."

"Virginia." Drew savored my name like a bite of the two-cent mints by the register. "What time do you get off?"

I tilted my head, my neck exposed by hair skimmed back into a ponytail. I didn't want to be easy, but this was Drew, the guy every girl wanted, even the ones with the best boyfriends. He was too old for me, and my dad had already cussed around the house about the "renegade hippie from Calafornyah."

"Four," I said.

Ding. Ding. Ding. Ding. Ding. "Quit your flirting," Mr. Anderson hollered at me. "Mr. Rafferty's eggs are gettin' colder than January."

I floated off to deliver the waiting orders.

Drew showed up at four and waited outside, perched sideways on his saddle and smoking a cigarette.

Seeing him outside, I smoothed sweaty hands down my pink uniform. I ripped the rubber band from my hair, yanking out strands with it. Shaking loose the sulfuric smell of the grill, I wished Drew had picked a different rendezvous, where I could pretty up beforehand, and where Mr. Anderson wouldn't see me hiking up my uniform to throw my leg over the seat. By tomorrow everyone in town would know, including my dad. But when opportunity knocks . . . .

Squeezed between Drew's denim jacket and the sissy bar, I lightly held his sides. When he tore out onto

Highway 14, I clutched his torso. The ride was terrifying and thrilling, my bare thighs gripping his pants, my hair snapping around like a flag and airing out quite nicely.

Fourteen miles down the road, about the time I started to wonder if I'd been abducted, Drew turned onto a gravel road into Cottonwood.

"Why are we stopping here?"

Cottonwood had a population of fifteen, a grain elevator and a steeple on a weathered clapboard church creating its sky line. The only operational businesses were a bar and a hall where the occasional country western band played. It occurred to me that he might be stopping for beer.

Instead he put down his kickstand in front of Grindstone Hall.

He looked around at the buildings sprinkled under the vast blue of Dakota sky. "It's like a ghost town."

We awkwardly disembarked and shambled around in the heat and silence. The prairie sprang green and lush around us, the clover fragrant.

"Back in the 30s my mom went to high school here," I said. "There was a bank and a general store with a post office."

"Far out." Drew wandered off the road to peek through a broken window. "The gutting of America."

That seemed like an astute remark for someone I'd pegged as blue collar, even if he did hail from California.

When Drew turned away from the building, a female killdeer pierced the air with a high dee-dee note. Her striped head lifted from the edge of the crumbling sidewalk and she ran in front of Drew, fanning her rusty tail and dragging her wing.

He stopped. "Is that bird injured?"

"She wants you to think so. She's luring you away from her nest."

"Seriously?"

I pointed to four speckled eggs resting in bits of stubbly straw parked in the concrete crumbles. The bird trilled louder, "Dee, dee, dee," fluttering its wings like it was a poor, helpless creature that couldn't fly.

I led Drew away so the bird could relax. Kicking a chunk of the broken concrete with my white tennis shoe, I asked, "Are you going to stick around Philip?"

He turned from watching the killdeer, his eyes big and brown and limpid. "I have more incentive now."

I was being sweet-talked. Not that I disliked it.

"I have a job at Little Scotchman."

Little Scotchman was the town's only industry. It built hydraulic ironworkers and kept Philip from shriveling up like Cottonwood.

"Doing what?" I asked.

"Welding. And you?" He lifted a brow. "You going to stay?"

"Just 'til I graduate. Ten months," I said. "But who's counting?"

"No time to waste then." He slid both arms around my waist, towed me to him, and planted his lips against mine. He was a delicious and dangerous kisser.

Our relationship progressed until I was strutting around Philip wearing Drew's jeans. They fit perfectly. He was taller but I was leggy.

On Friday nights, we slow danced in the middle of the Philip Auditorium to bad covers of "We Got to Get Out of This Place." The guys and girls on the sidelines cast us glances full of curiosity and envy, wondering why

Drew had chosen me. I was a poor girl—not prime dating material. And my dad was a larger-than-life character. Men played whist with him at the pool hall and listened to him holding forth at the Park Inn Café but they didn't want to end up related to him.

Daddy, for his part, didn't say anything about Drew and me. I was a girl, after all. The expectation was I'd meet a guy and get married, even if he would have preferred it not be a long-hair from Calafornyah. At least Drew had a skill and employment. He was an unknown, preferable, maybe, to some "goddamn uppity Democrat family" in Philip.

A common sequence for relationships in Haakon County was pregnancy, then marriage, followed by a life in the family business or on the family farm. That had been my mom's story, my oldest sister's story, the story of several seniors the previous year.

But I possessed a secret power—birth control pills. A doctor in Rapid City prescribed them to "regulate menstruation," and more and more girls in Philip suffered from irregular periods. I also religiously saved my money, planning to leave Philip the day after high school graduation.

Drew and I zoomed around on his motorcycle, drank beer, and had sex in his room at the Senechal Hotel. In August, before school started, with no malice or any sign he was tired of me, Drew announced he had to be moving on. "I'm sure a smart girl like you understands."

A romantic, he'd brought me back to Cottonwood for this announcement, giving our relationship a poetic circularity.

"When?"

"As soon as I can get together a little more bread."

"Why?"

He leaned against the red bricks of one of the deserted buildings. "Let's just say I was on my way to Canada when I stopped here."

There was one main reason young men headed for Canada. "Bad number?"

He nodded and pulled me against his body. I liked everything about it—the broad shoulders, narrow waist, the way we fit together. We cuddled. "Tempting to stay," he said, brushing my hair back and nuzzling my neck.

I couldn't have him sticking around and being sent to Vietnam on my account, especially since I never, even in our most intimate moments, envisioned "us" as permanent. My whole future hung before me somewhere far from Philip.

A small, nauseous feeling percolated up my spine. "How do you plan to get more money?" I wrenched myself away and stared coldly into his eyes. If he had any designs on my hard-earned cash, he could suck eggs.

He grasped both of my hands. "It doesn't really involve you."

I squinted at him. "What doesn't involve me?"

"The Park Inn Café."

I yanked my hands free. My history and blood soughed through these weeds, dried-up from the August sun. Both sets of grandparents had homesteaded here in Haakon County. My mother had "batched" in this ghost town when she came in from the country to attend high school. The first time I got drunk was behind the Grindstone Hall. I wanted to escape, but the Dakota plains would always ride with me and cradle me as home. "What are you saying?" I whispered.

"They don't go to the bank every day."

Just as most people didn't lock their doors, the café didn't worry about leaving money in the till, but I was surprised Drew had paid that any mind.

"You work nights on Tuesday and Thursday?"

"You know that." My voice came out full of starch. "So is that what our relationship has been about? A few hundred dollars?"

He snatched my hands again, tugged me to his body, and held me tight. "Come to Canada with me."

The offer made me smile into his shirt. That wasn't going to happen.

He rocked me in his arms and kissed the top of my head. "All you have to do is leave the back door unlocked."

"Okay."

"Okay?" He backed away enough to look me in the eyes. "Thursday, then?"

That Thursday, Mr. Anderson shooed me out the door while he was scraping the grill. "See you bright and early," he said.

Outside the August night was still, Highway 14 deserted, the black sky full of shooting stars. The temperature had fallen to a tolerable balminess. As I walked along our dirt road, a slight breeze drafted into the draw and the cottonwoods in Peterson's Dam sang to me.

When I reached our house, the only light on was upstairs. My parents, who rose with the dawn, had gone to bed long ago. I tiptoed into the front porch and snagged my brother's green canvas Rapid City Daily Journal bag hanging from a nail. Overkill, but convenient.

I walked back to the café. Mr. Anderson's car was gone.

What I had not told Drew was that I could enter the Park Inn Café any time I pleased. I had a key. On winter weekends after I post-holed through snow for a half mile at five in the morning, Mr. Anderson didn't want me to get caught outside waiting for him. It had never happened, of course. Mr. Anderson always had the lights on, the coffee brewed, and the griddle heating up before I arrived. Often a customer or two already occupied a table.

I unlocked the back door and slid through the dark kitchen—my path lit by gleaming stainless steel and muscle memory—the quiet broken only by an electrical hum. I peeked through the service window. During the day, Mr. Anderson had drawn the blinds on the big front windows and he'd left them down.

I crept forward, opened the till, and unhitched the bag from my shoulder. I stacked all the bills, then lifted up the tray and scooped out the big bills stashed underneath. Taking the rubber band from my hair, I stretched it around the bundle and pitched it into the canvas bag. I left the loose coins in their slots, but added the rolled ones to the bag.

Shrugging the canvas strap onto my shoulder, I picked up an order pad and a pen to leave a note for Drew.

You made it easy to say goodbye.

He'd imagined me as a sweet little girl. I was not.

Back home, I set my alarm clock. I'd need to rise and shine early to beat Mr. Anderson to the café and put the money back where it belonged.

[June 3rd 1989, California State University, Long Beach, California, USA]

S.L.U.G.
BY
THOMAS PLUCK

Stately, slender Joey Cucuzza was out in the dockyard for a broken container seal when he got the call. He let his phone ring in his pocket to piss off everyone involved. The yard foreman. The security manager.

Usually these visits were perfunctory, bullshit to satisfy management. Seals were tracked like registered mail. Everyone who touched the container was in the system. If someone broke a seal to rifle a container, they'd gotten the nod from bigger fish upstream.

But not this time.

"You gonna answer that?" Chimento said, examining the cut plastic ring like he was Sherlock with a flat top.

Chimento was the security manager for the company that operated the terminal on these piers. Joey was the union hiring manager, assistant to the dock boss. No union labor got hired without his approval. Which meant he had a lot of people kissing his ass.

And also that he dealt with a lot of bullshit when one of his workers did something stupid, like cut a seal and leave it hanging from an open shipping container door like a runny nose.

Joey took his phone from the pocket of his camel hair coat. The autumn wind coming off Newark Bay ruffled his styled, salt and pepper hair. The screen said "Ma."

Maddone, was more like it.

He sent her to voice mail. Bring bread from Vitiello's on Sunday, I'm making cavateel and broccoli. That, or somebody died, like your sixth cousin from over in Big Tree, which didn't have a tree no more, but a bus depot, and the buses parked too long by the corner and could you do something about it, mister big shot at the port?

Vaffanculo to that.

Joey snapped his fingers at the yard foreman, who was playing on his own phone. They had the area coned, but ninety-foot-tall straddle carriers—moving gantries that stacked and moved shipping containers like Lego blocks—rolled past them at speed. Step out of the yellow lines, and they'd cut you in half.

"Frankie. What's missing from the box?"

Frank Fournier put his phone down. "We're waiting on the bill of lading. And DHS. They got their fingers up our ass."

Homeland Security had a shack with mirrored windows at the exit. You could never tell when they were there or not. Most of the time they were playing video games, but they liked to hassle the foreign national sailors on the ships. The sailors loved going to the local outlet mall and spending money, but DHS acted like they were all terrorists, even though they had to pass through Customs to step off the ships.

"Scusi, Chim." Joey stepped around the barrel-chested security man to peek inside the container.

"What, you think the citrullo left their Waterfront card?"

Joey pulled on a pair of Solo Classe kidskin gloves, and gave him the Italian salute.

There was a gaping hole in the stacks where boxes were moved. Usually if something was stolen, it was smuggling. A pallet marked on the bill of lading as linens that were actually counterfeit Gucci purses—tourists in Chinatown still ate that shit up—with maybe heroin or banned Chinese phones stuffed inside. A smuggler operating without his boss Aldo's say-so was not to be tolerated.

Joey pushed a loose box aside. "Minghia."

The thief had left something.

A dark, dainty, pedicured foot dangled between two boxes. Joey had seen his share of bodies, but even a refrigerated container—which this was not—would have stunk like a butcher's shop if there was a body in it, living or dead, for the overseas voyage.

No stink. This croaker was fresh.

And blue.

Body paint? The foot was small, but not definitely female. Joey's own tootsies were pedicured inside his bespoke Italian loafers.

A murder investigation would shut things down. Bad for management, but good for overtime. It would also bring scrutiny, at a time when Aldo was in a vulnerable position, as New York applied pressure on the smaller New Jersey family for control of the docks.

Chimento was on his phone now, distracted.

Joey nudged the box, and the blue foot fell out of sight.

He conferred with Frank the yard foreman, who had paid Joey a year's salary for the position, and taken a street loan from Aldo to cover it. It was an investment, and the overtime had already paid off.

"There's a body in there, Frankie."

An eyebrow raised on his hangdog face, the low winter sun gleaming off his shaved and waxed mahogany skull.

"Get rid of it. I'll take care of the bill of lading." Joey found micromanaging offensive. He refused to depend on people with no imagination. Frankie would find a way. The vig on his loan would make sure of it.

"You got it, Mr Cee."

Chimento came back over. "My I.T. guys are getting the records and the camera feeds."

Joey nodded. "Call me when you know twat's twat."

Joey drove his electric blue Alfa Romeo Giulia Quadrifoglio off the yard, dodging straddle carriers. His phone buzzed again.

Ma.

He gave the car pedal and shot between a carrier's immense wheels, rocketing to a stack of empty containers where he could talk in peace. The straddle driver honked the air horn. They hated when he did that.

"I need you to get your computer from the attic," Ma said, breathing heavy, which meant she had tried to climb up herself first.

"Ma, that thing's thirty years old. It's probably full of spiders and shit."

"Your niece likes computers. She's all excited, and I want you to have it down when she comes over."

"When's that?"

"Lunch. I made cavatelli. Pick up a loaf from Vitiello's."

Minghia.

Joey skipped the line at Vitiello's because he could. A fat Nutley fuck gave him the stink-eye, but that only made it sweeter.

His Ma's place was in Avondale, the ghetto for Italians fresh off the boat a century ago. Other parts of town held columned mansions and classy, working-class homes, but Avondale houses were so close together you could borrow a cup of sugar by reaching across the alley and knocking on your neighbor's kitchen window.

The one-way streets were like bowling lanes. He parked on the sidewalk in front of the green aluminum-sided house, and waved to her neighbor, an old man pushing a manual lawnmower, wearing black loafers, knee-high black socks, and a guinea tee foxed with sweat at the armpits.

The screen door slammed behind him. Ma wouldn't let him send a guy to fix it. "I want to hear if someone comes to slit my throat," was her reasoning.

His mother stirred a pot on the stove in her housecoat, and 'Joey Ramone' slouched at the Formica-topped kitchen table, thumbing a phone.

"Hey, Unc."

His niece Nicolina had grown like a weed.

To be fair, he couldn't remember when he'd last seen her. Which was a disgrace on his part. He was her godfather. He sent cash for every occasion, but after she hit double digits in age, he'd been scarce. Kids were a pain in the ass once they stopped thinking the sun shined out of yours.

"Hey yourself," he said.

"Hay is for horses," Nicky said. "That's what you used to tell me." She neighed, then snorted at herself. She wore black Chuck Taylors, jeans shredded at the knees—and not bought that way—and a black tee-shirt emblazoned with some internet thing. And her hair was pure Joey Ramone. Her face was a mystery behind the mop.

"I did, didn't I?"

The Ramones. He hadn't listened to them since he was her age. The songs all came back. Catchy as fuck, funny and weird. When you listened to The Ramones, you were a Ramone. Inducted into their black leather, denim, and white tee-shirt bizarro army of street commandos who just wanted something to do, to sniff some glue, to be sedated, and who didn't want to hang around with you or to go down in the basement.

He grinned, despite himself.

There was a computer connection. It tickled at the back of his brain. Airplane glue and amyls had killed the cells that harbored that memory. Gay clubs in the '80s were a superfund site of nose chemicals.

Ma set out a serving bowl of cavatelli pasta and broccoli florets swimming in broth with whole cloves of garlic. He tore the heel off the Vitiello's loaf and dunked it right in the juice.

They ate in silence and mopped their plates with the bread. It was so good that the kid even put down her phone.

The attic was a crypt.

Nicky crawled up first, like a denim-leather walking stick. "This is like a museum. Or House of the Rock."

Joey had undressed to his undershirt and a pair of his old man's sweatpants that remained in his dresser, with the rest of his clothes, twenty years after his death. They had been washed recently. Ma didn't miss the old bastard any more than Joey did, but she hewed to routine.

The kid was right. There were clothes and decor from the '70s crammed up here. A vintage store owner would cream their capris.

"She doesn't throw out anything," Joey said, hunching beneath the pitched ceiling, avoiding the exposed nails. "Which is good for us black sheep, right?"

Nicky smiled. "She offered to patch my jeans."

"She used to sew band patches on my stolen motorcycle jacket, back in the day. It's probably up here somewhere."

Her eyes lit up. "Really?"

"Let's find the computer first."

Rooting through his past was both nostalgic and depressing. Like shoveling your own shit. But the kid raised his spirits, asking what the "hecc" was up with his dad's platform ankle boots, and oohing at the fondue pot.

Joey's own uncle, mother's side, had run gay bars in Manhattan for the Jewish mob. He'd bought the fondue set off the back of a truck, because his Ma wanted to try some recipes from a magazine. Except instead of the Scandinavian cheeses, she used aged provolone and mozzarella from the deli. The whole house smelled like feet. But they ate it in silence, spearing toasted pieces of Vitiello's bread on the skewers.

"Next time," his uncle said, "instead of fondue, let's fon-don't."

Joey laughed to himself.

"What's so funny? This stuff is amazing."

"Just memories. Here we go. The Atari." He pulled out a dusty cardboard box with pictures of a smiling white family, all staring at a little television screen connected to a black and white keyboard. The screen was painted with a space nebula, from which numbers, space ships, footballs, and letters flowed out. Not the white on blue screen with the block cursor—blinking for you to make shit happen—that you would actually see.

That blue screen held infinite possibilities, when he was a Nicky's age. Even if the world didn't.

Nicky brushed off the dust. "So cool!"

Downstairs, they went through the contents. Joey held up the converter that once connected it to his old 11-inch portable TV. "You're gonna need to find an antique shop to play this thing."

"No biggie, the instructions are all the internet."

Joey's phone buzzed. He walked into the tiny, chain-link-fenced yard to talk. He walked a circle around the stone bird bath.

"Mister Cee, you're not gonna believe this," Frankie said, over the wind. "I sent photos."

Joey flipped through his roll. The naked body was spread out like it was making an asphalt snow angel. A vibrant, dark blue, like those paintings by Klein. The only hair was a white Tina Turner wig.

Disgraciata.

"It's a sex doll," Frankie laughed. "The uh, detail is amazing."

"I hope you wore gloves."

"Yeah, it's nasty. Someone had a good time with Lady Blue and didn't even throw her a wash rag."

"Blue? Why is she fucking blue?"

"She's gotta be cold."

"Stick her in storage, for now. This gets out, I'm going on the warpath." Men were worse than the old Italian women of this neighborhood with the gossip.

"Okay, Mister Cee. I gotta go. DHS is sniffing around. Someone put a bug up their ass."

Sfachim. DHS were tits on a bull, a useless show agency created after 9/11. Joey had watched the Towers fall from atop a crane, and he grew up with them in his skyline, but the amount of useless security enacted in their name gave him agita. They put in radiation scanners at the port, which only went off when a container full of cat litter or bananas went through.

They set them off, for whatever reason, and DHS was never there to catch it.

When Joey turned 45, his doc told him to get a nuclear stress test. They shot him up with radioactive dye and made him run uphill on a treadmill, trying to wear him out. He was in good shape, his legs would have given out before his heart.

Aldo got a kick out of it, called him the Hulk and made him flex. And Joey set off the radiation scanners for two weeks straight.

DHS didn't stop him once. Not even to fuck with him.

Tits on a bull.

Inside, he found Nicky sitting on the lumpy green carpet in the parlor with his Atari in her lap, in front of Ma's wooden console television. The one with the broken knob you turned with pliers. The flat screen he gave her sat on top of it, tuned to Turner Classic Movies. Sidney Poitier and some British kids.

He poked through the box while she opened the Atari with a pocket multitool, revealing the green circuit board. She began touching connections with a voltage tester. She had a fanny pack full of tools, and was good with them.

The box held cartridges for Atari BASIC programming, Pitfall, a few other games. A floppy drive the size of a bread box, floppies labeled in blue ink, in his middle school penmanship.

And magazines.

Joey Ramone's tinted glasses looked back at him from one cover.

He rolled it up and put it in his slacks pocket.

"It looks like the video output is damaged."

"Yeah, it blew up on me." He ruffled her Ramone mop. "I gotta get back to the port. There's a situation."

Nicky touched bits of solder with the tester. "Come on, Unc. I need parts. There's a place in Jersey City. And I haven't seen you in so long!"

The kid was good with the guilt, too.

Joey took Heller Parkway through the swamp to Jersey City, fast.

"This car is disgusting," Nicky laughed, from the passenger seat. "Every time you start it, a polar bear dies."

He talked to his phone. "Play The Ramones."

After a moment, "*Blitzkrieg Bop*" began to play. Good driving music.

He didn't want the blue broad thing to get legs. Once it got out, work would grind to a standstill as the men came up with gags and pranks and betting pools on whose goo was in Lady Blue.

"Polar bears would eat your face for dinner."

"They're smart enough to cover their noses when they hunt people," Nicky said.

Joey didn't know that. It was the kind of stuff he loved learning as a kid, when he was programming the Atari.

The Joey Ramone article had you program a song that never made it onto an album. You had to type the whole thing in, and it supposedly played a never-released Ramones song while a little blob bounced over the lyrics, so you could sing along.

What the hell was it? Some monster movie shit. He'd typed it all in and the damn thing broke before he could run the program.

She took his phone and played "Cretin Hop" next.

Gabba gabba we accept you, one of us. He'd rented *Freaks* from Curry Home Video once he heard that was where The Ramones chant originated. Watched it with his uncle. They always watched the Sunday monster movie, like *The Mushroom People*, or some shit with a giant lizard having a conniption.

"How'd you get into The Ramones?"

"Nonna gave me your records, duh. The Dayglo Abortions? Pretty gross, Unc."

Minghia. He remembered that one.

"*'Dogfarts'* is pretty funny. Before you ask, I fixed your old turntable. The belt snapped. You replaced it with a rubber band and wore out the gears."

Sharp kid. He let her talk.

"Oh my God, Unc! Clear your browser history!" She looked at his phone like it was a clown dick. "Who's the hottie?"

He grabbed it from her, swerving into the debris-littered shoulder. "That's port business."

"I was gonna say. Mom said you liked dudes."

"I do, thank you very much. It's a doll. We got some sickos there. They sit in trailers all day looking at porn." He slipped the phone into his pocket and wiggled his hand. "Apparently, Rosie Palm and the Five Fingers isn't enough for some of them."

"Gross."

He double parked in front of Gizmo's, the maker shop she had plugged into the GPS. "We gotta be quick. I need to find out who dumped Smurfette in a container. We thought it was a body."

"That happens?"

"Sometimes."

The inside of the shop was crammed with shelves of 3-D printers, trays full of parts, kits, and gadgets. The owner was a little geek with a beard and no chin, wearing a tee-shirt over a long-sleeve tee like he walked out of the '90s.

Nicky introduced herself with a different name, and they talked like old friends. They must have known each other from online. Joey remembered dialing up Bulletin Board Systems on the 300 baud modem attached to the Atari. Downloading porno photos took all night. But he wasn't hiding muscle mags under the bed where his old man could find them. On a floppy disk, they might as well have been in Fort Knox.

The geek pointed Nicky toward a shelf and she dug into the junk with glee.

The shop was in Aldo's territory, under their capo, Heck Costa. Joey walked up to the counter.

"She's a friend of Aldo's."

The geek gave a cartoonish wink. "She's a friend of mine, too. On the maker forums."

Joey took a business card from the register. "Keep the trolls off her. You have any problems, tell Heck to call Joe Cucuzza."

The geek's eyes were his tell. Joey's name had weight, even with citizens. "Thank you."

"So, what's on my niece's wish list?"

He left cash and told the geek to deliver the 3-D printer on her birthday.

Nicky came back with a basket of parts. "Some spares. Just in case."

Joey's phone buzzed. He left more cash, and he took the call outside.

Traffic had built up behind his car. People swore as they cut around it.

"I wanted to give you heads up, Mister Cee. They hit a whale."

"They what?"

"The incoming ship, from Maersk? They hit a humpback whale. The Coast Guard's coming to clean up."

That meant a work backup while they waited for the ship to dock. Men loitering around, too much time on their hands.

"Where's Smurfette?"

"That's why I'm calling. I put her in an empty, but 'cause the ship's not in, they put the yard on location detail, and they moved it."

"You lost Lady Blue?"

"I know where she is, I just can't get her."

"Call Del in Locations."

"He's still pissed he lost to me in fantasy football. He won't answer."

Joey sighed. "I'll call him. Text me the box number."

He called Del and got no answer. That meant he was up in a crane. An empty that got moved around with a rubber sex doll inside would make noise, and someone would open it. Then the gossip would start.

Nicky came out to the car with a bag. "Thanks, Unc."

He looked at his Tag Heuer Monaco. "You got somewhere to be? Wanna come to the port with me a while?"

"Okay. I guess." The kid had a good poker face, but Joey saw the curl of her lip, the little shine on the peach fuzz. She liked her uncle.

He killed a few polar bears getting on the Turnpike. Weird Tales of The Ramones kicked in, the newest collection. The Atari song was on the tip of his tongue. The Bluetooth interrupted.

"Frankie. I'll get there when I get there."

"You two-timing me, babe?" Aldo said. The dock boss.

And his boyfriend of ten years.

Nicky snickered.

Joey pinched her cheek. "Ow!"

"No, babe," he said. "Just dealing with that broken seal. They found a blue fuh, uh sex doll in there, but nothing stolen. It's gotta be some sort of play."

"The DHS is in an uproar. I don't need this right now."

"I'll take care of it, babe."

"You better, or tonight—" Joey cut the connection.

Nicky bit her lip and snorted.

"Not a word."

"I was thinking, Unc. Whoever's doll that is must be into *World of Warcraft*."

"And why's that?" He didn't ask what *World of Warcraft* was. He could Google it later.

"Because hottie is a dark elf." She held up her phone. A bunch of blue people with white hair and pointy ears. Except these had dainty outfits on. One of the guys was kind of hot.

He exited the pike and zoomed around the outlet mall and onto the piers. They passed a Himalaya of road salt being readied for the upcoming winter, and lots full of cars fresh off the ships.

"Is that like Dungeons & Dragons?"

"Kinda. Whoa, you're into D&D?"

"Back in the day." All the outcasts were.

"It's cool, you get to be whatever you want to be."

Funny, that's what he thought the kids growing up these days had. At least in comparison to growing up in the '80s. If a girl dressed like Joey Ramone back in Nutley High School, she would have been called a diesel dyke.

Joey's tell was a double blink.

Jesus, sometimes he was capa dosta. A hard head. How could he not see it?

If his niece wasn't a baby gay, he'd munch Lady Blue's buciacca.

But whatever Nicky was, he was in her corner. And she needed to know that. Joey's Uncle had been on his side no matter what. And that had held him together through the worst.

"You can't be what you wanna be? Who says?"

She shrugged.

He pulled into the container terminal and waved at the security shack. They drove past the mirror-windowed hut for the DHS goons. He didn't set off the radiation scanner anymore, but he drove around the security gate just to give them the finger. He cut across the yard, flashers on.

"First of all, you're you. And you are fantastic. Anyone tells you what to be, you tell 'em vaffanculo." He gave a conspiratorial lean. "Except your parents, them you just nod and let it go in one ear and out the other."

"And secondly, you're Joey Cucuzza's niece. That carries weight, even out in Morris County." He pulled into a safe spot by the pier, where the gray chop of Newark Bay spread like a hammered pewter landscape out to the horizon. "Don't you drop my name, but gimme that phone."

She handed hers over. He dialed his number on it.

"Now you got my number. Text me whenever. For uncle shit."

She grinned. "What's uncle shit?"

"Whatever you want it to be."

He got out of the car. The wind flapped his suit jacket. Out on the water, the Coast Guard had a tugboat pushing the whale carcass out of the shipping lane. He scoped it with the set of binoculars he kept in the glove box. One sailor was a woman with her hair tied back, arms tattooed in sleeves, as muscled as the men.

Nicky stood next to him. He handed her the field glasses.

"Whoa."

Sailors walked the deck with flensing knives, huge hooks on poles. The whale had been carved up by a propeller, and it looked pretty bad. It was good for kids to see the blood and guts of the world, with a loving hand on their shoulder. As if to say, it's bad out there, but I got you.

"What happened to the whale?"

"A ship hit it."

"That sucks."

"That's the price of global shipping. Those parts you needed, they were made in China. Nonna's cavatelli? We ship the wheat to Italy, they make the pasta, then ship it back. And it sells for two bucks at the Shop-Rite."

"That's crazy."

"That's the world. Until you kids change it." He gave her shoulder a squeeze. She wasn't as jacked as Sailor Sue up on the tug, but he had a feeling she hit the weight room at her school.

"You swole, girl."

She laughed. "Don't ever say that again."

"I was being ironic. I'm Gen X. We invented that shit. Or at least perfected it."

"So where's the uh, dark elf?"

"That's the question of the hour. Let's go find out."

He drove to the Locations shack. Gilly was on shift in front of a nicotine-stained keyboard. He had a head like a brick, and complexion to match.

"I need a box found and moved." He gave him the number.

Joey had given him the job. Not out of the goodness of his heart, of which there was none, but for the seventy gee purchase price. So Gilly would play.

"It's not in the system." He tilted the screen to show his work.

"Then I need the team on it." Locations found missing containers. The union had fought the installation of GPS trackers on boxes as a "security threat," but mostly because every terminal had a Locations department in charge of finding boxes that weren't where they were supposed to be. With trackers, they'd be out of jobs, and everyone else would lose hours spent waiting for them to find them. It was only a matter of time before they were mandated.

"Del's got the team. Nothing I can do. DHS says it's MARSEC one."

"And nobody called me?"

He went outside to call Frankie. "Nicky, stay near the car. Don't go out of the yellow lines, or you'll be a Joey Ramone-shaped pancake."

Nicky sat on the hood and played on her phone. He grimaced at what her Levi's would do to the paint.

His phone rang before he could dial Frankie.

"What's this MARSEC one bullshit?" Aldo said. "They brought the Port Authority, and I had to wing it."

When Aldo got nervous he ate. Then he got angry at himself and took it out on Joey, saying he didn't love his old fat ass anymore. It would be a long night.

"Babe, I got this. Don't you trust me?"

Of course he did. If Aldo didn't trust him, he'd be in pieces in the Meadowlands, with all the other people who'd lost his trust.

"Go hit the sauna, turn off your business phone. I'll let you know what's up."

Aldo rang off. His babe had a temper.

Frankie answered like he knew his ass was in the meat grinder.

"I was with the cops, or I would have called. They stuck something in that box when we were gone, Mister Cee. Lady Blue was a ringer."

"What the fuck did they stick on us?"

"A crate of Kalashnikovs. No way that was in there when we scoped it."

"This stinks like shit on ice." Guns came in all the time. Customs snagged them. These were probably taken from the Customs shack. "They lost your box. Lady Blue probably took a swim."

"Del ain't lost squat. I saw the box on top of a stack. Someone has her for safe keeping."

"Gimme the row."

Joey flagged down a straddle carrier, the three story rolling cranes that stacked and moved containers six high. He couldn't see who was in the bubble up top, but if they stopped, they either owed him something, or wanted him to owe them something.

"Nicky, show me how strong those jacked shoulders are. You wanna ride this thing with me?"

"Hecc, yeah!"

She climbed the ninety-foot ladder to the top, with him close behind. The ladder had a cage on it, so you could catch yourself if you slipped. Her Chuck Taylors handled the rungs better than his loafers. She was huffing at the top, but smiling, showing off for her uncle.

A driver named Imaya was driving the crane. She didn't have a vig with Aldo, but she knew the game. To be a woman in the Stevedore's union, you had to.

"What's this, bring your daughter to work day?" She was pure Newark, tough and proud. And ballsy enough to make fun with the mobbed up gay hiring manager.

"Leave the jokes to Wanda Sykes. Nicky's my niece, I wanna show her that you broads can do anything the swinging dicks can."

"You damn right, we do twice as much for thirty percent less."

He told her where the container was, and where to put it.

She navigated the rows with care, since her move wasn't in the system. Nicky gawked out the hazy plastic bubble of the control room, sitting in one of the harsh metal seats. "This is wild!"

Imaya rolled the straddle carrier over the row, and they felt the counterweight shift as the crane locked into the container and lifted it up. As they rolled out with the box, a DHS squad car came into the yard, lights flashing.

The squad parked diagonally in the lane to block their exit.

Imaya gave him a look.

"Keep going," he told her.

She sounded the horn and stood to get a better view. They passed over the car with a foot to spare at each corner.

"Star Wars-ed 'em," Imaya said.

Joey knew how scary it was to be in the squad car's position. Aldo had him pranked right after he made dock boss, to test his nerves. The guy probably pissed his pants.

Nicky missed it, looking out the window with the binoculars.

"I got a better place to drop this box," Joey said.

Imaya laughed when he told her. "You better keep my name out of this."

"Today's roster won't have your name on it, but you'll get paid for OT all next week."

She had to take a roundabout route to exit the yard without tearing down phone lines, but she knew the way. They rolled next to the DHS trailer and dropped the container in their squad car parking space.

Down on the asphalt, he showed Nicky how to open a container. This one was rusty, and the locks squealed as they cracked it open.

Lady Blue's lapis lazuli ass mocked them from the rusty corrugated floor.

The DHS shack door wasn't even a deadbolt. "And this is how you pop a door with a credit card. You need one of the good metal ones."

It took a few tries but he popped it, and sure enough, the shack was empty of agents. He put Lady Blue in an office chair, facing the computer screens with the DHS shield as the screensaver, and snapped a few photos with his phone.

Then he turned off the breaker to the computer closet, and locked the door when he left. The terminal I.T. department would get an alarm, and find Lady Blue. From his experience, they would have photos on the internet before dinner. And if they didn't, he'd get Nicky to show him how to post them anonymously.

The guns would be forgotten. The Port Authority would get a photo op. It was immigrants and drugs the government cared about.

It kept them working. Like keeping GPS out of the containers. A bullshit excuse to log more hours.

He got a security guard to drive them back to his car, and told Aldo the deal. He was predictably pissed that he would have to talk to the cops, but laughed his ass off at the diversion.

"Relax, babe. I'm bringing home my momootza's cavatelli."

"And Vitiello's bread?"

"Of course."

He told Frankie the play while he raced his niece back to his mother's house to The Ramones.

"I don't need to tell you that this is all between us," he said.

"Duh."

"Thank you for the skinny on the dark elf." She hadn't solved anything, but helped him get his head around things.

"Those dolls cost like five thousand dollars."

Something clicked. No one bought that on a government salary. He'd have to take a close look at Frankie and Chimento when he got back to the docks.

A song kicked up with a carnival organ sound to it. Unlike any other Ramones tune, it almost sounded like the tinny speakers on the Atari. Joey Ramone broke into a short sweet repetitive verse about a cursed romance with a monster slug girl.

The words all came back.

"You know this one? It's a rare demo," Nicky said, singing along with him.

Joey took the magazine out of his pocket and dropped it in her lap. "When you get my Atari working, you gotta type all that in. I gotta hear this out of those shitty speakers."

"Aw, Unc. It's probably on YouTube."

"Do it for your uncle. I've got a surprise for you."

They stopped at a hot dog truck parked outside of a cemetery in Lyndhurst. On the Christian side, Joey's father and his uncle shared a plot with space left for Joey and his mother.

Joey and Nicky took their dogs and cans of Chocolate Cow to a tombstone on the Jewish side that was covered in memorial pebbles and guitar picks.

The grave of Jeff Hyman.
May 19, 1951 - April 15, 2001
Loving Son and Brother
A. K. A. Joey Ramone
Rock and Roll Hall of Fame

Nicky stared in silent reverence. She held her hot dog over her heart, and her right hand high, showing the horns.

Joey took a bite of his dog, then did the same.

"Gabba gabba, we accept you," Joey said, and Nicky tilted to rest her head against his shoulder.

"One of us."

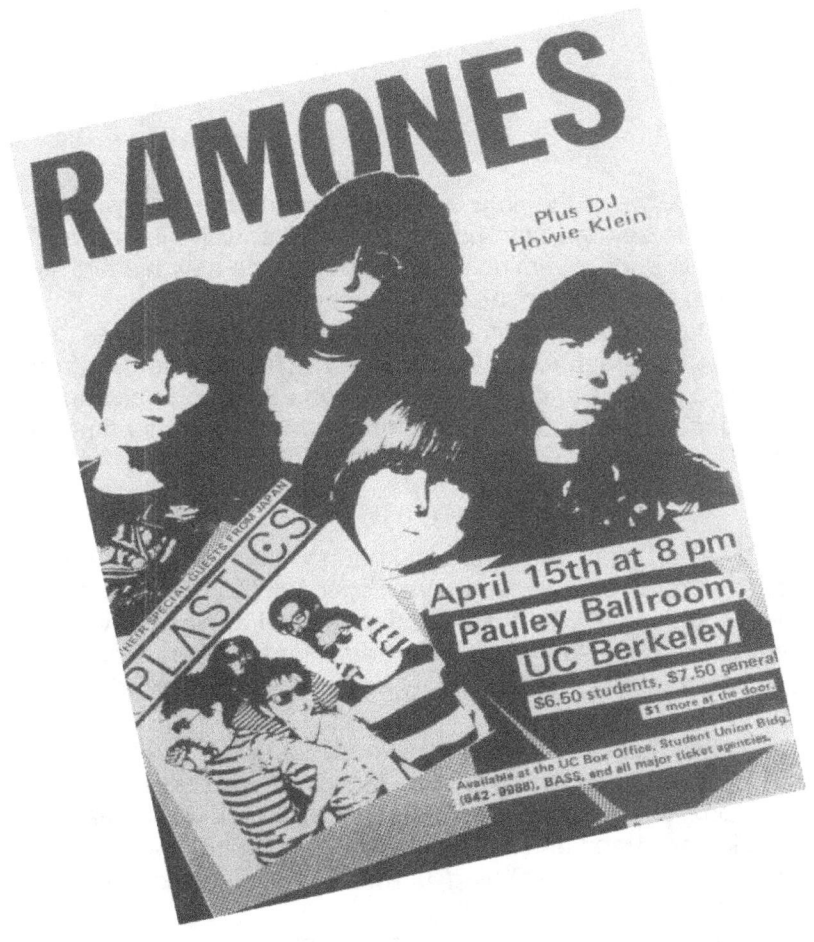

[April 15th 1980, University of California, Berkeley, California, USA]

DANNY SAYS
BY
HANNAH O'DOOM

It was only a couple of seconds between the time that Paul saw the bus and when it hit him. But in those two seconds, he saw his entire life. He saw learning how to ride a bike, with his dad pushing him from behind, he saw his first kiss with the girl next door at a middle school dance, he saw his high-school graduation, he saw himself standing next to his mom's coffin after she died. He saw Danny.

He saw every moment with Danny. The first time he saw her, playing pinball at the arcade. Their first kiss at the drive-in while a late-night creature-feature played on screen. Their first fight, in front of Danny's locker, when Paul tried to convince her to skip Algebra to drive in his old Trans Am to a punk show on the north side of town. Their first make-up, which led to another first for both of them. And Paul had time to make a wish in that two seconds; to see Danny again, somehow, someday.

The bus slammed into Paul.

It should have been a closed-casket affair, but Paul's mother had been distraught at the thought of it. His father insisted that she wouldn't have proper closure, so the mortician did the best she could.

Danny stood over the body, looking down. It didn't look like Paul. It was easy enough to believe it wasn't. It was some knock-off dummy made up to sort of look like Paul. Her Paul was off somewhere, playing his guitar.

A hand slipped onto Danny's shoulder and she nearly screamed. She looked up and into eyes that were just like Paul's, only older.

"He was going to give this to you for Christmas. I know he would want you to have it." Paul's father slipped a box into Danny's hands and kissed her on the forehead. "He loved you very much."

Danny looked down at the box, too afraid to open it. She was afraid it would make her heart literally burst out of her chest. She felt Paul's father's hand on her lower back, guiding her away from the coffin and back to her seat. From somewhere far away, she heard sobbing, unaware that it was coming from her.

Danny sat on the edge of her bed with the box in her lap. She stared at it, trying to accept the finality of Paul's last gift to her. It was small and square and wrapped in paper that Paul had decorated himself with doodles.

Paul had been rough around the edges. A wannabe punk rocker with big plans for a life in music. He also had the biggest heart that Danny had ever known. She thought about the first time he came to the house to pick her up for a date. Her dad nearly had a heart attack when he saw Paul's spiked Mohawk and torn jeans. Within fifteen minutes, Paul had her dad laughing and patting him on the back.

Danny smiled a little and wiped away a tear. She took a deep breath and carefully opened the box, careful to not tear the paper that was his last love note to her.

She carefully pulled a silver locket out of the box, gleaming under the light of the lamp in her room. The front of the locket was engraved to look like a record album. Inside was a picture of her and Paul, smiling stupidly at a camera from a booth down on the pier they had visited over the summer. On the back was the inscription "*One day, Idaho.*"

Danny closed her eyes, clutching the locket, remembering the day that Paul had told her he would eventually have the money to take her anywhere she dreamed. She had said the first random place that popped into her head. Without missing a beat, Paul promised her all the potatoes in Idaho.

Danny tipped the box and a cassette fell out. She inspected the hand-drawn logo, featuring the A symbol for anarchists. Paul had written the title "*Anarchists of Idaho.*" Other doodles adorned the front of the cassette cover. She opened it and slid out the cassette, labeled with just the words "*For Danny*".

Danny slid off the bed and over to her dresser and popped open the door to the cassette player on her boom box. And as she hit play, she made a wish to see Paul again somehow, someday.

The rough guitar riff and driving drums were exactly what Danny expected from Paul's band. They played in one garage, and then another, with speed and deafening volume. But the lyrics were soft around the edges. Even as Paul screamed them into the microphone, they sounded tender. He'd left her a love song.

Danny braced herself with her hands against her dresser. The air felt thick and shimmered before her eyes. Things started to spin a little and she shut her eyes tight and took a deep breath.

"Danny."

Danny stopped breathing for a moment.

"Danny. Look at me."

Danny lessened her grip on the dresser, still afraid that her legs might give out. She slowly turned.

Paul was standing in front of her, wearing his leather jacket and Mohawk. Danny thought to herself that she had finally cracked. The grief must have been too great for her brain.

"I'm sorry. I should have been paying attention. I didn't see the bus until it was too late. I'm so sorry." Paul held his arms open, his face twisted with grief and longing.

Danny stepped forward, into Paul's arms, and then through them.

"I'm a ghost, silly girl."

Danny stared at the ghost of Paul, still sure she had lost her mind.

"I can't stay long. Only as long as the song. But anytime you need me, play this song at 5:02 and I'll come to you."

Danny finally found words. Even if it was a hallucination, she had to say something. "I can't live without you."

Paul smiled a smile full of love and tinged with sadness. "You can and will live, and you are never without me."

The song ended and the boom box clicked as it reached the end of the tape. With the sound of the click, Paul was gone.

Danny sat on her bed, her legs crisscrossed, and her boom box in front of her. It had been almost a week since her hallucination. She had been afraid of playing the tape since that first time. But the ache in her chest was becoming too much. She longed to hear Paul's voice again.

She also couldn't help herself. She wanted to make sure it was just a hallucination. She didn't believe in ghosts, but still, if there was any chance of seeing Paul again…she waited until 5:02 and then hit play.

The choppy guitar riff broke the silence, followed by the driving drum beat. Danny closed her eyes. Paul's voice filled the room and the air began to feel heavy around her. Her head spun and she opened her eyes.

"Hi, silly girl."

Paul was standing in front of the bed.

"How is this possible?" Danny asked.

"I don't know. I made a wish. You made a wish. You said you wanted to see me again, somehow, somewhere. This is the how and where. But we don't have much time."

"I miss you. I miss you so much. I miss you too much," Danny said. Her chest heaved as grief tore through her again.

"You don't have to miss me. I'm with you. I'm cheering for you. Live your life. Live it big. We'll be together eventually."

The tape ended and Paul clicked away. Danny hit the rewind button on her player. "Come on, come on," she said to it.

She hit play again and the guitar riff started again. She looked around frantically. Paul was nowhere to be seen. Danny listened to the song as tears streamed down her cheeks.

"I've been accepted to Brown!" Danny danced around the room, waving a letter over her head. Paul leaned against the dresser, as much as leaning was possible in a non-corporeal form, grinning.

"Baby, I'm so proud of you!" He wished he could hug Danny, kiss her. But he was happy enough to see her moving on and growing. Danny was smart, and Paul had always been kind of afraid he wasn't smart enough to keep her.

The song started for a second time. Danny had figured how out to loop it three times back to back by re-recording it at the end of the first run. It gave them a little more time each visit.

"Me and you, we're going places!" Danny said.

Danny twisted the ring on her finger, her brow furrowed. Paul's heart swelled, and he wished, once again, he could hold her.

"Dans, it's a good thing. I'm happy for you." And he was. Of course, he wished it was him, but it couldn't be, and Jarred was a good guy. A big, goofy farm boy who had come in and melted Danny's frigid heart after years of mourning for Paul. It was time. She deserved happiness.

"You know that I will always love you, don't you?" Danny asked.

"Of course. And I will always love you. But this is a good thing. Live your life," Paul said.

"Can I still see you?" Danny asked.

"Always. 5:02, play my song. The ring looks nice on you," Paul said. The boom box clicked as the tape ended, and Paul disappeared.

Danny twisted the ring on her finger again and stared down at it, tears gathering in her eyes. She put her hand to the locket around her neck and smiled.

Paulie had been crying all day. Danny walked the floor, bouncing the baby boy in her arms, trying to calm him. His face was red from the effort of screaming. Danny was exhausted. She had tried everything she could think of to calm her son.

She walked up and down the hall. The grandfather clock downstairs chimed five times. Danny stopped in her tracks. Why hadn't she done it sooner?

She shuffled to the spare bedroom, Paulie screaming with every step. She went to the old boom box from high school that she had dragged to each place she had lived since then and watched the digital clock next to it. At 5:02 she hit play.

The guitar riff started and Danny swayed in time. Her son stopped screaming, staring in the direction of the music. Both mother and child could feel the air changing in the room. Danny smiled down at her son.

"He's quite the looker. Just like his mother."

Paul grinned down at the baby, standing next to Danny. She looked up at him, and how young he looked really hit her. His high-school carefree grin made her heart ache, and a little self-conscious of her harried, new-mother look. She hadn't slept well in weeks and there was vomit on her shirt.

"I'm not looking my best these days," Danny said.

"You always look perfect to me," Paul said.

"I can't believe I haven't shown you sooner. His name is Paulie." Danny turned a little, angling the baby toward Paul. The baby stared at the ghost wide-eyed and cooed. "He likes you," Danny said.

"I like him too." Paul beamed down at the baby. He stuck out his tongue and the baby laughed. For a moment, Danny's heart felt tight at the loss for Paul. He never got the chance to be an adult, let alone a dad. She smiled up at him. He would have made a great father, she thought.

"The name is a solid one too," Paul said.

"I named him for my first love." Danny smiled tenderly at Paul. She no longer felt the young-love passion for him. Grief, time, and age had softened her memories of them together in high school. Just a couple of dumb kids. Her feeling had deepened into tenderness, touched with nostalgia.

"The tape is almost done. Don't wait so long next time, silly girl. I want to keep tabs on this kiddo."

"I promise we will see you soon," Danny said.

"Keep living this great life," Paul said as he faded.

Danny sat in the swing on her back porch. It overlooked the little garden Jarred had planted years ago. She took a deep breath to inhale the sweet smell of honeysuckle. It grew like wildfire, and Jarred had always fought to keep it from overgrowing through the garden, but now crawled across the garden and climbed up the side of the house. The smell reminded Danny of all the summer nights she and Jarred had spent on this porch, drinking wine and talking, and now that he was gone, she didn't care if the plant grew over the house entirely. It kept him close in her memories.

She had just returned from dropping off her youngest at college. She was officially an empty nester and a widow. Danny watched the sun as it began its slow descent to set, and was filled with bittersweet happiness. She thought about the time she had left, and what she should do with it, and she heard Paul's voice. "Live your life."

"You should have seen the look on the TSA agent's face when they pulled this old boom box out of my luggage. I think he was all of twenty years old and I don't think he'd ever seen one." Danny was laughing, but Paul honestly didn't know what was so funny. How could someone have never seen a cassette player before?

"Look out the window, we are in Switzerland." Danny pointed to the large bay window looking out over snowcapped mountains. Below, lights twinkled.

"It's beautiful. But not as beautiful as you," Paul said over the drumming beat of the music. At one point, Danny would have blushed, but she was too old for such nonsense now. Paul looked more like her grandson than a boyfriend. But she had wanted to bring him with her in this last stage of her life. Her final adventure after raising a family was to see the world.

"Tomorrow we will be in Milan. I will probably be jetlagged, but I'm very excited," Danny said.

"Anywhere I get to see you happy is a good place for me." Paul smiled and the music clicked off. Danny watched as he faded away.

"She asked that it get played at the funeral, so we're doing it and that's that," Paul Jr. had said. Rosalie, his little sister, had balked at the idea of closing out their mother's funeral by playing some old musty tape. She was shocked that it, and the cassette player they had found in their mom's bedroom, even still worked. She had listened to the tape, its sound weak and wobbly from age, of some song that looped over and over that sounded like some high school kid's garage band.

Even though she had wanted to honor her mother's wishes, she thought this request had maybe been a touch of dementia setting in. Closing out the funeral with a song was a nice idea, but this? She couldn't understand. But her brother had got his way, and as the people in the pews stood to file out of the funeral home, he watched the clock, and at 5:02, he clicked on the cassette player.

"Hey there, silly girl."

Danny could feel Paul standing right behind her. She turned to look at him.

"It was a really nice service," Danny said. Her eyes, now bright with the gleam of youth, were filled with tears, but she smiled.

"You were very much loved," Paul said. She had felt him enter the room when the music started. It was an odd sensation to feel it this way, after all these years, on the other side. He laid a hand on her shoulder and she turned, thrilled to throw herself in his arms.

"You look like the day we met," Paul said, smiling down at her.

"I'm going to miss them the most," Danny said, watching her children linger as the crowd thinned.

"You can always visit them."

"And I will. But for now, I would like to spend some time with you." Danny smiled up at Paul and linked her fingers in his, waiting for the end of the song.

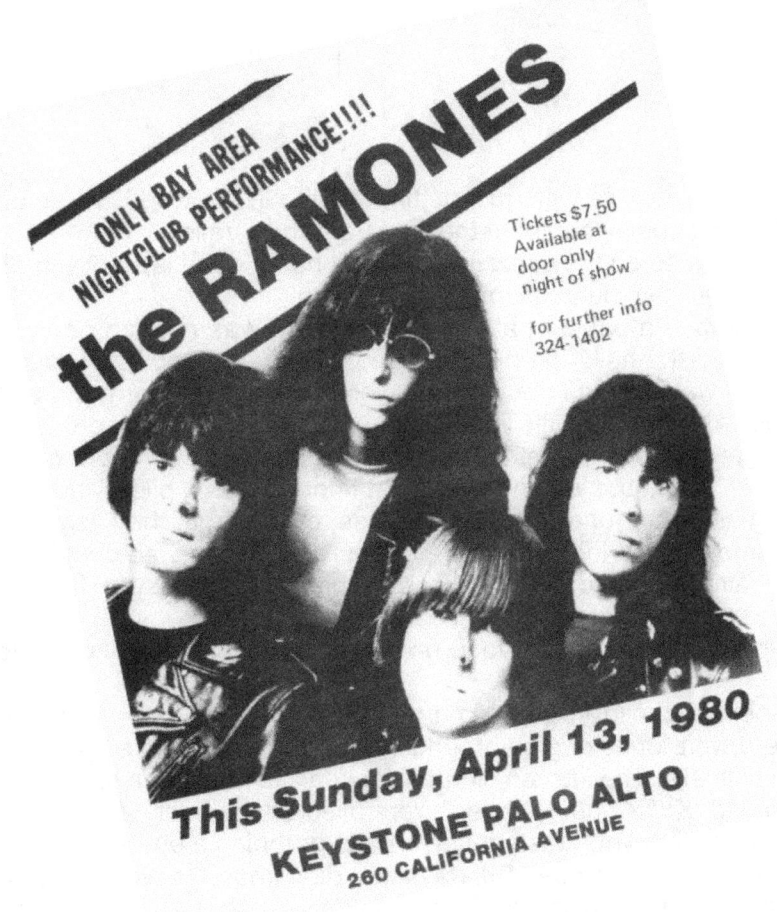

[April 13th 1980, The Keystone, Palo Alto, California, USA]

MY BRAIN IS HANGING UPSIDE DOWN (BONZO GOES TO BITBURG)
BY
BRET NELSON

The eighties were halfway done, but we were just getting started in the world. Three of us renting a tiny house in Reseda, California -- the soft, chewy center of the San Fernando Valley.

You can always tell which house on the block is a rental, it has a dead lawn or a broken fence. Ours had the dead lawn. The fence wasn't broken, but most of it was missing.

Sunday mornings were always a pageant at our little place. It was nearing noon when I gathered enough strength to make my way down the hall. The night before, we were at Madame Wong's seeing Agent Orange, and from what I could recall it was a good time. My ears were still ringing and my legs were inexplicably bruised. We'd seen them the previous November with The Ramones, drove all the way out to Pomona for that one.

I was hit with a tangy, greasy odor that stood out from our usual assortment of foul smells. "What is that stench and how do we kill it?" I asked, stepping over what I hoped was a pile of laundry.

"Chunky Ham Spread," said Terry, one of my roommates, calling from the kitchen. Terry Dodds was a year younger than me, but this morning he looked older. He had recently reached drinking age and it was taking its toll. He was crunching on saltines coated with nasty meat, chasing it with beer. The radio was playing whatever was on KNAC that morning, might have been reggae.

I joined him at the table. "You're eating cat food on crackers," I said. "The whole house smells like a spicy petting zoo."

"Not spicy. Look, the label says 'mild' in a calm, purple script. No boldness in this can. This is a smear of pork that knows its place." There were drips of grey around Terry's forehead and ears because last night he'd dyed his hair jet black to match his nails. The kitchen sink still looked like he'd been cleaning squid. Empty boxes and bottles of hair coloring labeled "*Kulur Sabih - Iswed*" were piled on the floor.

"That sink is a wreck. C'mon, sort your trash better," I said, grabbing a bottle of Spaten Pils beer from the six-pack on the table. The bookstore was closed Sundays so I didn't have to work. Even if I had a shift, breakfast beers were common. "Are those dye boxes written in code?"

"They're from Malta. Got them at the Dollar Shed along with a case of this ham stuff," said Terry. He was very smug about his bargain finds, even though he didn't need a job. His parents sent him monthly support checks while he worked on his communications degree at Cal State Northridge.

"Where's fucking Walt?" I asked.

"Out there," said Terry, pointing to the front of the house. I leaned back so I could look out the living room window. There was Walter Tillson, my other roommate, asleep in a beach chair on the front porch. All six-and-a-half feet of him was oddly contorted and he hadn't moved since three in the morning.

Terry and I stepped onto the porch cautiously, beers in hand. Waking Walt was an uncertain business. "Is he dead?" asked Terry. "I have to get rid of some things if the authorities are coming."

"No, I can smell his breathing," I said. "He needs messing with, though. He's got to work tonight."

"We can't mess with him too much," said Terry. "He's getting us into Club Lingerie for the Circle Jerks, so we shouldn't piss him off." Terry thought for a moment, then ran back into the house. The boy was hatching a plan.

As I waited for Terry's return, I noticed the neighbor across the street staring at me while he tended his lawn. He was on his knees poking out the dandelions with a screwdriver. I raised my beer, toasting him, making sure that my terrycloth robe kept any vital bits covered. His eyes went back to his weeding.

That was our only interaction during the three years I lived there.

Terry returned with a small pink box, another Dollar Shed triumph. "Fashion Girl Bandages," he said. "The label says, 'Barbara First Aid Strips.' She's a creepy Mattel knockoff, but she'll help your boo-boos." He was right, the character on the adhesive strips had off-center eyes and a chilling smile.

Terry carefully stuck a Barbara First Aid Strip on Walt's forehead. Walt didn't move, didn't flinch. "We'll tell him he banged into the door frame last night."

"Genius!" I said. "Our work here is done." With that, we went back to the kitchen. Terry turned on the small TV set on the counter, adding a layer of sound over the radio. The house had television sets and speakers everywhere, each connected to a single cable box and a giant audio system in the living room. Coax cable and speaker wire ran all over, no attempts were made to tuck it away. Tripping was common.

Anchorperson Jane Akre was on the TV, with a smaller image of Ronald Reagan hovering to the right of her head. "I told you, didn't I?" said Terry. "Second term and now he's gonna peel off that creepy old guy mask and we'll find out he's a crazy super-villain. Like he's one of Hitler's children." Terry was hooked on Headline News Network. It was always on. If he couldn't see it, he'd blast the volume so he could hear it from anywhere in the house.

"We should have voted for Bingo, that gorilla he made movies with," I said. "At least he had a college education."

"His name was Bonzo, not Bingo. And he was a chimp, not a gorilla. And you're a dick," said Terry.

"He did go to college, though," I said. "That was in the name of the movie. They should make a movie about this crap in Germany and call it 'Bonzo goes to Bitburg.'"

"What are you guys even talking about?" asked Walt, reaching for the last Spaten on the table. We hadn't seen or heard him come in. Moving undetected was a spooky skill of his. He hadn't noticed the Barbara Strip on his head.

"Reagan," said Terry. "You know, the president? Just got reelected? He's in Germany making a speech at some graveyard for soldiers."

Walt was more interested in his beer. ". . .and?"

"They're Nazi soldiers," said Terry. "It's like he's honoring the SS."

"That can't be right," said Walt. "Besides, if he's in Germany, he should be honoring the Reinheitsgebot! Prost!" With that, he drained his beer.

"Ja! Like we do, each day," said Terry. "Prost!" Down went his beer.

"When I first heard about this Bitburg thing, somehow it really bothered me." I said, moving a new six-pack from the refrigerator to the table and opening a bottle. "Now I just try to see through it. Oh, you can't watch Headline News tonight. Cutting Edge is on MTV. And prost!"

"You'll have to tape it," said Walt. "We're criminals tonight."

He was right. I'd completely forgotten about the robbery.

Walt worked at Kreeger, a poor-people's version of a department store. Weak furniture, odd clothing, strange linens, and creepy dolls. The lighting was so bright that you could hear it. The merchandise was way better than you'd find at Dollar Shed, but it was still shabby.

Recently, Walt asked for a raise. His manager turned him down, but also gave Walt a remarkable bit of information. The wages were so low that they anticipated 4.5% of their merchandise would vanish due to employee theft. An allowable loss.

Walt hadn't been doing his part. The manager said, "Just don't make it obvious."

That was a problem. Walt was six feet, five inches tall and stick thin. His head and shoulders were always visible above the shelves that divided the aisles, plus he had a tight, bleach-white mohawk that reached even higher. He looked like a broom.

He was noticed, all the time. How was he supposed to shoplift without making it "obvious?"

He needed help, the kind of help that only we drunken idiots could provide. A scheme was hatched to steal Walt's portion of the merchandise at Kreeger. Working together, we'd facilitate his participation in this low-rent profit sharing plan.

We needed to go over the final arrangements for the robbery, but everyone was starving and couldn't think straight. The only food in the house was that ham ointment of Terry's, so we ended up heading for a cheap, dreadful coffee shop in Sherman Oaks called Rusty Morgan's. Walt and I were shocked that Terry had never eaten there, as the place had been around for decades.

We rode in my Honda CVCC, mainly because it was fun to watch Walt squeeze his ladder-like frame into the back seat. On the way, we felt the need to prepare Terry for the lunch terrors he was about to experience.

"They've been open forever, serving the same food," I said. "I mean literally the same food. They acquired it, all at once, back in 1973. They made one big batch of tuna salad and they've been selling it off ever since."

"We're going to have abnormal tuna melts with your choice of an unpleasant side," said Walt. "I recommend the ptomaine tots."

We could feel Terry's unease growing. "Can't I get something plain? Like just some soup?"

"They call it soup, but the mucous content is too high for that title to be legal," said Walt. "I'd bring it to the attention of the police, but they eat there all the time so they must not care."

"Rusty Morgan's is a front," I said. "It's a place for dirty cops to exchange drugs and runaways for stacks of cash and snuff movies. The cops get to eat the real food that Rusty keeps in the back. He uses fancy stuff like refrigeration for the law enforcement meals."

By then we were pulling into the parking lot. There was no turning back.

Careful reconnaissance and planning for the heist had taken place over the last few weeks.

The main doors were too risky. The only security cameras in the place were pointed right at them, and the manager's station was at the customer service desk under those cameras.

We needed to find a location inside the store where Walt could move the goods, as if he was just pushing stock around. Then we needed a safe place for him to pass those goods out of the store to Terry and me.

We had to find a hole in Kreeger.

We checked every spot where doors, pipes, flashing, or windows were reachable. It was slow going, partly because we didn't want to get caught but mostly because Walt was working and we were wasted. But by the end of that first week, we'd found it.

All the way around the back of the store, Kreeger had a tire center. You could get a set of crappy steel-belted radials for your crappy car at crappy prices. The work was done by people who learned automotive repair as part of their County Corrections Vocational Program, so you knew it was going to be a quality job. And since your address was on the invoice, you also knew that your house was going get robbed while you were waiting for them to get your car off the rack.

The big, roll-down doors for the tire center dropped at 6:00pm, it closed three hours earlier than the rest of the store. And those doors, like most things at Kreeger, didn't work well. There was a gap between the bottom of the door and the pavement. A hole.

The Kreeger Hole.

The next step was to find something that Walt could push through it.

Walt had finally noticed the Barbara First Aid Strip on his head when he got out of the car. He didn't buy our tale about him hitting a door, but he left it there hoping for some sympathy from the female staff at Rusty Morgan's. That wasn't looking likely, as the hostess who seated us didn't pay any attention to him.

"You'd think she'd show a little concern," said Walt as we settled into our booth.

"Why would she?" asked Terry. "Your head is misshapen and upsetting. It's normal for people to avert their gaze."

"I've clearly been wounded. A vicious attack or horrifying accident, I may have a brain injury. No one cares." Walt started picking at the Barbara Strip as we reviewed the menus.

"Everything has some amount of mucous," I said, continuing Terry's briefing. "It's mixed in, there's no leaving it out or putting it on the side."

"What about these onion rings?" asked Terry.

"Mucous."

"French Toast?"

"So much mucous."

"House salad?"

"Fatal quantity of mucous," said Walt, still picking. "The last three people who ate a house salad are dead. No charges filed, because there were no bodies found. The victims popped out of existence like soap bubbles. Instantaneous dissolution at an atomic level. Ouch!"

He was really tugging on the bandage now. We could see a great deal of his skin move with it. "Wow," said Terry. "Those things are strong."

"Hell's monkeys!" said Walt. "What have you done to me? You pull some stupid prank about me hitting a door and now I've got this freak-ass fashion tramp stuck on my face forever."

"Terry, he's right," I said. "When you gonna turn yourself in?"

Walt scooted out of the booth. "Don't deflect. I know this was a two-man job, you rancid little goblin. Order me a tuna melt with tots and a beer," he said. "I'm going to soak this thing free." He stomped off to the restroom.

The robbery plans got solid just a few days ago. If he held his palm flat against the ground, Walt could move his hand through the Kreeger Hole, the tips of his fingers just showing on the other side, like four big beans all in a row. So, he prowled through the store looking for something one-hand thick. Hopefully something one of us wanted. Or maybe something we could sell.

There was a hallway inside the store that led to the tire center. It was a gathering place for carts with lost merchandise and returns. Walt would stash the goods there and, at a designated time, Terry and I would take our positions outside.

Terry's post was in the Honda, parked close and on lookout. I would wait by the roll-down doors. Walt would grab the stuff from the cart, walk through the tire center, and push the stuff through the Kreeger Hole. Outside, I'd grab it and hop in the car, then Terry and I would drive it back to the house.

We decided to test the process with a single item, just to see if it worked. So, last Thursday at 7:55pm, Terry sat in the car and I stood outside the tire center. Right on time, I heard Walt on the other side of the doors.

"Gabba gabba, we accept you," he said.

"We accept you, one of us," I replied. Passwords are an important part of any criminal enterprise.

Then, I saw an awkward, filthy piece of cloth snaking its way out of the Kreeger Hole. "What the hell is this?" I asked.

"Jeans," said Walt. "Pull them through, they're bunching up on this side."

As I pulled them through, it felt like we were flossing the building. The pants were deeply streaked with grease and dirt. The bottom of the roll-down doors hadn't been cleaned in years.

"You ignorant, pointy giraffe," I said. "These aren't jeans anymore, they're a dirty mop."

"What are you talking about? These were the only ones in my size," said Walt. "Do you know how hard it is for me to find clothes?"

"Then you shouldn't have murdered them. I'll bring this mess home so you can see, but the Kreeger Hole is hard on clothes. We'll have to think of something else."

We had ordered and were waiting for our "food" when Walt returned to the table. The Barbara First Aid Strip was gone.

"It came off, but there's a new problem," he said. With that, he picked up a sugar packet and pressed it to his forehead, where it stuck firmly. "I used a ton of soap and most of their paper towels. No good, the adhesive is still there."

"That's handy. I'm going to use you to post useful reminders," said Terry.

Walt peeled the sugar packet off his face and replaced it with a spoon, which also held strong to his forehead. "When we get home, I'll try some rubbing alcohol. Then I'll use whatever's left in the bottle to set you two on fire."

"Don't be cranky," I said. "Besides, I want to see if this water glass sticks to your face."

It didn't.

After the misfire with the jeans, we figured out a better thing to steal: Records.

They were shrink-wrapped to protect them from the horrors of the Kreeger Hole.

They held their shape for the journey.

And Kreeger had a surprisingly decent selection of albums. All we had to do was wait for Walt's next shift.

Which brings us to that Sunday night. Terry and I arrived a little early, parked behind Kreeger, and waited for 7:55pm to come. Terry's stomach was making odd sounds.

"That lunch is on a rampage through your digestive track.," I said. "Be warned, when you feel it enter the staging area, you won't have much time. As that terrible heap breaks free, you may think it will never stop. Your pile will breach the water in the bowl. Be ready for that but know that it will stop eventually."

"Please be quiet," said Terry. "We need to concentrate on crime. Is there more beer?"

"Yes," I said, handing him one. "Remember to hold on to your knees as you push that load through," I said. "Monitor your breathing. It's the only way to get through it."

It was time. I went to the roll-down doors and spoke slowly and clearly. "Requesting access to Master Control Program."

Walt's voice whispered from the other side. "Password?"

"Reindeer Flotilla."

"Access granted," said Walt. And seven feet away from me, a twelve-and-a-half-inch cardboard square spun out of the Kreeger hole and glided across the asphalt.

"I'm not there, dork," I said. "I'm here, where I'm talking."

Another record twirled out and joined the first one. I heard Terry laughing from the car.

"Cripes," is all he said, jumping to the newly active part of the Kreeger Hole. I got flat on my stomach parallel to the doors in case there was some play in Walt's throws.

He had a rhythm going now. Walt was whipping records frisbee-style. My body was stopping them from skating across the parking lot. "

FWIP! Elvis Costello, *Trust*.

FWIP! Soundtrack for *Temple of Doom*.

FWIP! Ramones, *Road to Ruin*.

FWIP! Neil Diamond, *I'm Glad You're Here with Me Tonight*.

"Woah, what the hell is this?" I said. "Who are you and what have you done with Walt?"

"It's for my mom. So is this." Out came a People Magazine with Nancy Reagan on the cover. It was thin enough that to stay clear of the Kreeger Hole's grease.

"That makes me sick," I said. "She's wearing a $50,000 dress she didn't have to pay for and I'm lying on my belly in front of a greasy door because I can't afford records."

"It's a land of opportunity," said Walt.

We got eleven records that night. And as long as we didn't get greedy or selective, we'd never have to pay for music again. Most importantly, Walt was finally doing his share at Kreeger. We were all active parts of the Reagan economy.

The next morning, I woke to find Barbara First Aid Strips on my forehead, the bridge of my nose, my chin, and the back of each hand. I was late to the bookstore.

[June 28th 1985, Barrowland Ballroom, Glasgow, Scotland, UK]

BABY I LOVE YOU
BY
TINA JACKSON

'This way Dolly. Give it to me.' The photographer is a sweat-stained wanker tripping over his cock, but she knows what to do. She pouts and blows out clouds of smoke and looks at him through her false lashes as if he was the only man on earth who could find her sweet spot. 'That's it Dolly. Straight at me. Give it to me.' He's so turned on by who she used to be. The honeydripper with the voice of an angel. While there's dogs in the streets, thinks Dolly. She's had it with men who treat her as if she's not an actual human but she can switch it on for the dough-faced no-mark if she has to. Her body remembers the moves, the poses. Her brain thinks fuck you but her body goes through the motions.

There was a once upon a time for Dolly Nectar. A hard-time once-upon-a-time when sharp-suited boys walked on the shady side of the street. Boys with sticky fingers in no-good pies. If a girl got those boys' guard down, she might touch his heart and find the sweetness that made him ashamed of himself. But when the struggle to survive hand to mouth in a poisoned pit got too much the kiss might turn to words and then to blows. They wore their battle scars with pride, the girls in the tight skirts and the big hair and the eyeliner that took their eyes out all the way to there. 'He wouldn't do it if he didn't love me,' they told each other. Everyone needs to believe in fairy tales.

Dolly looked like those girls but the boy she liked was Donny Daydream. He saw the world a different way from the hard-faced sharksters that the girls on her stairwell swooned over. He used to sit in the bus shelter with Dolly after school and share his chips and silly stories that made her smile. 'I went to the bingo with my mum last night,' he said. 'The ghost of Joey Ramone was sitting at the table opposite. He won £200 and when they called his numbers he didn't say over here like everyone else. He said hey ho let's go.' 'Joey Ramone isn't dead, Donny,' said Dolly. 'He doesn't usually play bingo at the Mecca on a Friday night, but I swear I saw him,' said Donny. He started singing *Baby I Love You*, true and low in a soft, sure tenor. Dolly joined in on the chorus and when they finished everyone waiting for the 54 broke into a round of applause. 'You've got a good set of pipes, girl,' said Donny. 'You ought to try out at punk night at the Dog and Ferret.'

Dolly knew that Donny would never say a cross word, or raise his hand to her. Soft, that was what Donny was. She might have had a soft spot for softboy Donny but she still kept him a secret. He was a hopeless case, off his face, mooning around in his big boots and his leather jacket, strumming his clapped out guitar and singing songs and saying things that didn't make sense. And she wasn't going to scrabble around in the cinders waiting for a fairy godmother to come along. She didn't want to be Dolly Daydream. She was going to sing her heart out at the Dog and Ferret, and fly away from this concrete nest where everything was blighted and dreams turned to shit and the air stank of hopelessness. With her skimmed milk skin and her peroxide crown she wasn't going to be one of those girls who got kissed and then got hit and then waited outside Wandsworth with a VO, 'property of' tats and a pram. Dolly wasn't just going to be queen of the gutter, she was going to be queen of the world.

The Sidewalk Cinderellas were the girl group for the children of the night, and what sweet music they made. After their first outing, they were offered a regular slot at the Dog and Ferret. She was the streetwise chanteuse that thrilled the boys all the way to their groins with that pounding vibrato that made them imagine the noises she'd make in private. Behind her were Kelly and Chanelle, the backup singers who were her best mates from her block.

At least, they were until people started calling them the Ugly Sisters. That was Len Nectar's doing. He was the best looking boy on the estate and he had his fingers in all the pies. 'I'll be your manager,' he said. 'I'll take you places beyond your wildest dreams.' 'In your red Cadillac?' said Dolly. She liked the picture in her head, her sitting in the passenger seat while Len, with his black moustache, drove her the hell out of loser-ville. The way Len looked at her made Dolly think she could be somebody. 'Just you mind,' he said. 'You'll have to lose the Ugly Sisters.'

Dolly went solo. Kelly and Chanelle were yesterday's chip wrappers. 'You don't need friends now you've got me,' said Len. Donny started using. 'Just chipping,' he said. 'Just a little taste.' 'Donny's a loser,' said Len. 'I'll tell him to sling his hook.' So Donny slunk into the shadows with his guitar, and Len had a name strip made for the windscreen of his red Cadillac. Dolly and Len, it said. 'Let's drive along the highway of dreams, baby,' said Len. And then he kissed her, with wide-open razzle-dazzle eyes that promised her so many stars she didn't notice the sharks circling in their dark grey waters.

Len said he'd take her places, and he did. He knew people. Opened doors. One moment she was singing into her hairbrush and the next she was at the Marquee. Then it was Dingwalls, The 100 Club, the Music Machine. A recording studio. Sayonara, Dog and Ferret. There was a single, in dayglo plastic. A Rosie and the Originals cover, Angel Baby. That was for Len. Letting people know she was spoken for. She sang it on Top of the Pops. 'The camera loves you,' said Len. 'But not nearly as much as I do.' He was the possessive sort, didn't like other men talking to her. He asked if she'd do him the honour, and they rocked up to the register office, cutting a dash in the finest that Kensington Market had to offer. Len was cock a hoop. 'You're all mine now. My songbird.'

They were a punk rock power couple. Len and Dolly Nectar, him all Flash Harry and her the little sparrow from the gutter. Sometimes Donny would be on the bottom of the bill that Dolly was the top of, strumming his guitar and singing his shambolic lullabies, but Len always kept them apart. 'Look at him, falling all over the place. What a wreck. I call him Donny Blunders,' said Len. Dolly didn't dare risk pissing Len off by talking to Donny but she tried to stand up for him. 'Don't be rotten, Len,' she said. 'He's just Donny, that's all.' Len didn't say anything, just smiled and said Donny was lucky to have such a good friend.

The next time she bumped into Donny she said hello. What a car crash and she didn't see it coming. When they got to the dressing room Len stamped on her makeup bag. 'You still fancy him don't you?' he hissed. 'You're carrying on with him behind my back, aren't you? With that shitty little junkie. You two-timing bitch.'

A few days later Len dobbed Donny in for dealing. 'It's just a joke,' he taunted Dolly when she cried. 'Can't you take a joke? You're not just worthless, you're pathetic. Even Donny Blunders wouldn't want you if he knew what you were really like.' Dolly learned the hard way that the fairytale existence Len Nectar offered was more

Bluebeard than Beauty and the Beast.

The bouffant backcombed beehive is a weave these days and she knows what they want, the sidewalk Cinders who got away when the frog prince she kissed turned out to be a toad who poisoned her life. And she gives it to them. She sometimes feels like a dog from the pound who doesn't know who it belongs to and trips over her tail to give people what she thinks they want. It got beaten into her. Years of it. She knows that now. Every sneer, every insult. Every time he kept tabs on her, asked where she'd been, who she'd spoken to, what she'd being doing. And then accused her of seeing other men behind his back. Every moment when she felt she was walking on eggshells, waiting for the bomb to drop. She'd sent out smoke signals, hoping someone would understand, and help. One night she'd sung *It's In His Kiss*. Changed the lyric to 'it's in his hit.' 'You're worthless,' he sneered at her later. 'And you've put on weight. If I threw you out no-one else would want you.'

There was a song of her own she wanted to sing. Sparrow. 'Why would anyone want to hear that?' sneered Len. 'It's shit.' The first time Len raised his fist to Dolly, she walked. He came after her. Cried. Said he was sorry. He'd never do it again. So she let him come back. The second time he did it, he said it was her fault. And the third, and the fourth. He said it so many times she started to believe him. There wasn't anyone who could tell her any different, because Len kept her to himself.

It was Kelly who helped her to escape. More than helped. Bumped into her in the street and saw the bruises. Didn't listen to the excuses. Came round with the car and packed all her stuff while Len was at work. 'I haven't got anywhere to go,' said Dolly. 'Yes you have,' said Kelly. 'I've got a spare room.' 'He'll come looking for me.' 'Let him,' said Kelly. Everyone knew who Kelly's brothers were. When Len came banging on the door shouting the odds Kelly opened it and Terry and Wayne were standing right behind her.

After Len, Dolly didn't think she'd ever sing again. Who'd want her? She was a washed up old has been with the stuffing knocked out of her. She thought about singing in public, which had used to be the place she felt most alive, and every time she thought about it, she felt sick. 'I can't do it,' she said. 'I've proper got the fear.' 'You can still carry a tune,' said Chanelle. She'd offered Dolly a job in her nail salon as soon as she'd heard Len was out of the picture. 'You want to get out there. We could do it together. I bet Kelly would and all. Len was a tosspot. He was about as much a Prince Charming as Kelly and I were the Ugly Sisters. He didn't want you to have any friends, that's what that was all about. He's gone now. The best thing you can do is take back what he took away from you. You thought you'd fallen for the leader of the pack didn't you? Well now he's gone.'

Other things happened after Len. Donny kept popping up in Dolly's thoughts. She asked around. He's in rehab, said someone. He's selling the Big Issue, said someone else.

'The boys saw him on TV a couple of months ago,' said Kelly. Kelly had a good life. She could afford to spend her days on social media because her twins, Elijah and Elisha, who learned to chat on the mic of the family soundsystem at the same time they learned to talk, had their own dubstep channel. It was the pride of their hearts that they could look after their mum. 'He thought the world of you, did Donny,' said Kelly. 'He always was daft. He's got loads of views on YouTube though. Look.'

Donny in the video still resembled a human pipecleaner with big boots at the end of his bandy legs. Under his trilby his hair had been dyed pink and looked like it had been chewed by rats. The song was called *The Ghost of Joey Ramone Haunts the Mecca Bingo Hall Every Friday Night*. The chorus went 'Joey's got a dabber/Goes gabba gabba hey.' Same old Donny, thought Dolly, and it made her sad. She could have had someone that thought the world of her, and she'd thrown him away because Len Nectar had made her think she was too good for him. She'd hurt him and it made her ashamed of herself.

And now here she is, after all these years, back on the bill. Playing to the camera. Talking to a reporter. The old bird who soundtracked their adolescent sex. Once upon a time. She's glad they changed their name though. There was never any fairy godmother and the handsome prince was Len and he'd have ruined her life if he could. She looks in the mirror and sees the lines, and the weave, and the extra weight she's carrying, and she knows she's not the same girl who gazed out from the covers of all those dayglo seven inches. But she's here, and she's survived. She's singing again. And it's showtime soon.

Tonight's the big one. That's why the local rag had come down. 'Go on girl,' Kelly said. 'We'll do it with you. Not just for old time's sake. For us. For a laugh.' There was a time she never thought she'd sing again. And here she is. The buzz has been building and it's a sellout show. Waiting in the wings to make her entrance, Dolly feels the flutter. She knows that feeling. Remembers it. She can do this. She can be that person, the one the photographer saw. She can be Dolly Nectar. She can put on a show.

The MC steps up on stage. This is it. Showtime. Dolly and Kelly and Chanelle straighten up. Look at them all, back together, dressed to kill, ready to sing their hearts out.

'Before our mystery guest we've got something special for you,' says the MC. 'They started out singing here and they're ready to remind us why we loved them. They were legends as The Sidewalk Cinderellas. They made us proud and we know you've all been waiting for them. It's Local Heroes festival time at the Dog and Ferret and local heroes don't get much bigger than these. Let's have a great big Dog and Ferret welcome as they come up to the stage – under their new name - The Ugly Sisters!'

The band strikes up and the three old girls sashay out. A bit battered round the edges, a bit broader in the beam, but still themselves. They look out and there isn't a face they don't recognise. Their intro blasts out, they open their lipsticked mouths and their tune takes over – the one they'll never forget, the one they'll be singing when their minds have gone and they can't remember their own names and their teeth have fallen out. Ooh I love you, baby I do... and they can feel the love, as the Dog and Ferret crowd, every one there, is on their feet with their hearts in their mouths. Swaying. My angel baby, my angel baby. Remembering what it felt like, the first time. Way back when. Three voices, singing as one, Dolly's lead making the throwaway lyric sound like pure soul poetry and the harmonies from Kelly and Chanelle transforming them into the most heavenly host the Dog and Ferret have seen since... since the good old days.

As the old numbers pour out the years fall away, and even though she's singing her heart out, Dolly looks into the crowd, scanning all the old faces, because there's someone missing. A face she wishes she could see. And as she sings, the yearning in her voice fills the room, and several punters find a tear falling into their pint, and a lump in their throat.

And there he is. After all these years. Shouldering his guitar, pushing his way through the crowd, clambering up on stage with his pipecleaner legs with great big boots on the end. Showing up for showtime. And Kelly steps up the to the mic and says, this next one's for the ghost of Joey Ramone. And the band strikes up, and Dolly goes to the mic on autopilot and the words fall out of her. Have I ever told you? And Donny swings his guitar round his neck, starts strumming, sawing away at the chords. He picks up the chugging riff, sways his way over with a great big grin plastered over his face. And just in time for the chorus, he joins her at the mic. Baby I love you, he bellows, and she bellows it right back. Baby I love only you.

It brings the house down. After the show, a lot of people want to talk to Dolly and tell her how great she is. She isn't at the bar though, or in the dressing room, or outside having a fag. Dolly Nectar is nowhere to be seen.

But anyone who takes the trouble to look just round the corner would find Dolly and Donny sitting in the number 54 bus-shelter, sharing a bag of chips and singing in perfect harmony. And anyone looking particularly closely might just spot the ghost of Joey Ramone, leaning against the wall of the shelter, counting his winnings.

[November 18th 1984, Montezuma Hall, San Diego, California, USA]

CHAINSAW
BY
GREGORY NICOLL

"I escaped out of a window in Hell," Sally told him yet again. She ran her hand slowly down the ugly patchwork which the shattering glass had etched into her flesh on that hot afternoon 13 years ago.

The doctor nodded and scratched another brief entry into his little brown notebook.

"I've already told you that," she added quietly, "a hundred times."

She glanced around his office. The room smelled deeply of dark leather furniture and varnished wood. Tall bookcases lined three of the walls, with a large hardback copy of *Face Your Fear: A New Look at Psychotherapy* by Dr. Daniel R. Melnick prominently displayed -- her doctor's latest best-seller.

A wide window on the fourth wall gave a view of the asylum's sprawling grounds. It was cracked open very slightly and the scent of fresh-cut grass occasionally wafted in. Sally remembered how, as a child, she had loved that aroma. But for more than a decade now, the sound of the lawnmower mostly terrified her, dragging her back into her most hideous nightmare.

It sounded like a chainsaw.

She wondered if Dr. Melnick had been aware of the groundskeeper's schedule. Had he deliberately arranged her session today for this particular hour, perhaps as part of his *"Face Your Fear"* manifesto? Briefly she recalled seeing him chat with the keeper a day or two before, out in the asylum's serene gardens.

Dr. Melnick nodded. "Of course, Sally," he said gently. "The repetition – saying those same words – it's part of what we psychotherapists call 'Imagery Exposure.' You replay your bad experiences often enough – you face your fears -- and they will ultimately hold no power over you."

He lowered the notebook to his desk and pushed it aside. "You and I, we've made significant breakthroughs together in the past several months. I'm very encouraged." Swiveling in his chair, he turned to a large stereo boom box on the bookshelf behind him and began rummaging through a pile of audio cassettes, looking for one in particular.

Sally let her breath out slowly, trying to ignore the sound of the lawnmower. There was a time when the snarl of a small gasoline engine would have made her drop to the cold hardwood floor, sobbing and paralyzed with fear by flashbacks of *The Man with the Human-Skin Mask*. Dr. Melnick was right. She was getting better. At least a little. But facing her fears never became any less unpleasant.

The doctor located the desired cassette and inserted it into the player. "This should pep you up a bit."

"Another of your famous mix-tapes?"

He grinned. "No, not this time. It's the new album by The Ramones."

Sally nodded. She knew this was his favorite band, some scruffy-looking guys from New York who rocked pretty hard.

A powerful electric guitar figure ripped from the speakers, drums kicked in, then vocals. Sally was immediately captivated. She'd heard various Ramones songs dozens of times on the doctor's compilation cassettes – he was always pointing out which ones were their "classics" – but for the most part she found them too blunt for her taste. She suspected the doctor loved The Ramones mainly because so many of their songs were about characters with mental problems, taking Thorazine, requesting shock treatment, or getting sedated. There was even one called "Psycho Therapy."

This was different. The track rocked just as hard, but its lyrics were more contemplative, as if the vocalist was processing inner demons and confronting secret weaknesses. Then it erupted into a beautiful, forcefully sung chorus in which the singer repeatedly declared, "I wanna live!"

For a band with so many negative songs – she had once laughed at how many of their titles included the word "don't" – this was a pleasant, unexpected switch. She noticed Dr. Melnick was tapping his desk blotter in time with the drumbeat and mouthing the lyrics. She began to sing along herself.

When the song ended, he switched off the boom box. "I thought immediately of you when I heard this one. It could be your anthem. You've been moved from asylum to asylum for over a decade now, and that's no life -- it isn't living – not for someone like you, who's still young."

She scoffed. "I'm 33."

"That's still young. You could live three times that long."

Sally shrugged. She gestured at the boom box. "So, this is the band's new album?"

"Yes. It came out in September." He slid the cassette case across the desk toward her. "You're gonna love the title."

She picked it up and smiled. The album was *Halfway to Sanity*.

Dr. Melnick took the unusual step of escorting Sally back to her room after the session. Normally this duty was entrusted to one of the orderlies, Matt, but apparently the doctor had some business with the big guy and used the occasion to talk with Matt as they walked.

Sally preceded them down the long echoey corridor, but she turned back to glower at the pair several times when she heard them whispering conspiratorially behind her back. She wondered what they were up to. Upon opening the door of her room, she drew a sharp breath and stopped cold.

In the middle of her bed was a chainsaw.

Smelling of polished steel, motor oil, and gasoline, it looked almost exactly like the one carried by The Man with the Human-Skin Mask when he had chased after her all those years ago. The panels over its small motor were painted light green but were marred by numerous scratches from long use. It was obviously heavy, making a deep impression in the bedspread and mattress.

Sally let out her breath and flexed her fingers. She took a step forward toward the bed and reached down for the saw. The front handle's rubber coating yielded slightly to her fingers as she wrapped her left hand around it. The metal throttle handle was cool to the touch of her right hand. The bed creaked slightly as she lifted the saw off of it.

She turned to face Dr. Melnick and Matt, who were standing close together just outside the door, and extended the saw toward them.

"I wanna live," she said.

Without taking his eyes off Sally, Dr. Melnick whispered two words to Matt. There was both resolution and pride of accomplishment in his tone.

"She's ready," he said.

The sign said, "WELCOME TO TEXAS."

The doctor's red Chevy Camaro soared past it.

"So why is this your 'Little Camaro'?" Sally asked, stretched out in the front passenger seat. "It's the same size as your silver-colored one."

Dr. Melnick smiled. "The silver one has a bigger engine. I call this the 'little' one because it's only got four cylinders." He patted the dashboard affectionately. "Better mileage on long trips."

The car had no air-conditioning. Sally was unaccustomed to this inconvenience after the comparative luxury of the ambulances and institutional vehicles which had transported her between facilities since 1974. Warm wind from the gap at the top edge of the window whipped her long blonde hair back and forth.

The rural Texas highway provided an endless rogues' gallery of intense aromas, from assorted roadkill – mostly deer and armadillos, with the occasional cow or horse – to the lingering odor of manure as they passed farms and stockyards. She cranked the window up tight several times, only to lower it again when the heat of the sunlight against the glass became too much.

However, the Camaro did have a cassette tape deck. Dr. Melnick brought a small vinyl case stuffed with his mix-tapes and had taken great delight in loudly cranking up *"Way Down South"* by The Fleshtones as the car crossed the state line.

Sally spotted by the roadside up ahead a group of hitch-hikers, thumbs extended. She worried Dr. Melnick might stop for them – she didn't want to pick up any hitchers ever again, after what had happened 13 years back – but realized with great relief, as he didn't slow down, that the Camaro's rear seating couldn't accommodate them.

As she watched the group recede in the rear view, she noticed an old dark-colored pickup truck following at a considerable distance behind their car. She shuddered, recalling how, during her ordeal here in Texas, one of her tormentors had transported her as his captive in a similar vehicle.

They drove on without saying a word for a while, until the doctor finally broke the silence.

"So, Sally, tell me again about the man you call The Hitcher."

She took a deep breath and let it out rapidly. "We picked him up on a road just like this one. He was a strange guy. Really strange. A bit older than me at the time, maybe in his late twenties. He smelled bad, as if he never washed. His face was awful, with a weird birthmark or something, and his lower lip drooped open like it was partly paralyzed."

"You said he'd worked at a slaughterhouse . . . "

She nodded grimly. "Yeah, he told us that was the family profession. He and his brothers worked on the killing floor, slaughtering cattle. But then the slaughterhouse brought in a new, special machine to do that kind of work. It put them all out of work."

Dr. Melnick nodded. "Have you ever seen one of those machines?"

She shook her head. "No. Oh, God no. Never even heard of such a thing, except when The Hitcher told us about it."

"Would you like to see one?"

Sally's brow furrowed. "Why?"

The doctor shrugged. "I believe it might be helpful for you, facing in real life – in the daytime - another component of the story that's driving your fears. I made some calls last week. It's all arranged."

He braked the car, slowing its speed considerably, and switched on the turn signal.

The smell of cattle manure wafted through the Camaro's open windows, stronger now than ever.

"It's up here," said the strange little man.

"Up here," he repeated, straining to be heard over the cacophony of bawling cattle. He pointed along a narrow, inclined alley separating two long wooden walls. There were lights dangling from the high ceiling – bare white bulbs surrounded by protective steel cages – but heavy shadows dominated the space and, even on this sunlit afternoon, it felt eerily like night-time.

The smell here inside the big, loud room was awful, a mixture of putrid cow shit, rancid puddles of urine, and drying blood, all of it peppered with a distinct element of rotten meat. When Dr. Melnick offered Sally his clean white soft-cloth handkerchief, she snatched it from his hand and pressed it tightly over her nose and mouth.

Their slaughterhouse tour-guide was a scrawny, weasel-faced fellow dressed in filthy denim overalls. He had introduced himself only as "Shaw" and boasted with obvious pride that he had worked at the facility non-stop for the last ten of his thirty-five years. Apparently the grisly labor suited him. He mentioned he had forsaken other employment opportunities, concluding his informal autobiography by adding, "but here I am, still pushin' a mop."

Shaw pointed at a large, rusty mop bucket mounted on wheels, filled halfway with a sickening cocktail of blood and cleaning solvent. A few soap bubbles floundered around the edges of the grisly mix. It reeked of rubbing alcohol and Pine-Sol. "Takes a mighty strong combo of cleaners an' grease cutters to tidy up the ramp after we've been running the machinery for a while," he explained.

He gestured for them to wait at the bottom as he rolled his mop bucket up the ramp toward its peak. Sally noticed that in the partial shadows, silhouetted against one of the dangling lights, Shaw almost looked like an image of the Ferryman from Greek Mythology, poling a little boat across the River Styx toward the gates of Hades.

"Straight into Hell," she whispered.

The huge, thick-handled mop dripped foul liquid as he hoisted it from the bucket and began vigorously applying the mix to the surfaces of the cattle chute. Sally worried a river of gore would come rushing down at her and the doctor, but Shaw wiped and pushed skillfully, channeling it all into drainage slots so the floor of the ramp remained mostly dry.

Eventually, his chore complete, Shaw splashed the mop back into the bucket and beckoned for them to join him at the top of the chute. "Watch your step."

They made their way carefully up to where Shaw was waiting.

"There it is," he announced proudly, pointing at the machine. "This here piece o' pure genius is called a 'captive-bolt pistol.'"

The device was suspended on a large, flexible overhead armature which hung from somewhere up in the shadows of the ceiling. The bolt gun resembled an oversized power drill. Rubber hoses connected it to tanks of compressed air stashed back in the shadows. In stark contrast to everything else so rough and grotesquely stained around it, the surfaces of the gun were smooth and gleaming, bright as a mirror.

Dr. Melnick took a step toward it and examined a tiny imprint along the edge of the device. "It says it's made in Solingen," he observed. "Fine German steel."

Shaw nodded. "It was mighty expensive, yep. But the bosses tell me it was worth it. They used to have to go an' hire a whole crew of big strong guys to whack the beeves with hammers all day. But this here bolt pistol?

Hell, anybody can run it. Faster too."

He stepped over to the air tanks and began cranking the valve on one of them. There was a loud, brief hiss of escaping air and then the needle began to move around the dial of a large pressure gauge on the wall nearby. Shaw watched until the needle reached a spot marked with a piece of red tape. The valve hissed out another blast of air as he tightened it back.

He turned to them, grinning. "So, you wanna see how it works?"

The motel was nicer than Sally had expected, and she looked forward to a decent night's sleep after their long, eventful day. The sheets were soft, smelling faintly of bleach, and the thick orange corduroy bedspread was heavy enough to serve as a comforter. She bunched it around herself.

Still wearing her blue jeans and white T-shirt, she wondered if perhaps now she should fetch the nightgown from her duffel bag. But no, she was just fine like this, the caress of the corduroy too pleasant to forsake.

Dr. Melnick had left the door to his adjoining room partly open. She could see him working at the small desk, hunched over maps of the area. Although the authorities never located the exact site of the horrors she had witnessed – there had been much speculation she just fabricated the whole story – Sally still recalled enough of the general area where it had happened. The doctor's plan was to drive those roads, crisscrossing the territory. He said he hoped it would bring back to her a "sense of place" and would like to see what memories that might trigger.

After settling into their motel rooms, they had enjoyed a delicious takeout dinner of chicken vindaloo – by mutual agreement, they emphatically did not want beef – but the spices had been strong. She gulped cold water from a wobbly plastic cup in which two melting cubes of ice floundered against the side. It felt good going down her throat. Soothing.

Switching the bedside lamp off, Sally let her head sink into the soft fabric of a cotton pillow. She was soon adrift in sleep.

She woke at the sound of the chainsaw.

The room was illuminated faintly by the first purple rays of dawn through the gap at the top of the cheap motel curtains. At first, she thought she was dreaming, caught up in the swirl of her nightly flashbacks of being pursued by The Man with the Human-Skin Mask and his roaring, sputtering power tool. The saw's sound was muffled at the start, distant in a dreamlike way, but when chips and splinters of wood began flying at her, nicking her face and catching in her hair, she knew this was no dream.

The saw's guide bar now protruded through the main door of her room, its chain chewing the cheap plywood and pressboard, spewing needle-like fragments. The sound was monstrously loud, louder than it had ever been in her dreams, and was accompanied by the smell of gasoline, clouds of sawdust, and oily smoke. Bright white-hot sparks flew as the blade struck the small metal frame of the Motel-Rules-and-Checkout-Times sign posted on the back of the door.

Two hands grabbed Sally's shoulders. She let out a shriek but realized it was only Dr. Melnick, tugging her into the next room. She noticed his roadmaps were still spread out on the little table, the same desk lamp beaming down on them, as if he'd been up working all night. Still fully dressed, he had his car keys in his right hand. Without a word he eased open the outside door of his own room, revealing his red Camaro in the space just beyond it. Sally could also see a dark-colored pickup truck parked in the distance, not in a parking space but stopped perpendicular, in the open dirt of the motel's courtyard. It looked as if it had been hot-rodded, with custom oversized chrome exhaust pipes under the running boards along its sides.

The doctor sneaked a quick look outside in the direction of the saw. Judging that its operator was still distracted by the demolition of Sally's door, Dr. Melnick made a quick break for his car, wordlessly pulling Sally with him.

To facilitate the load-in of their luggage, he had backed the Camaro into the parking space so that its trunk faced the rooms. Its front end pointed to the highway, which proved helpful in making their escape. In seconds they were both aboard, doors slammed and locked, throttle-body injection thundering the Chevy's little engine to life, rear tires kicking up rooster tails of gravel as they spun in the dirt.

Sally had not dared to look in the direction of the chain saw when she exited the room, but now, fighting against the G-force of the car's powerful acceleration, she turned in her seat and stared back toward the motel. She saw a huge, hulking figure at the trashed door of her room, swinging the saw wildly, left and right. His face was hard to make out in the dim light and the clouds of engine smoke, but she knew immediately it was The Man with the Human-Skin Mask.

Her nightmare was real again.

Dr. Melnick pounded his fist on the dashboard as the car skidded onto the highway and picked up even more speed. "Go, Little Camaro, go!" he shouted.

Sally looked back toward the motel again and saw the pickup truck's headlights light up. They became two glowing eyes as the truck followed the Camaro, bumping its way up onto the paved road in eager pursuit. The truck itself was nothing but a black silhouette behind those two beams. Overhead, a few fading stars twinkled amid the glowing purplish canopy of the pre-dawn sky.

The truck drew closer.

Stunned by the ferocity of the crash, she had no memory how or why it had happened.

Did the truck ram their Camaro off the road, or did Dr. Melnick instigate the accident himself, in some frantic attempt to undo the truck's pursuit?

The pickup lay upside-down in the gravel a few dozen yards away, engine dead but wheels still spinning. Its roof was partly collapsed, all windows shattered, broken glass spread in glittering puddles surrounding the wreckage.

The Camaro had skidded into the side of the building and struck hard at a 45-degree angle. Steam hissed from its shattered radiator, filling the air with the smell of hot anti-freeze. The car's left front end and hood were now crumpled back so they nearly met the windshield. A spiderweb of cracks glistened in the glass on the passenger side.

As she wiped a thin stream of blood from her eyes, Sally slowly realized the windshield had been broken by her own forehead striking it. In their panic to escape from the motel, neither she nor the doctor had taken the time to fasten seatbelts.

Dr. Melnick lay sprawled over the steering wheel, his right arm draped along the dashboard. He was unconscious but still alive, his chest rising with each rough breath, and the fingers of his right hand moved slowly, in a strange gripping, clawing motion.

With great effort, Sally pushed the car's passenger-side door open. The bent metal creaked and groaned. She climbed out, struggling to get to her feet, drawing a deep breath and feeling dizzy, greeted by the lowing of cattle and a strong odor of manure. Stabilizing herself against the wreckage of the Camaro, she turned and looked up at the building their car had struck.

It was the slaughterhouse.

She barely registered that detail when, from back behind her, there came the sound of a chainsaw sputtering to life.

It was him - *The Man with the Human-Skin Mask* – standing by the overturned truck and gunning the saw's snarling, smoking motor. He waved it at her. Then he charged.

Despite the blood running down her forehead and compromising her vision, Sally ran straight for the slaughterhouse door, remembering the path from the previous day. The main entrance – an immense sliding corrugated steel panel – had already been rolled open for the day's first shift. She ran through it, the sound of the raging saw growing ever nearer, ever louder behind her.

At the peak of the cattle chute she found Shaw's rusty mop bucket. The liquid in it was clear, apparently fresh, reeking of strong solvent. She swirled the end of the mop around in it and then hoisted it, dripping as she turned to face the saw.

The Man with the Human-Skin Mask struggled to ascend the chute, the weight of the sputtering motor making it difficult for him to balance. He climbed slowly, taking careful, deliberate steps, watching and measuring each footfall of his massive leather boots.

But he looked up when Sally screamed at him, "I wanna live!"

It was just the moment she had hoped for. She lunged forward with the mop, thrusting it, shaking it, flinging it, directing a hard rain of solvent into the ragged eye-holes of the monster's mask. The hulking figure let out an inhuman squeal and dropped the saw onto the cattle chute. It struck with a fearsome bang, the chain spewing bright sparks as the engine died.

His big, meaty hands rubbed madly at his burning eyes. He whipped his head back and forth, desperately trying to shake off the aggressive chemicals. Then he froze in place and looked up – his eyes now red as blood – when he heard the hiss of air from the valve on the tank up above.

Sally had cast the mop aside and commandeered the captive-bolt pistol. She watched the big pressure gauge on the wall as she continued to crank the valve. Its indicator needle passed the red mark and kept going. Gripping the pistol, she stepped forward, pressed its muzzle into the forehead of The Man with the Human-Skin Mask, and pulled back the trigger.

The monster's head exploded in a shower of gore.

Outside, in the smoldering wreckage of the Camaro, Dr. Melnick's twitching hand drifted from the dashboard and slumped down to the controls on the cassette desk. Reflexively, he pressed "PLAY" before collapsing limp again.

The tape began spooling. It was a track from The Ramones' first album, a cut which until now the doctor had carefully avoided playing in any circumstance where Sally might hear it.

The song was "Chainsaw."

[September 14th 1986, El Dorado Saloon, Carmichael, Sacramento, California, USA]

HERE TODAY, GONE TOMORROW
BY
JAMES RYAN

Paul had to laugh at everyone on St. Mark's Place whose dress and demeanor screamed "bridge and tunnel."

As that was everyone, he kept it to himself; as that included himself, he suppressed it deeply. Solid dark blue blazer under his trench coat (a steal, a big name from an outlet store doing closeout), thin striped three...color tie that kind of worked with the blazer and the light blue shirt, slacks (from another outlet store), black laced dress shoes; Paul's sense of horror at what he'd become grew with every second.

He dared not look at his own reflection in the window of the pizza place he was slowly walking by.

He did take a second to make sure he had everything, though. Portfolio still in hand, his thin laptop secured, check; wallet, not yet lifted by a pickpocket, check; ticket back on the Metro North in the inner blazer pocket, uh... huh.

Yep, he thought to himself, definitely very "*bridge and tunnel*," and still in the same shape for the most part as he'd been before he left the house. On St. Mark's Place, to boot; he wondered if this was an act of insult to injury, which would apply to whom, the insult or injury, between him or the street.

The cold irony smacked him one that not only the people in the East Village didn't feel like they belonged here, neither did the businesses. There were so many ramen restaurants and bubble tea boutiques that it felt more like West 46th on a non-matinee day. Except that the last time he was on Restaurant Row there were not as many 'For Rent' signs in the windows.

Manic Panic, St. Mark's Books, St. Mark's Sounds, St. Mark's Comics; even Trash & Vaudeville was gone, though it only moved a short way off. The changes...

No, the obliterations; this was no longer the neighborhood he'd been in. The neighborhood he'd sneak out of the house to go to when he was too young, and the place he went as often as possible when no one cared. The energy, the possibilities, gone, all of them.

This hit him hard as he stood in front of where *Gem Spa* used to be. The sign was gone, and all that was left of the place was a boarded-up open wound.

"Egg cream fugit," he said aloud. Given he was at the place a bit late and how many others there were not with him to grieve the dead, he thought, it was the best he could say. And if there was one thing this neighborhood could do as it did back in the 70s, maybe the only thing, it gave people a chance to say aloud what was on their mind in peace. Just another voice on a street that never listened to you as you spoke your mind, spilled your guts, opened your heart up...

"Paul?"

He heard her behind him, and just assumed this woman was talking to someone else.

"Paul, is that you?"

Her voice was familiar; it sounded exactly the same, which shouldn't be the case from that long ago, after the end of the century. Remarkable coincidence, that someone would sound like her...

"I'm open all night too, you know, and I can give you more than a fucking egg cream."

His blood froze. Sounding a lot like her, maybe it was someone else, but the same pick-up line...

He turned to see her, not believing but unable to deny it. She still had the same hair, a faux hawk dyed neon yellow but not trying to hide her dark roots. The same single earing in her left ear, a bronze infinity loop hanging to look like an '8'. Black cherry lipstick. Nails painted iron spike black. And those eyes...

He could never forget those eyes. They were more exciting to look at than the rest of her, even when she took her clothes off.

"Paul Colvin; it is you," she said with a smile. She added in sweet baby girl voice, "Oooh fuck, you look horrible."

"Suzy Nacht," Paul replied. "Unless you changed your name."

"A few times, but hey, that works. I liked that one; those were good days."

"I thought you couldn't stand sunlight."

"You know I don't die if I'm up, but I feel like crap until sundown."

"Oh, right, yeah, forgot," said Paul, looking around to see if anyone else could see who he was talking to. And then wonder how he'd explain to someone who was looking at them what was going on.

"But seriously, look at you. When's the last time you rocked drainpipes and a ripped tee? It must be, how many decades since you looked hot?"

"So you were wrong, you did miss me, despite what you said."

"Oh, I think of everyone that's gotten away, even the dozen or so before you came along."

"And how soon did you find a replacement?"

"It's easier than you think," Suzy said with a smile, a flash of teeth briefly there but gone.

Paul sighed. "Tell you the truth, I might have taken you up on it if I thought I could do that."

"If you're begging me now, the offer's off the table, flabbo."

"Oh, I'm not begging..."

"Not now."

"Not for that, no..."

"But you did. The slight whimper in your voice as you wanted to get me somewhere quieter where we could..."

"Like you ever said no for more than a minute."

"Hey, I have desires, too." Suzy added, "All kinds of hungers, in fact."

Paul took a second to center himself. The mindfulness training from those classes were probably never meant for a case like this, but it was the best he had.

Paul continued, "So did you ever stop being a punk rocker? Wouldn't that have given you away after a while?"

"You'd be surprised how easy to blend in it was after everyone embraced the scene. A change of clothes this decade, flatten the hair a year here or there, and sometimes, like now, everyone wants the whole package again."

"I suppose the package is the important part."

Suzy gave a few slight twists, opening the jacket to show off more.

"So what about you?" she asked. "What did you do when you left the scene?"

"You mean when I left you, don't you?"

"Like this was any fun when you were alone. You told me that, remember? On this spot, all those years ago?"

"Yeah, okay, I did. But I got a life."

"Is that supposed to be a dig?"

"Take it any way you want." Paul added, "Like you did me."

"Now that's not fair. Who was driving us the whole time?"

"I had time to look back and realize it wasn't me. You're great at getting people to do what you want and make them think it was their decision."

"Except for once."

"So," Paul said as he started to smile for the first time since Suzy showed up. "You can't just have someone join you for decades; they have to want to be by your side forever, huh?"

"Oh come on! If I did that, we'd be killing each other in a few hours."

"Did you say 'killing'? Really?"

"Oh, you know what I meant! A whole night of bitching and moaning over how many years, really? It's not like your wife was dragged home after you tied her up at the altar, right?"

Paul's smile died as Suzy mentioned his family.

"Hello?" Suzy replied as she pointed to the gold ring on his finger. "Not exactly hiding you're off the market, are you?"

Paul looked at his wedding band and started to breathe again.

"And hey, good senses, remember? I can still get her scent after she pressed against your clothes this morning." Suzy twitched her nose slightly, "Daughter, too, mid-teens, right?"

Paul just stood there and looked at her.

"Oh don't worry, I'm not after any of them. I don't like going to the suburbs, you know that."

"The tag you wrote in CBGB's woman's room, 'Fuck the Cleavers.' Yeah, you told me."

"And I've never come across either of them down here. In fact, there's almost none of the neighborhood on you; why the visit tonight?"

"I was, just…"

"Oh, stop it," Suzy said as Paul hesitated. "Okay; I'm just curious how you turned out when I said no…"

"You said?"

"Semantics; so if I promise I'm not going to go after you and your family, at least for old time's sake, I really want to hear how it turned out, okay?"

"And why do you need to know?"

Suzy drew in an unnecessary breath. "I always wonder, everyone who says that they don't want to spend a few years with me... okay, decades, yeah, whatever, whether anyone thinks it was for the better or not."

Paul examined her by sight; it was not the same way he once looked at her, as a temptation or as a predator, but those considerations were still there, still part of it.

"Okay," he said. "If you really want to know, I was here for an interview at Cooper Union. They had an open position for a writing associate, and I came in for that."

Suzy took a few beats to say, "Wow, you really did become a writer like you wanted. And you have a wife; just one daughter, I guess?"

"Yes, Lucy and Mina. And no, I didn't really get to be a writer, not like that. I became a high school English teacher, which yes, I'm happy with."

Suzy nodded along, a slow head banging, as her hair moved up and down to the rhythm of Paul's words.

"And no, I don't think about or regret turning down what you promised. Eternal youth, constant energy, all of that; I may have said then I wanted to just keep head banging forever all night, but I don't regret not doing that, no."

Suzy banged her head a few more times before answering, "Okay, I can get that, sure."

"I really think that for me, when times changed, they got better. I could say I missed them, that I'd missed those days, but I'm happy I got out. I don't think I could have been with you forever, and I bet on some level you're glad you didn't convince me to give it all up, to pay the price that would have cost."

"I guess we'll never know, will we? We don't know whether you could have been head banging forever or not."

Part of Paul wanted to just say goodbye right there and get on with it, but he couldn't go without asking, "So what guy did you choose to spend the rest of your nights with?"

"Oh, I had three since then."

"Three, huh?"

"You remember Ross Hyman, the guy whose place we used to go when we needed to?"

"Oh God, Ross."

"You're sound like you're having a panic; I can hear all that blood rushing through you, you know."

"I hadn't thought about him in, oh..."

"It's okay if you wanted to forget that; you wouldn't be the first guy in a three-way that couldn't handle it being two guys in the same bed."

"So you went with him, then. Uh."

"And after that there was Christine Cummings."

"Christine? Never met her."

"That was long after Ross was gone. She was there to look for the old haunts, the ones that were still around. She claimed she was just studying the history, but I think she wanted to go back there to that time herself."

"And the third?"

"Steve Bell. Now that was a disappointment; he talked a better game than he gave." Suzy added, "Hey, even I can fuck up every few years."

"So what did they say when they met each other?"

"Oh they never did, th..." Suzy stopped herself.

"Now hold on; if you promised someone eternity with you, and you had three other people who could live forever with you, but none of them met? How'd that happen?"

Suzy looked down, trying to hide her eyes from Paul for the first time since this began.

"Did they, what, go somewhere else? Go with someone else, get their own friends with benefits to replace you, what?"

Suzy finally said, slowly, "They could never replace me."

"Is that a boast?"

"No, I just... I..."

"What is it you're trying not to tell me? What happened to them?"

When she told him, he backed away, first slowly, then a few feet further away he turned into a trot. He picked up the pace as the 6 came into Astor Place, and paced the subway car as the train went uptown.

He was nearly running by the time he caught his train at Grand Central, and didn't stop turning to look at who got on until the doors closed at 125th Street.

He forced himself to focus on Lucy's face, on Mina's, anything to scrub Suzy's burnt-into-his-retinas' visage.

He tried to erase her from his mind, especially those eyes that he could have said yes to if she had asked again, those nails long and sharp enough that they could have sliced through the plywood over Gem Spa.

He especially tried to forget her answer:

"You were kind of on the right track when you said you wanted to be head banging forever."

"But how do people who live forever…" he started to say before it hit him.

"Well, forever can end pretty quickly, if I think we'd be better off if it were over…"

[November 15th 1978, Minstrel's Alley, Highwood, Chicago, Illinois, USA]

MERRY CHRISTMAS (I DON'T WANT TO FIGHT TONIGHT)
BY
JOSHUA L. JAMES

Sleet pelted the steel roofs of the cars parked along Third Street. Snow had blanketed the ground for days, but this was cold, hard ice. It was like something in the heavens had taken a turn for the worse.

The overcast sky mirrored the sheets of snow and ice on the street, so the whole world was just a gray fog. It was late afternoon, though, which meant the Christmas tree displays in the park had been turned on. Reds and greens and silvers broke through the monotony. Busy people bundled in layers and wrapped in colorful nylon winter coats, rushed in and out of the shops, grabbing last minute gifts.

Maggie Sharp stepped out of the passenger side of the Ford Econoline onto the cracked asphalt and slipped, stretching out into a near perfect split, barely keeping her ass from slamming into the pavement.

"Goddammit," she said, gripping the door handle and pulling herself back to her feet.

"What's up?" Steve said.

"Goddamned ice," Maggie said. "I about busted my ass." Maggie tiptoed and slip-slided to the back of the van, pulled open the double doors. "Hey, Steve. I forgot the set list. Can you grab it from the doghouse?"

Steve was Steve Windsor. The best lead guitarist Maggie had ever played with. Definitely the best lead guitarist you could find in this shit hole town these days. The 90s sucked but you could still find real rock 'n roll if you looked hard enough. The problem wasn't that it wasn't around. Guys like Steve, guys from the bad old days, were still around. Steve could've made plenty of money as a sessions guy or taught classical guitar if he wanted to. He could've gone toe-to-toe with Eddie Van Halen or Steve Vai. But he was a punk rocker in its purest form. "Better scrounge with the roaches and keep your soul," he'd told her once, "than to feed from the golden trough with the pigs and die empty anyway." Yep. He always had some mixed-up melodramatic bullshit proverb to say. But she knew what he meant, and more important, she knew that he meant it.

The problem was people didn't know the good stuff if it slapped them in the fucking face. Disco and dance pop had corrupted the collective sense of taste. Hair bands had heavy metal-poisoned the airwaves, and 90s radio showed little sign of recovery. Punk wasn't dead—it just wasn't on MTV. It lived here, in places like this shithole biker bar on Third Street. Dante's it was called. The Splinters were playing Dante's on Christmas Eve for two hundred bucks plus beer. Rock 'n roll lived here.

And Maggie lived there: an old high school that had been converted into apartments about six blocks away from Dante's. As part of a gentrification program, the city renovated the campus, sold it to an asshole slumlord who already owned half the city, and passed it off as an *"artists' village."* The owner, Vik Shwartz, overcharged for rents, but gave discounts to people who worked in the arts as his deal with the city required. They called it the "Culture Campus." The only culture at the campus involved being broke, patchouli, rats, and dope. Lots of dope.

Maggie was working on it though. She'd been clean for two months today. She even shared at her NA meeting. There was no chip for two months, but clarity was its own reward. Two months with no heroin, no alcohol, no weed, no nothing. She couldn't say she didn't miss it, but she was glad she'd done it. She didn't think Rick had even noticed. Maybe it was that he was so into the drugs, but she didn't think so. He was so into himself that he couldn't tell where he ended and she began. All addicts were selfish. She'd learned this. Was there anything more self-centered than dedicating your days to a chemical because of how it made you feel?

With Rick it was different, though, it was deeper than addiction. He believed everything—everyone—existed for him. It was narcissism. They'd been together for one fast year, but the last two months, the sober months, had dragged by. Their relationship had been a passionate one, a fire that burned so hot it snuffed itself out. They'd argue and pick at each other, anger building and fuming and exploding into a screaming match. Sometimes worse. Then they'd fall into each other's arms and into bed, pleasure building and fuming and exploding into screaming, self-loathing orgasms. Love really was like a drug, Maggie thought. The higher the high, the lower the low.

Now, standing there staring at her guitar case, lost in the memory of her soon-to-be old life with Rick, Maggie couldn't wait to get on that stage and take her aggression out on all six strings of her Mosrite. Rick didn't know it was over yet. He would tonight. She just had a feeling. It would be a Christmas miracle.

"Maggie?" Someone said this like they'd been waiting awhile for an answer.

Maggie spun around to see her drummer, David, standing there, probably waiting to unload the van. "Hey," she said.

"You okay, Mags?"

"Yeah." She put on a smile to discourage questions. "I'm good. Just zoned out. You know."

David studied her a moment, then nodded. "Right. But like, are we good?"

Dammit. She should've known this would be a thing. He was a rebound. She needed to let him down but now wasn't the time. She had to get through this night.

"Yeah," she said, laying a hand on his arm. "We're good."

"Good. Cuz you look fucking hot." He smiled, his eyes tracing her figure.

She rolled her eyes, playing coy. Really, she did look hot though. She went with the black leather pants a la Joan Jett. They looked better on her though. Not to be cocky, but they did. Maggie's ass was nicer. She had her black hair pinned up. It was messy but sexy. Her pink tank top rode up just enough to offer a glimpse of her flat stomach. You could see just a little of the stem of her rose tattoo that stretched from the left side of her navel down to her pelvic region. She wore dark eyeliner and not much more makeup than that.

"Thanks," she said, flippant. "Dave, always with the compliments."

"You make it easy."

Jesus he was cheesy. He was so good looking though. The Splinters had groupies just because of David. She hadn't met a woman who didn't swoon at the sight of him. Maggie didn't find him especially attractive to be honest. Sure, he was objectively hot, but she wasn't into him. First of all he was young. She was almost 30 now and Dave was like, what, 21? She couldn't remember exactly. He was talented as hell but a little dumb. A good guy but not her guy. The real reason she'd hooked up with him, and she had to admit this was a little messed up, was that Rick was so adamant that they were already fucking. Seriously. He never stopped accusing her of it. It was like he wanted it to be true.

So last night, on the eve of Christmas Eve, she stormed out after the fight and went straight to David's apartment, pushed him down on his queen-sized mattress that rested on the floor (yeah, seriously) and screwed his brains out. Poor kid had feelings now. She could see it in his eyes. She almost felt guilty. Then she thought about all the women who men had used for sex over the last 12 millennia and she got over it.

"Charlie's got some guys to help us unload," David said. Guess he realized she wasn't going to keep flirting.

"Cool." She cracked a smile. "I'll keep my eyes on Johnny though."

"Right." David did his surfer, Keanu-like laugh. He actually kind of looked like Keanu. His shaggy dark hair framed a pair of gorgeous almond eyes and he had a lanky but strong body. "Wouldn't expect you to let Johnny out of your sight."

Johnny was her 1965 blue Mosrite Ventures II, just like the one Johnny Ramone played in the early years. The Mosrite was her pride and joy, and Johnny Ramone her guitar idol. Well, next to Steve. There was no doubt that Steve was the better guitarist in The Splinters, but Maggie loved to bang out the rhythms on the Mosrite. Power chords, down stroke only, legs stretched out, channeling her hero. She liked to think she kind of played like him. Her vocals, though, were original and melodic. A local music critic wrote that The Splinters sounded like "Blondie on speed." Maggie both appreciated and resented the comparison.

The Splinters had a little commercial success at one point. Maggie and Steve had started the band with a couple of Maggie's high school friends. They weren't really cut out for life on the road. They were on their third rhythm section now. Maggie still held out hope the best days were ahead of them.

Dante's had a backstage where they could leave their gear. Two bands were opening for them. The Splinters would take the stage about 9. They were a regular act at Dante's. They wouldn't do it for $200 just anywhere these days. In the bad old days, they were lucky to get booked much less paid.

They always went out to lunch whenever they played Dante's. They were comfortable, and the nerves didn't get to them. It was like they were the home team. Today was different though. Maggie was definitely nervous.

"Mags?" David said, catching her zoned out for the second time today. She looked at him quizzically. "Your order." She could see concern on David's face. Was he suspicious? No way. He's a dude. He couldn't see past the fact they were in bed together 12 hours ago. If he's worried, he's worried about that.

Maggie followed the server's red apron up, past the pen and order pad, and found her eyes. "Sorry, Bailey."

"No worries, Mags," Bailey said. "Drink? Maker's?"

"Yeah... wait. No thanks. A Coke is fine."

"Maggie's sober," Gina said. "Tell her, Maggie. You should be proud."

Maggie cracked a smile, gave Gina an appreciative look. Gina was The Splinters' newest bass player. She hadn't been around for very long, but Maggie had taken a liking to her. It was nice to have another woman in the band.

"Two months today," Maggie said.

"Congratulations, Mags," Bailey said, shifting her hips from one side to the other in her excitement. She wore a Santa hat with a bell on top that jingled when she moved. "That's awesome. And on Christmas Eve too." Bailey had a Southern drawl and an innocence about her that put you at ease.

Bailey turned to Steve and asked for his drink order. "Miller," he said. "That okay?" He was looking at Maggie, not Bailey. Maggie was with these people almost every day, and she'd been slurping soda while they had adult beverages for two months, but Steve still asked every time. She loved that about him.

"I'm good."

The conversation went on while they ate, but it was just a fuzzy haze in Maggie's peripheral. Her mind kept going back to Rick, to what she knew had to happen. It wasn't like she just suddenly realized he was bad for her. She'd known that. But something about the sobriety, the clarity. She'd always seen their relationship as a toxic mess, but now she knew it was abuse. Her mind flashed to images of him screaming, punching holes in the wall. Images of herself grasping him, begging him to stay. Images of herself apologizing, always taking the blame. She got sick to her stomach. The woman in those images—that was not Maggie Sharp. Maggie Sharp was fierce and independent. Maggie Sharp was a fucking rock star.

"Hey, Mags," Steve said. "Can I see the set list?"

Maggie passed it over, waiting for Steve's inevitable suggestions.

"Is Rick coming to the show?" Gina said.

David's eyes dropped to his half-eaten cheeseburger. His face reddened, not enough for anyone else to notice. But Maggie noticed.

"He'll be there."

Gina nodded. "I didn't know if they were playing or on the road or what."

"They're on a break till March I think." Maggie had met Rick out on the road. He fronted a band called Toxin. They had a much more pop-rock sound. Rick was a gifted vocalist. He was destined to be a star. Maggie remembered a thing she learned in middle school. Her science teacher told her that the stars she saw in the sky had already burned out. Better to burn out than it is to rust.

"Just one cover?" Steve said.

Maggie smiled. "That's all I had planned. That okay?"

His lips tightened and his head tottered like he was considering. "I guess."

"Aw, Mags," David said. "No showing off for *Windsor the Great*."

Steve admonished David with a look. For the second time, David's beautiful face was pinkish. The Splinters wrote punk songs. There were guitar solos, but they were short, just to stretch out the bridge. Steve liked to throw in some metal covers so he could play longer solos.

"We can do another," Maggie said. "Scratch one and put in what you want."

"The Devil Cried?"

Maggie nodded her consent.

"Sabbath." David said, his surfer bro voice proving he'd recovered from his facial scolding. "Nice." He started air drumming, already imagining the crowd at Dante's in front of them.

A few hours later, Maggie tried to relax as The Splinters did their sound check. The anxiety had festered and fumed though, her head a pressure cooker filling with steam.

A tacky red garland lined the sides and top of the stage. Maggie looked to her left and saw the requisite tacky artificial tree on the stage. It looked completely out of place. She had to laugh, letting some of the pressure escape.

They opened the show with "*Hammer Down*," a hardcore song from their garage days. It was a Dante's tradition. After a few songs from the latest record, they played "*Crimson on Satin*," a tongue-in-cheek ballad Maggie wrote about losing her virginity to a douchebag in high school. The crowd, many of whom she recognized, were loving it.

Maggie had been scanning the crowd all night, but she couldn't see Rick. Why wasn't he here? This wasn't going according to plan. She had to stall. "We're going to take a short break," Maggie said into the mic. "We love you, Dante's!"

"You okay?" Steve said when they got backstage.

Maggie smiled, reassuring him. "Yeah. Throat just got a little dry. I thought you guys would want to get your share of beer in too."

Steve didn't look convinced.

"Mags, if there's something up." He let his voice trail off.

Maggie shook her head. "Steve," she said, a little sharper than she meant to, "I'm good. I just needed a break."

Charlie played music over the PA and used the break to remind people to tip the staff. Maggie had killed about ten minutes with the break. "We're going to play a little Sabbath," Maggie told the crowd when they returned to the stage.

David counted them off and Gina and Maggie picked up the rhythm behind him. Right as Steve started his Tony Iommi impression, the back door cracked, spilling street light into the dive bar.

Maggie caught Rick's eyes just as a snowball pelted him in the back of the head. He whipped around and yelled at someone she couldn't see. Probably just the street kids. They loved to accost adults going in and out of the Third Street shops and bars. It was almost as much of a Christmas tradition as The Splinters playing Dante's.

Rick looked up at Maggie and smiled, still wiping the snow from his long dark hair. He made his way through the crowd. Already she could see he was limping a little. People stepped out of his way. They all knew who he was. Maggie returned the smile, but there was no warmth in it.

Anger rushed through Maggie and it came out in her vocals. She played everything faster, and David and Gina had to keep up. She never took her eyes off Rick. She thought about the constant accusations. She thought about the manipulation, always making her feel like it was her fault. Her anger was fuel for the music. And then it happened. A Christmas miracle.

The left slide of Rick's face went slack. His cheek and even his eye drooped. Panic set in on his face. Into the mic, Maggie said, "It's that time, Dante's! It's Christmas Eve. It's time for our favorite cover song. Merry Christmas!"

The crowd cheered. People who were sitting at tables stood and gathered around the stage. The sudden cluster of people pushed Rick farther forward. He was in the front row now, Maggie staring down at him.

Rick tried to get control, but he just looked panicked. Maggie could see that he couldn't move his left arm now. It just hung loosely at the side of his body.

"Merry Christmas, I don't want to fight tonight," Maggie sang melodiously into the mic. The band picked up the rhythm right behind her. The crowd danced like it was compelled to. "Merry Christmas I don't want to fight tonight," she sang four times, eyes locked with Rick's. He was still panicked, but she saw something else in his little abusive face now too. Realization. He got it, and she knew it.

"Where is Santa at his sleigh?" Maggie sang. Rick began to drool and foam at the mouth. "Tell me why is it always this way." He fell forward, catching himself on the guard rail with his working right hand. Maggie knew he'd lost control of his left leg. This was ataxia. She knew it'd happen because she'd researched it extensively.

By the time they got to the chorus, the crowd was moving so rhythmically, so frenetically, that you couldn't tell one person apart from another. They were just background for Maggie's message to Rick. Just backup dancers in her own little rock opera. *"Cause Christmas ain't the time for breaking each other's hearts,"* Maggie sang into Rick's soul.

She was just thankful it finally worked. She'd been lacing his dope with thallium for about two weeks. Last night, sometime between the back of his hand meeting her lip and her rushing to David's bed, she'd grown impatient and thrown it on heavy. All day she'd hoped the poison would do its job. It finally did. A Christmas miracle.

As The Splinters brought their cover of The Ramones classic to a close, Rick was in full seizure. Probably he no longer knew what was even happening. People around Rick noticed now and started yelling. Maggie didn't stop playing until she finished the song though.

"Merry Christmas, I don't wanna fight tonight with you," Maggie sang to Rick and Rick only. She meant it too. She didn't want to fight with him. Now she wouldn't have to.

[July 17th 1988, The Graduate, Santa Barbara, California, USA]

SHEENA IS A PUNK ROCKER
BY
WENDY DAVIS

The I.D. clearly wasn't Sheena's, but the fat bouncer didn't give a fuck. He barely glanced at the photo. She handed him a five-spot, and he ushered her in with a pat on the ass. She stifled the urge to punch him, to break his dirty teeth, and instead marched around and waited for Lydia. He inspected Lydia's I.D. more closely and then frisked her, running his hands over her bare legs, his thick fingers slipping under her miniskirt. Lydia looked unbothered as he stood up and smirked, nodding for her to go.

"If that's how he gets his kicks," Lydia said.

Sheena grinned. "Don't worry. I stole his wallet."

They giggled and walked into Gryphon's — the blighted laundromat that was also a bar. On the laundry side, a sun-scorched woman folded clothes with rough hands. A Capri cigarette hung from her blistered lip. She shoved her laundry in a pillowcase and glared at everyone as she left.

Sheena plucked the few dollars from the stolen wallet and tossed it in the trash. They made their way to the laminate bar, shimmed with phonebooks, surrounded by stools repaired with duct tape where Mac stood sentry. He never had a night off, and it showed. His weary eyes glazed over the patrons, the day workers and bums, the streetwalkers and the unmedicated, anyone who'd scraped up enough to earn a seat and drink cheap booze.

Mac didn't speak — just eyed the girls. "Two rum and Cokes," Sheena ordered. He poured with a heavy hand and slid the flimsy cups across the bar. Sheena paid him with the stolen cash just as shrill feedback raked their ears. The annoyed regulars flinched and rose to go. They'd had enough of these punks.

On the slumped stage, Cheap Shot was playing a sloppy version of *I Wanna Be Your Dog.* The lead singer, Billy Mercy, was carving his chest with broken glass. He fancied himself a shaman, like Iggy Pop, but his spirit world was soggy, his antics tired. Now, streaked with blood, he was humping his amp, his pants at his knees, a pathetic erection. His pinhead friends were marching and shoving each other, slapping their own faces. The rest of the crowd looked bored.

"They couldn't play their way out of a toilet," Sheena said.

Lydia nodded. "That should be us up there."

"Fuck Big Ed and his boys' club."

"It wasn't Ed's fault. You know he offered us the gig first."

"Then he should have stuck to his word."

"Well, he got wasted and lost his ass to Billy in some bet. Billy told him he'd forget about it if they could open for The Gone Dogs."

"Stop defending Ed. Just because you tickle him a couple times a week doesn't make it right. He fucked us on this one. The Gone Dogs are on their way up. They got a great deal with Superlative Records and just booked this gig to fill in dates between D.C. and Atlanta. This could have been big for us."

Sheena tossed back her drink and scowled. She was tired of the same bullshit. It didn't matter that the Cadettes would torch the stage, stirring up the degenerate crowd. Lydia, with her teased red hair and fishnets, singing, dancing, and swaying the bass with her hips. Jules in a tank and denim cutoffs — her surfer-girl hair flying as she attacked the drums, and Sheena, peroxide blond and tight, furiously down stroking her Silvertone guitar.

It didn't matter because bands like Cheap Shot got first dibs, even if they fumbled their way through a show. But The Cadettes had to be great to get any gig. And they were great because they'd been playing together since high school. After Sheena's brother left for the Navy, she'd discovered his records — the Stooges, The Ramones, the Dolls. His walls plastered with xeroxed flyers — Black Flag, Bad Brains, the Misfits.

But it was The Runaways poster that struck her heart. When she slid the record from the sleeve and gave it a spin, her life changed. Her destiny became clear. She swiped her brother's Squire Strat from a dusty corner and began strumming along with the records. Instead of Teen Vogue, she bought Guitar Player.

And when the new girl Lydia walked through Central High's doors wearing leopard tights and heels, a t-shirt scrawled with Blank Generation, Sheena found her lead singer. Jules was a natural fit, too. Hyperactive and athletic, drumming on desks. A card-carrying member of the KISS Army.

They practiced in Jules' basement every day — a sick yellow lightbulb hanging from the ceiling. But they were a girl band, and no matter how good they got, the boy bands dismissed them. Didn't take them seriously. Were amused or aroused but somehow unconvinced.

The music stopped, and Billy Mercy ended the set with a stupid spoken word piece.

"What an asshole," Mac muttered and looked at Sheena's empty drink.

"Want another?"

"Nah," she said. She was out of money but not out of booze.

"Don't let me see that pint in your pants, or you're out of here."

Sheena shrugged. Mac knew everything.

From out of nowhere, Jules, breathless and flushed, bounded up to the bar.

"You'll never guess what happened. Tim nodded out in the bathroom. Ed's so fucking pissed. They're trying to wake him, but no luck so far."

"Gun Crazy's supposed to play next — right?"

"Yeah, and The Gone Dogs aren't here yet." Jules' eyes flashed, and all three smiled.

"Does Ed want us to play?"

"You got it. You know Ed. Doesn't want to lose bar business."

"He should have booked us in the first place."

"No shit. Serves him right."

Upstairs, Billy Mercy was being a real prick about sharing his band's gear.

"If you break it, you're gonna buy it."

"Whatever, Billy. Your speaker's already busted," Sheena said. "You haven't noticed because you're fucking tone-deaf."

"Fuck off, Sheena. Just because Lydia gets up there and wiggles her ass doesn't make The Cadettes better than us."

Sheena wagged her pinky finger at him and said, "Better than wiggling your tiny cock."

Billy sneered and lunged at Sheena. She stepped back and then landed a sharp punch to his throat — just like her brother taught her. Billy grabbed his neck and began coughing. His boys laughed.

"Get our gear off stage," he ordered. "I'm not letting these cunts use it."

"The hell you will," Ed quietly said. He stepped between Sheena and Billy. He stood like a refrigerator, a veteran, a former cop.

"You take that gear out of here, you don't come back."

Billy knew better than to challenge Ed. Gryphon's was the only place in town that let Cheap Shot play.

Billy threw a tantrum, punching the wall and stomping downstairs. In the back, the bathroom door slammed open, and Larry emerged, carrying Tim over his shoulder.

"Is he O.K.?" Lydia asked.

"Yeah. He's fine. But I'm gonna fucking kill him when he wakes up," Larry said.

He threw Tim on the filthy couch. He groaned and rolled over and was out like a light.

"You guys playing in our place?" Larry asked.

"Yeah," Sheena said.

"You can use our guitars. You know Cheap Shot's gear is shit."

Sheena was surprised but grateful. She and Larry were a thing for a minute. He considered himself a punk intellectual — believing having something to say outweighed having chops on the guitar. But when his pals teased him about Sheena playing circles around him, suggesting she was the alpha, he became resentful, his ego bruised. He quit seeing her — never explaining why — but later telling others The Cadettes relied on tits and ass to draw a crowd.

"Thanks, Larry," she said.

"Yeah. Stuff's in the corner. I'm leaving Tim here — roll him over if he pukes, will ya?"

Sheena tuned the borrowed guitars while Lydia retouched her Egyptian eyeliner, slid off her shirt, leaving on her sequined bra. Sheena watched her stretch, kicking her legs up the wall in a handstand, balancing a minute before slowly coming down.

"Sheena, come here," Lydia said, and Sheena put down the guitar and wandered over. She shut her eyes as Lydia tousled her cropped bleached hair and set it with hairspray. Her soft hands tipped Sheena's chin and painted her lips coral — like a Hitchcock blond.

"You look hot," Lydia said with a wink. They smiled as if sharing a secret.

Jules was ready. She always was. She didn't get dolled up — she sweated so much it would be for nothing anyway.

The Cadettes took the stage to a restless crowd. Catcalls and whistles pierced the room, and someone yelled, "Show us your tits, Lydia!" Lydia slid her thumbs under her bra straps, shimmying her shoulders. She turned and bent over, circling her hips, giving a peep show of her ballerina ass.

Sheena plugged in and strummed, the amp vibrations tingling her arms, while Jules impatiently twirled her drumsticks. Sheena gave Jules the signal, counted it off, and *Lose That Girl* jolted the room. Beer cans spewed as the frenzied crowd bounced and bashed, romping in their debased playground.

Three songs in, Lydia's bass thrummed as Sheena lit a cigarette and said, "Somebody get me a shot." An outstretched arm handed her a bottle of 151. "Not fucking around, are ya?" she said and plucked the bottle from the guy's hands. She turned it up and handed it back. He drank and set it on the stage.

From the corner of her eye, Sheena noticed some fellows at the side — a lanky guy with eyes like Lurch and a couple of others holding guitars. They looked like they needed a meal or a fix. Probably both. The Gone Dogs were here, and they were watching them play.

Jules launched into *The Roadhouse*, a slinky number that veered outside the machine-gun rhythm of most of their tunes. An instrumental with a spooky guitar from some dark, haunted highway — Sheena's new thing since discovering Link Wray. Lydia set down the bass and danced, snake-charming the crowd, threading the mic cord between her thighs, leaving them breathless as the last note washed over the room.

Sheena took another swig of 151 and lit a cigarette while Lydia slung the bass over her shoulder. Jules clapped the drumsticks, and Sheena's guitar fired off.

The fevered crowd exploded —frantically banging their heads. The Gone Dogs continued to watch, dumbstruck. But midway into the song, Billy Mercy stumbled onto the stage.

He waved a broken drumstick in the air, like a busted conductor directing a band. Sheena narrowed her eyes. She mouthed keep playing at Jules. Jules nodded back.

Billy slunk behind Lydia and began thrusting his bony hips — the crowd thrilled, egging him on. Suddenly, their sleazy fantasies were real. Somebody was gonna fuck The Cadettes. It was about goddamn time — these girls had tortured them for too long.

Billy pumped faster. Unfazed, Lydia wiggled closer, and with an uh-oh look, playfully bumped him with her hip. Billy stumbled back, miraculously catching his balance. He grinned and threw his arms in the air. The crowd whooped as he crept to Sheena's amp and began twiddling the knobs. Her guitar cut out. She slid it off her shoulder, placed it on the stand, and coolly smoked. This asshole was not going to break her. Not now. Not ever.

Billy's eyes landed on the 151. He swiped the bottle and chugged the liquor. It ran over his face and soaked his clothes. He turned toward Lydia, unzipped his pants, pulled out his cock and began jerking off. Lydia feigned surprise and motioned come and get me. He stepped forward, but Sheena had had enough. Billy Mercy wasn't going to steal her show.

Sheena flicked her cigarette at Billy's chest. The ember ignited his liquor-soaked shirt, lapping him in flames. Terrified and on fire, he dove off the stage as the crowd scurried like roaches. He landed with a sick thud. A couple of fellows ripped off their shirts and beat down the blaze as a scorched stench filled the room.

Lydia was stunned. Sheena was pleased. Jules stopped playing. Angry eyes burned, and angry fists clenched as the crowd grew dead quiet. The Cadettes, those bitches, had gone too far.

Over the hush, Sheena spoke into the mic.

"Fuck you."

The mob rushed the stage, but The Cadettes were already running. Big Ed had the side door open, motioning for the girls to follow. They sprinted toward the parking lot, tumbling into Ed's beat-up Nova. He cranked it up, squealing the tires as they hit the road.

Sheena turned and watched the furious silhouettes grow smaller. She burst into laughter.

[February 17 1978, Armadillo World Headquarters, Austin, Texas, USA]

I DON'T WANNA GO DOWN TO THE BASEMENT
BY
CHRISTINA DELIA

I don't expect anyone to believe me, but Mick and I were angrily dividing up our record collection (as is customary at the end of a turned-shitty relationship) when that thing he'd been keeping in the basement ran up the slat stairs and into our living room and bit Mick's fucking head off. So I stood there staring at the now-ghastly uneven neck stump of my lover-turned-hater. Obviously, I was in shock. I'm still in shock. My fiancé is a dead man. I'm next.

If a lifetime of slasher movies prepared me for anything, it's don't run up the fucking stairs. The killers that hunt hapless teens in slasher films are slow-stalking humans. This creature is a fast moving mound. It looks like a cross between that ranting brain Krang from the Teenage Mutant Ninja Turtles cartoon and Pizza the Hutt from Spaceballs.

Yes. I'm a child of the Eighties.

And this is what I get for dating a scientist.

I hit the venomous flesh-colored blob in its face (if you can call that regurgitated lunch meat a face) with a bucket. I dump a bottle of Bona on its head. I am meticulous about my honey oak hardwood floors, but as I wildly look around our living room for objects to defend myself with, I realize all that shit I fretted about doesn't matter.

Hardwood, my injured pride at finding out my man cheated on me, that sham the poets call love…they all seem absurd. How ridiculous to care about anyone or anything other than myself when this world is so clearly about survival!

I spy a bottle of Windex next to the coffee table. Grabbing it, I spray that nasty sucker right in its big solo off-center milky white eye. Its dark pupil narrows on me a second before being temporarily blinded. It howls in muffled agony; sounding like if someone using voice-changing technology had their pinky toe hacked off.

This thing has no toes.

Tentacles, sure. Weird body stumps, tumorous lumps and mush. The thing is a gelatinous lard pile, but it has what look to be toeless feet with long, pointy coal-colored talons jutting out of them. Like a devil made an unfortunate snowman in Hades. Those hideous puppies would shred a pair of canvas sneakers to bits. Hounds of hell, my dogs are barking indeed.

As I am fighting for my life, I think about the hounds of hell, and if they too are going to appear and drag me down, down, DOWN past the basement and to a cosmic crawl space where neither God nor anything holy or sacred ever dwelt. The thing's feet stink, and it's not the usual type of foot odor that can be remedied with some baby powder.

No, they smell like a cross between festering hamburger and feces. Is that the sickening aroma of rotting flesh? I close my eyes and swallow hard to avoid breathing out my nose.

It breathes on me and its breath is oddly cold but just as foul as its foot odor. I shake with chills and sweat, and I silently curse myself for ever allowing Mick to bring this "*work project*" into our home. "It's harmless, it's science," he'd laughed, and I'd just shrugged. What did I know? I wasn't the scientist in the room.

The scientist in the room has lost his head. I aim to keep mine, so I push past the behemoth (oh God! I touched it! My FINGERS!) and run like my life depends on it down the basement stairs, like a demon's chasing me.

It does. It is.

I don't know if the monster sees where I'm headed, but I have no doubt that it can sniff me out with those flared nostril cavities. The vomit goblin! I've never used that phrase before, but holy shit if it isn't accurate! It looks like Sloth from The Goonies had a baby with aspic.

The basement is pitch blackness (that's why I refuse to paint down here; I need natural light). I slump shaking on the side of a wardrobe that I wish could transport me to Narnia.

Fuck this, I'm a proud gay man, and I'm not going to hide in a closet. I have come too far in my life. I have to kill this thing.

I can discern that it's moving around overhead. It was so fast when it was slurping Mick's skull, but now it sounds like it is moving slow…dragging something.

I taste bile, and I know that it's dragging Mick's body. Why? Is it a trophy?

My dad was a deer hunter. My mom liked to stick pins in butterflies (she amassed quite a collection). I never hurt anyone or anything, except for myself. Maybe it's because I was raised by parents who liked to hunt down and trap other living things, but I've spent most of my life stuck in bad relationships.

I had thought that Mick was different. He had a great career, and seemed to love me back. Things changed when he brought that thing home from the research lab.

It was so small then; the size of my mother's breast cancer tumors before her mastectomy. Yes, she had shown them to me. Yes. She had cried in my arms. I was a caring son. I can be strong for other people when they need me, but I couldn't stay in that house in the wilderness where my dad kept sneering, "I know what you are."

I know what I am, too: a good person.

A survivor.

But it would be nice sometimes to have someone to hold onto.

Like the distance between Mick and me, like Ma's malignant masses, the thing that Mick brought home GREW.

At first he'd said, "James, you're imagining things!" I wasn't. That's what he said about his affair, too, until I caught him in bed with Gray from the gym.

"Jimbo, you can watch," Gray had laughed, and I just stood there stupidly (I feel like I'm so good at that!) remembering how I'd thought his name was Gary, and how I didn't like him when we first met.

I'm usually spot-on about people. Except my lovers—I have terrible taste in men; sexy intellectuals with Oscar Wilde wits who take me to the opera and hand me rose-colored glasses.

All of the operas Mick took me to were tragedies.

I should have known.

I don't believe in coincidence, and I find it very strange that this malformed mutant glob attacked Mick at the exact time he was blasting The Ramones self-titled studio album. Like, it was literally on track seven, *"I Don't Wanna Go Down to the Basement"* when the goober came up from the basement and murdered my ex-fiancé by chomping his head like someone famished in a TV commercial hocking a satisfying Snickers.

No amount of television viewing could have prepared me for this.

So I'm freezing in my cold-terror-sweat-dripping muscle tee, praying to a God that I'd always envisioned as looking like a cross between Olivia Newton John at the end of Xanadu and Iggy Pop in the "I'm Bored" video (I don't know why… now's not the time to judge me!)

From the darkened corner, I pray and rage cry through my gritted teeth (is this the death lead up? Am I next?)

My soon-to-be basement tomb is where I silently dry heave (that stench is still stuck in my nostrils! That bubbling road kill might as well be tattooed onto my eyelids… I can't stop seeing it and what it did to Mick) and try to retrace the events of the day.

Having caught Mick in the act just last week, I'd opted to stay at our mutual friend Bonnie's place. She likes me better, even though she's known Mick longer. (Bonnie had told me this months ago, but I never told Mick because I didn't want to hurt him.) Mick however, had no qualms about hurting me, when he knew I'd be home at five-thirty, and he'd elected to fuck Gray at five-fifteen.

Timing is everything.

And just then I catch the unmistakable boom of Gray's voice. Always the life of the party, I guess Mick had made him a key. Is he already so comfortable strolling into the shambles of our shared life like a sitcom neighbor looking for gossip to delight in, money to borrow, a fridge to raid, or, in this case, a relationship to destroy?

I'm glad that I never liked Gray. How could I? His body language is that of a taker. He is not the sort of person who will hold the elevator for anybody. He never cleans up after using the free weights at the gym.

He thought he had my fiancé. Now he's left alone with his rotten self.

But really he's alone with that rotten thing

I doubt that Gray has come to make amends with me. More likely he knew I'd be moving out, and that we were splitting up our stuff. He wants to cuddle Mick, comment on my belongings, and make me feel uncomfortable in my own apartment.

Too bad for Gray he never gets the chance. His hysterical screaming makes me wonder if he's found Mick's headless corpse, or if the monster has gotten him? This question races through my pounding head like a morbid "*chicken or the egg?*" scenario.

I'm not certain of the order of events, except that Mick died first and Gray dies next.

Much like the echo of his orgasm, I also wish I could un-hear the reverberations of Gray's demise. His shrieks are pure agony, like his skin is being scraped off of his carcass; pulled pork personified.

I have to cover my own mouth to keep from screaming, and I do, digging my fingernails into the sides of my face. I feel something wet and sticky and realize I am puking uncontrollably into my hand.

Gray is a shitty human being, but he doesn't deserve to die. And anyway, I don't want to listen to any more of it. Watching Mick get T-rexed by that ball of snot and cauliflower was awful enough.

Eventually, Gray's screams subside. God, how I wait for a whimper, hoping he is still alive. No, I don't want him to suffer, so in this case death must be necessary. Yet I don't want to be someone who has just listened to the torture and murder of my love rival.

I don't want to lose my humanity.

All I hear is sudden silence, and I never knew silence could be so loud.

I'M NEXT! I'M NEXT! I'M NEXT!

I think about the horror movie tropes. I was so focused on not running up the stairs, that I ran down to the BASEMENT.

NOT BETTER!

I hear its entire weight shift on the slat stairs, and I know. There's nothing like the feeling of knowing you're about to die. It's trauma beyond trauma. I feel myself outside of my body. My therapist has referred to this as dissociation, but I have only experienced it once prior, in college.

I was beaten in the street for being gay. They had punched me in the back, kicked me in the face and torso over and over again, and spat on me. How had it happened to me in bustling Center City Philadelphia? And not in the wilderness I'd known my entire life? I was left on Lombard Street in my own blood, concussed with multiple skull fractures and broken ribs. I lost three teeth. And I knew I couldn't tell my parents; not with my mother hooked up to monitors. My father would have said something along the lines of, "What were you doing out at that hour? Prancing down the street like a big shot? What'd you expect?"

I hadn't expected to be the victim of a hate crime, and if there's one thing I loathe being, it's a victim.

I don't want to die.

Does anyone want to die when death nears? Do you just drown with it? Soak it in?

I hear it coming toward me…hunting me.

Prey, prey, PRAY.

I'm not godless, but I'm not much for prayer. I consider myself to be spiritual, and that's what I'm contemplating when I experience divine intervention.

Chirp, chirp, chirp.

The squeak of an Easter chick.

And then the monstrosity is upon me. I head-butt into its mush pile excuse for a stomach, and it is taken aback, I think, because it begins howling. The sound and smell combination is nauseatingly ferocious; like a festering head cheese on helium gargling a high-pitched sea shanty over a crackling middle school loudspeaker.

Covering my ears, I attempt to avoid its shrill blubbering, but not before I catch the chirp again.

I fumble over in the direction of the noise, and notice one of Mick's incubators. The bulb is out, but I see them: two little flesh-colored blobs.

Twins.

And then a third.

Triplets.

I know what they need. It's what we all need.

Lifting the three brain matter-like lumps from the useless incubator, I carry them upstairs in the palm of my hand. The creature wails, but then I believe it realizes.

I am not going to hurt them.

The monster follows me upstairs, careful to ease itself over the broken slats. I hear its devil's talons scratch against the remaining wood, and know it just used these to peel Gray.

My tense gut is telling me that my life depends on saving these baby blobs. And I want to save them. I can't bear the thought of any more death; human or otherwise.

The creeping carbuncle moves gelatinously behind me, and I dully recall Drivers Ed class *(keep a safe following distance.)* Maybe I am finally losing my mind?

I lead the oozing lump upstairs, past Gray's smushed-in corpse and Mick's headless one. I think about love and loss, and how in the end we're all just pinned butterflies.

We enter my studio. I cringe at my portrait-in-progress of Mick; my never-would-be wedding gift to him. His sharp blue eyes reassure me from my easel in a way that real-life Mick never could. Maybe in love we create what we want to see. That's all a relationship is: sitting for a portrait. Only I'd had to paint from a photograph, since Mick had refused to sit for me; he was too busy screwing Gray, and lording over odious scientific abominations.

The natural light streams in, and seems to relax the beast. I carefully place the tiny tumor triad in a Frankenstein collector's plate I keep on a shelf next to my art books.

Full circle fright irony.

I hold the plate in my hand, and take in the view one last time. So breathtaking: the trees are just budding white blossoms, both the flowering plants and sun promise springtime after a harsh winter.

Compared to the basement, this is heaven.

The thing seems to think so, too; it topples to its side in a sort of reclining position. It seems relieved; grateful.

One day I am going to die, but I don't think today's the day.

Why are you letting me live? Because I'm kind?

I don't say it aloud, and I don't need an answer. I put the Frankenstein plate on an end table next to my Dali, Magritte and Keith Haring books. I walk out of my studio, and then the front door. Once outside, I keep moving, break into a run, and I don't think I'll ever stop.

I don't tell a soul. Who would believe me? I stay at Bonnie's, and she somehow assumes I'm this pale, jumpy and traumatized from seeing Mick again so soon after the breakup. She doesn't ask me any questions, and I wouldn't have answered them, anyway.

Three days later, my landlady Mrs. Falvoa gets in touch with me. She says if I don't pick up my record collection and the rest of my stuff, she'll donate it to Goodwill. Knowing me well, she accurately perceives that the way to get to me is to threaten the existence of my vinyl.

I am afraid to go back there, but of course I can't tell her this. Mrs. Falvoa says she's been showing the apartment to prospective tenants, and seemingly nothing's happened to them.

How do I know this? I've been checking news feeds obsessively, but finding nothing. So then I stay up all night Googling phrases like "*Flesh-colored blobby monster on the loose*" and "*Thing eats man's head.*" All the search results I'm getting are ads for Halloween masks and porn sites.

When Bonnie, her friend Stephanie and I enter the apartment, I am in awe. The place is immaculate; all natural light gleaming off of my honey oak floors.

We load up my vinyl collection in milk crates, just like when I moved in: The Ramones, Misfits, The Clash, Bad Brains, Iggy and The Stooges, The Germs, X-Ray Spex, Black Flag, The Cramps, X; my beautiful on and on punk record hoard I never thought I'd see or hear again.

Turning around in the space, I can't believe the looks of the place now compared to the veritable slaughterhouse I had frantically exited. The fiend took its babies and left the scene, but not just that. It had cleaned up all the carnage; somehow no trace of Mick or Gray.

Just my empty Frankenstein collector's plate as a grim souvenir.

It is assumed that Mick and Gray have run off together. I receive a lot of jilted lover sympathy, and all I can do is nod and wonder if that massive earth-quaking-third-cousin-once-removed to the Jell-O mold swallowed the rest of Mick and Gray's murdered bodies whole?

I hope they are finally at peace.

Where is the creature now? And its offspring? Will the oozing infants return? Or wreak havoc somewhere else as a full-grown terrible trio?

Just as with my mother's cancer, we'll have to wait and see.

I will never take natural light for granted again. It saved my life, and the life of those baby blobs, too. I will not worry about future horrors, but live in the present.

Stepping into the sun, I feel the light on my face; thinking about Iggy Pop, Xanadu, and how I survived the basement.

[September 27th 1987, The Roxy, West Hollywood, California, USA]

MAIN MAN
BY
JOSEPH S. WALKER

i

It's hard to say when we first became aware of The Main Man. He lived on the edges of lives already lived on the edge. The earliest sighting we can be sure of was at a loft party in the village, thrown by a conceptual artist, in the process of being evicted, who wanted to do as much damage to the place as possible before he left. He had a dozen sledgehammers, and everyone who came was invited to take a swing at the walls. Someone walking around being insistently retro with a Polaroid camera caught The Main Man in the process of doing it. In the picture the sledgehammer is a blur. The Main Man himself is shirtless under his jet-black leather jacket and the first thing you notice is the giant number 13 tattooed on his chest, blood-red block numerals stretching from his collarbone to his navel. Most people were content to crack a brick or two and get back to the drugs and music. It was The Main Man who went after the load-bearing pillar outside the loft's toilet. When it came down, the couple who'd been fucking on the bathroom sink were trapped for hours.

ii

Sure, The Main Man did time. Refused to give a real name even to the cops and they came up empty on fingerprints, so they called him John Doe. He had a prison tattoo artist turn the tracks on his arm into a skull. Spent hours sitting on his bunk just laughing, at nothing anyone could figure out. They had to assign him a new cellmate every few weeks. The Main Man could make you lose your shit. Sit there laughing all day and then you'd wake up in the middle of the night with his brown eyes inches from your face, staring like he wanted to tie your guts in knots.

One of the rattled cellmates was in with a gang, so they came after The Main Man one day in the showers. A captain backed by three gym rats, their arms swollen from spending all their yard time with the weights. Everybody else backed away. The Main Man stood there and watched them come. He was lean, his naked body snaked with ink from ankle to shoulders. The captain shoved his chest. "You're gonna learn some manners or die," he said.

The Main Man grinned the way a wolf grins. "Can't kill a man already in hell," he said, and he reached up lightning fast and mashed the captain's eye with his thumb, gouging into the socket. Son of a bitch screamed so loud that even the crooked guards couldn't pretend they didn't hear it. They came in and broke it up.

The captain ended up losing the eye. When he came out of the prison hospital The Main Man was waiting on the yard to show off his new tattoo: an eye, right at the base of the thumb. "Got room for another," he said. The way the captain slunk away from him was a death sentence. He should have known you don't back down, inside. One of those gym rats killed him a week later.

iii

When he wasn't behind bars or crashing with a woman, The Main Man lived on the streets. At least that's what we assumed. Sometimes you'd see him propped up in a doorway, arms crossed, so still it seemed like he was just something painted onto the building. Always in that leather jacket. In the summer he went shirtless under it but he never stopped wearing it. Maybe he just didn't have anywhere to put it. If he had a place of his own none of us knew it.

Once at three in the morning we saw him pushing an empty wheelchair down the sidewalk. Didn't know where he got it or where he was taking it, but we figured there was somebody in it when the evening started. We followed him down to the docks and watched him push the wheelchair all the way down a pier, right to the end and into the water. The Main Man never broke stride. He watched it until it sank out of sight in those nasty waters, then turned and came back, moving at exactly the same pace. We parted silently and he walked through like nobody was there.

iv

Women either hated The Main Man on sight or wanted him immediately. There's women around to this day who would push their husbands in front of subway trains if The Main Man came back and took them by the hand. None of them could explain what was so special about the way he fucked. They wouldn't even try, really, just said that once they were hooked on him they couldn't find a way back. It confused us because he didn't seem like somebody who'd be particularly sensitive or giving or whatever the hell women are supposed to want.

If any of them ever meant anything to him, he didn't show it. He didn't seem to care about them any more than he cared about anything, which was not at all. Some of us admired that about him, the way he seemed untouched by the world, utterly indifferent. Since he didn't care about anything, he didn't much want anything either. He'd take what was offered.

Fiona worked the midnight shift at a diner where The Main Man hung out sometimes in the predawn hours after whatever party or club he'd been at had closed down. Fiona was a sweet girl. Everybody called her Fee. She played bass, but not well enough to get a regular gig. She got to where she was taking The Main Man home with her after her shift two or three times a week. Mornings when he didn't show at the diner, she'd get a hollow look in her eyes and hang around until noon, hoping he'd show. One day she heard that The Main Man was getting hot and heavy with a stripper at a place a couple blocks away from the diner. She sweet-talked her way backstage at the place and shot the woman three times in the chest, only it turned out to be the wrong stripper.

Fee's lawyer came around to try to get The Main Man to testify. When he heard the story, The Main Man didn't stop laughing for hours.

v

Don't let anybody tell you The Main Man had friends. Scorpions don't have buddies. He'd run with a group for a few weeks, seem all in. Well, his version of all in. Hard to be all in for real when you won't even tell anybody your fucking name. He'd be up for anything, though, from street brawls to hijacking trucks. And what the fuck, you gotta figure that a guy who won't tell the cops his own name isn't gonna come up with yours, either.

Problem was that at some point he'd decide he was bored. Or maybe he just didn't want to be predictable. Some of us thought that there was a level of rage in him that never went away, and every once in a while it had to boil over. He'd be walking down the street with guys he'd been hanging with for weeks and suddenly turn and punch one of them in the nose, then start kicking him in the ribs once he was down. Pull stunts like that a few times and it starts getting hard to find anybody who will walk next to you. Seemed to be how he liked it. He was The Main Man, after all, not A Main Man. He was his own.

vi

The Main Man was ready. For anything. Always. He had to be just to survive, with all the people he pissed off. He was ready, and he was fast.

There was a neighborhood boxer, Andre Maple. Everybody called him Tree, not so much because of his name as because he was built solid and broad. People said Tree was going places. He'd won a bunch of amateur fights, was on the verge of going pro. He was in a pool hall shooting one night and The Main Man was on the next table. We never knew what went down between them. Some words went back and forth and then Tree stepped forward and threw the right hook that had ended his last three fights. Except there was nobody there for the punch to connect with, and by the time he'd finished the motion, the neck of a broken beer bottle lodged in his throat. We never even saw The Main Man break it. Tree lived, but his vocal cords were severed. He never fought again.

Something like that happens, everybody tells the cops they didn't see shit. This time we didn't have to lie. We hadn't seen what The Main Man had done. One second he was standing there about to be a human punching bag, the next Tree is grabbing at his neck as blood pours down his chest.

Couple weeks later we noticed the new tattoo on The Main Man's side, just above the beltline. A broken beer bottle with blood dripping from the shards. Another trophy. People started saying the 13 must be the number of people he'd killed.

vii

If he wasn't on the streets or in some girl's bed, The Main Man would be in a club. The faster and louder the music, the better. He got kicked out of plenty of places. He would hurl himself onto the dance floor and bounce and jump around until, inevitably, what was a dance had become a brawl. One night when this happened the band stopped playing to watch. The Main Man didn't care for that. He liked to have a soundtrack to his fights when it was possible. He jumped on the stage and kicked the guitarist in the balls. The drummer charged him and The Main Man threw him into the sound board. Sparks flew as the board broke. The bassist wasn't doing shit, but The Main Man spun to him anyway and started choking him with his own amp cord.

Looking back I guess The Main Man was sheer hell on bass players.

viii

The Main Man would steal anything that wasn't nailed down and most things that were. Every woman who took him home ended up reclaiming some of her own shit from a pawn shop. In clubs he was known to walk behind the bar, pick up a bottle and just walk off with it, generally while bartenders looked confused about what the hell they were supposed to do. The Main Man was no pro. He couldn't crack safes or bypass alarms. He didn't worry about shit like that. Broke plenty of shop windows, though. There were people who said the leather jacket was in a window display when it happened to catch his eye. He threw a metal trashcan through the glass and just walked away with it, brushing away shards that put little cuts all over his hands.

One night we saw him driving down the street in a cop car. There was a uniformed cop in the back seat, shaking the grill and yelling. The Main Man just idled along like he was sightseeing. That landed him inside again.

We never knew where the jacket went, the times The Main Man was locked up. It would just appear again when he got out.

ix

We don't know where he came from and we don't know where he went. One day somebody said, "Haven't seen The Main Man in a while," and we all realized it was true.

Most likely somebody killed him and his body is in the river or some shallow pit, or just in the sad graveyard where the city dumps the unclaimed. Maybe he moved on to another town and he's raising hell and pissing people off in a different time zone.

Some of us like to think he's living in some quiet town somewhere living a normal life. He puts on a suit that covers most of the ink and spends his days behind the counter at a car rental place or managing a grocery store, his greasy, tangled hair tamed into a disciplined buzz. Maybe there's a wife. Kids. The leather jacket is in the back of a closet in a guest bedroom. Waiting.

Some of us like to think that anybody could be The Main Man.

[September 27th 1979, Hillwood Commons Lecture Hall, Long Island, NY, USA]

TOO TOUGH TO DIE
BY
JON PARK

Arthur cannot recall the last time he was on these streets. He watches from the back of his limousine as they glide through Manhattan. Down into East Village. Recognising nothing. He knew these streets when they were grim and intimidating. The buildings like broken teeth, stained and crooked, have been cleaned and crowned. Now they sparkle. The perfect smile.

The limo reaches the corner of Bowery and East Street. Peter, his driver, slows so he can glance up to the heavens. Levitating, a sign. "Joey Ramone Place." He smiles. The years fading.

Onto Bowery Street, the mean bars and music venues are long gone. Expensive boutiques, trendy art galleries and gleaming coffee shops now exist in their space. He looks for the white awning that used to hang here, CBGB written on it in blood. Where his life began within its smoggy womb. CBGB's is long gone. Its doors closed and boarded up in 2006 over a rent dispute. So many times, Hilly had reached out to him for help. But he was lost. Fighting his own battle with drink and drugs. The only calls he was excepting were from his dealer.

Hilly eventually lost CBGB's. Then his life. He owed Hilly so much. Yet he had failed him. A burden he has carried all these years. Today, he hopes to make amends.

"Peter," he calls, "Can we stop just here?"

"Sure Mr Jones, but you do know the venue is a couple more blocks."

"Yeah, I know, I just need to check in on an old friend."

He steps from the limo. 315 Bowery. Where CBGB's once stood. He recalls its windows smothered in flyers for bands, its exterior white walls lost beneath graffiti. When the doors opened the heat and smell of weed would slap you dizzy. A designer clothes store stands in its place. He peers into its windows, seeing the twenty-year-old student, whose life was yet to begin. He feels a tear run down his cheek and brushes it away. He wishes he could speak to this kid and tell him of the mistakes he will make, the loved ones he should have held close and the friends he should have been there for. He smiles and whispers, "You did alright kid."

A stumble. "You okay Mr Jones?" Peter asks stepping forward. He waves a hand, looking down at the pavement where someone has scratched "*CBGB73*" into the concrete. He remembers the night his life began. August 1974. Him and his buddy Stevie standing in the main aisle of CBGB's drinking warm beer while sweat dripped from the ceiling. He often accompanied Stevie to CBGB's. Stevie loved folk and blues music and CBGB's provided this in abundance and was renowned for it.

They order another two beers as the next band began to emerge onto the stage. Twenty or so hippies, the love generation are gathered at the front, a greenish smog hanging over their heads.

He can see the four members of the band he will come to love and adore, on stage, getting ready to blow a hole in his life. A hole he will attempt to fill for the next forty years. Each member wore a black leather motorcycle jacket, faded jeans and sneakers. Battle fatigues for the war they were about to wage.

The lead singer looms out of the shadows into the spotlight. Shoulders stooped. Eyes lost behind a pair of black Ray Ban's; his long fingers curled around the microphone stand. Menacing.

It begins with a call to arms. "ONE! TWO! THREE! FOUR!". And his world explodes. A tsunami of sound submerges him. Dragging him under. Driving the air from his lungs. The assault on his senses relentless. No mercy. No prisoners taken here, mother fuckers.

Each song rips away at his very DNA. The tectonic plates of his life shift as the band blows his world apart. This performance is like nothing he has ever experienced or will ever experience again. It is like witnessing the Four Horsemen of The Apocalypse, wearing leather jackets as they storm the walls of Rock and Roll. It ends after ten minutes with a cry of, "WE ARE THE RAMONES, GOOD NIGHT," the microphone drops to the stage and they are gone. The revolution has begun. His world changed forever.

Someone is screaming. Stevie, beside him, is pissing himself laughing. Then he realises, its him screaming. "FUCKING YEAH! FUCKING YEAH". Every fibre in his body alive. Wanting more.

"What the fuck Stevie. What was that?"

"It sure wasn't the blues" Stevie replies, still laughing.

"Who the fuck were they? They were fucking awesome."

"I think he said they were The Ramones, but I couldn't really hear over the screaming. Ask one of the bar staff. They'll tell you."

And so, he does, standing at the bar, buzzing, alive. "What can I getcha?" the barmaid asks.

"Would you happen to know the name of the band who've just finished?" he shouts, ears still ringing.

"I don't, but Hilly will," and she calls down the bar to a middle-aged guy who is loading beers into a fridge. "Hilly, kid here wants to know the name of the last band."

Hilly looks up, wipes his hands down his shirt and comes to where Arthur stands.

"Guess you mean the speed freaks. That's The Ramones. Tall geeky kid is Joey. You can do us both a favour, take them these beers and you can introduce yourself". Arthur takes four bottles of beer from Hilly. "Take the door to the right of the stage. The dressing room is at the bottom. You'll smell them before you see them. And, hey kid, tell Joey to stop dropping the fucking mike. Those things ain't cheap."

So, he makes his way backstage, Stevie following. He finds The Ramones sat in the small dressing room. "Hi, I'm Arthur. Hilly asked me to bring you some beers."

"Cheers kid", said Tommy, The Ramones drummer and acting manager, relieving him of the beer he hands them out to his band mates.

"I thought you guys were awesome," he finds himself blurting out, embarrassed. The four band mates raise their beers in unison. "Fuck Yeah," hollers Dee Dee the Ramone's bass player, "the revolution has begun, and we've got our first recruit."

"Where are you playing next?" he asks.

They all look at Tommy. "Nothing firm yet kid, but I'll speak to Hilly before we leave tonight."

"Well, listen, if you're interested, our Uni puts bands on every Friday night. I can ask about getting you a gig."

"If it pays, we play,", cries Dee Dee and again they raise their beers with a "Fuck yeah!"

Two weeks later, The Ramones are on stage at his university, watched by an audience of bemused students. Again, they blaze through their set. Arthur stands with Stevie, mesmerised. Absorbing every note, feeling alive. Then they are gone.

The band are back in the dressing room when Sarah the Student Treasurer seeks him out.

"Arthur, can I have a word?" she asks.

"Sure," he said stepping out into the corridor.

"What the fuck was that?" Sarah shouts. "We agreed thirty dollars for your buddies to play at least thirty minutes. They managed ten. Every fucker is complaining. Now, if your buddies expect to get paid, they better get back out there and give me what I'm paying them for."

He heads back into the dressing room. "You got our money?" Tommy asks.

"Not yet, the treasurer wants more for her thirty dollars. Like twenty minutes more."

A moment of silence, then Tommy speaks. "Okay troops, let's get the fuck back out there and give the lady what she wants." The Ramones march back on stage, play their set two more times and Sarah begrudgingly pays up.

Arthur booked them a couple more gigs with ambitions to manage them, but they always refuted his requests. Eventually the band gave him a simple explanation. "Listen Arthur, you're our friend. We don't want business to fuck with that." He loved them even more.

Although he never got to work with The Ramones on a professional level, through them, other bands soon began to approach Stevie and him to arrange gigs for them. They were soon spending most days searching for venues, making bookings for The Misfits, Blondie, Television and many more he no longer remembers. Him and Stevie took a small fee for their time. After a few months this had become so lucrative that they both quit university, rented a small office not far from CBGB's and thus was born East Village Management.

Within five years, East Village Management had become one of the biggest agencies in the world. A stable of bands under their tutelage, but much to his regret, The Ramones were never part of it.

In 2015 Stevie passed away from a heart attack while holidaying on his yacht in the Caribbean. By then, the world had also seen the departure of the four original members of The Ramones.

His mobile phone rings and brings him back to reality. It's his wife Karen, "Hi love. Yeah, I'm on my way now. I was just checking in on an old friend. I'll see you in ten."

He gets back in the car and they set off for the venue.

For the first time he feels a sense of unease. He recalls the countless conference calls with John Atkinson, their head of legal. "Listen Arthur, this is not illegal but as to whether it is ethically correct is a matter for you and your conscience." He knows that if he wants to keep East Village Management ahead of its rivals then they need to keep innovating. Take the odd risk. Record sales have plummeted and most of their acts income now comes from touring and merchandise. To survive and thrive they must find new revenue streams to exploit.

"We are here, Mr Jones", Peter calls to him. Arthur steps out in front of "The Tunnel Club." This was the nearest venue they could find to CBGB's. Two heavies squeezed into dinner jackets guard the entrance. Fiona his personal assistant steps between them.

"Arthur, so pleased you could spare us the time," and they air kiss. "Come on, we don't have much time before the big event kicks off." Fiona leads him into the club.

"Are we expecting trouble?" he asks, nodding at the two heavies.

"Precautions, Arthur. Precautions. Golden ticket only for this gig. This is the biggest day in the history of our firm. We can't afford any unwanted guests."

Fiona leads him through the bar area. The smell of food suddenly making him feel hungry.

"This will be where we will be hosting our esteemed guests. Everyone has accepted. Safe to say from some of the calls I've been receiving, we have grabbed their attention. Oh, Tommy wanted to know did you want to sound check?"

"No, I'm good thanks. How are the band?"

"All good. Sound checked and raring to go. Karen's with them."

"Well?" he asks.

"What?" she asks, pencilled eyebrow raised.

"How did they sound?"

"Good, Arthur, really good."

He relaxes a bit, knowing Fiona would have been brutally honest.

Two more heavies guard the next set of doors. Fiona leads him through. "And this is the room where we will be blowing their freaking minds." He sees the stage with a black curtain pulled across it. Its smaller than the one he remembers at CBGB's. Tommy is stood at a mixing desk in the far-right hand corner of the room. His sound and lighting team are making their final checks.

Tommy waves. "He's all good, Tommy," Fiona shouts across to him. Tommy gives a thumbs up.

"Has everyone signed an NDA?" he asks.

"Yes, all taken care off and no one is allowed in this room with a mobile."

He glances round. Soon, thirty of the most influential people in the music industry will be gathered here in this room. Journalists, record executives and television producers all makers and shakers in the industry. All gathered here to witness his rebirth.

Fiona looks at him. "Now listen Mister. Today you will change the face of rock and roll. This is your day so enjoy it. Now I will love you and leave you and get back to welcome our guests. Now go say hello to your better half," and he sees Karen his wife has appeared through the curtains and stands at the front of the stage. He makes his way over to her.

"How are you?" Karen asks bending down to embrace him.

"Nervous. The boys?"

"Yeah, they're excited. The sound check went well. They just want to get on with it."

"What's with the curtains?" he asks.

"Build the suspense. We'll open them as you finish your piece."

He smiles, between Karen and Fiona he has a formidable team. He just wishes Stevie could have been here. Just a pity his wife had him cremated.

Fiona appears at the doors and waves. He leaves his wife, who disappears back behind the curtains.

"Patrick is here, he wants to know can he have an exclusive."

"I'll come and say hello."

He follows Fiona back into the bar. Patrick Smith, *The Rolling Stone* editor-in-chief is stood with a photographer drinking a glass of champagne.

"Arthur you devious old bastard."

"Less of the old, Patrick". They hug.

"Okay, you got me here, so come on give me something to work with. "

"Patrick, I wish I could, I really do but if I did Fiona would cut my balls off. All I can say is what you will witness today will change the face of rock and roll for ever. Now, you must forgive me I need to love you and leave you and get back and I promise you the first interview after the event. "Okay, it's a deal. But let's have a photo before you go."

"Sure", and they stand arms around each other like old friends while the photographer snaps away.

Back in the main room he spends the next thirty minutes chatting to Tommy and his team. Trying to remain calm as the minutes tick away. Then Fiona is at the door. "It's show time. Everyone is here and already getting impatient. Tommy can one of your crew alert Karen and help her get the band in position. Arthur, get your arse on stage and blow their fucking tiny minds. Oh, and we love you. "

He heads to the stage. Finds his spot, watches as the double doors open and the invited guests are ushered in. Friends and business colleagues who have always supported him and Stevie over the years. He nods and smiles as they spread out across the room. Tommy brings down the room lights and the spotlight hits him. He can see movement behind the curtains. It is time to make history.

And so, he begins. "Esteemed friends and Rupert from Rolling Stone," they laugh. "I've known most of you in this room for thirty years. We have shared the highs and lows together. I thank you for being part of mine and Stevie's journey and for your continued support. Our industry continues to change and evolve. Record sales continue to decline. We must innovate to survive. Those who know me well, know my life began two blocks from here at CBGB's. In August 74, Stevie and I were lucky enough to witness a moment of musical history. A night that changed my life. And tonight, I want you to relive that night with me and witness the future of our industry."

He pauses as the curtains begin to slide open. "Ladies and gentlemen, I give you the greatest rock and roll come back of all time. "

Powerful spotlights hit the stage. The lead singer, black leather motorcycle jacket hanging lose across his stooped shoulders, steps forward. Eyes lost behind Ray Bans. His long skeletal fingers slowly wrap around the mike stand. "It's good to be back", he coughs.

And so, it begins, "ONE! TWO! THREE! FOUR!" The opening beats of Teenage Lobotomy blast out. Arthur smiles. He can see the banner stretched across the back of the stage, announcing the dates for the "*Resurrection Tour*".

Then someone in the audience begins to scream.

[December 7/8th 1985, Brixton Academy, London, UK]

CONTRIBUTORS

Kevin David Anderson: The KKK Took My Baby Away

Kevin David Anderson's debut novel is the cult zombie romp, *Night of the Living Trekkies* from Quirk Books. His latest is the horror-comedy *Midnight Men: The Supernatural Adventures of Earl and Dale*, from Grinning Skull Press. Anderson's stories have appeared in more than a hundred publications from anthologies, magazines, and podcasts. His stories can be heard on podcasts like Pseudopod, Drabblecast, NoSleep, Horror Hill, and The Chilling Tales Network.

Shaun Avery: The Crusher

Shaun Avery has been published in many magazines and anthologies, normally with tales of a horrific or satiric nature, and has co-created a self-published horror comic. He sadly never got to see the Ramones play live. He did see a tribute band called Ramona once, though. They were awesome. (Sidenote: he has a tendency to go on tangents sometimes).

CW Blackwell: Somebody Put Something In My Drink

C.W. Blackwell is an American author from the Central Coast of California. He has been a gas station attendant, a rock musician, and a crime analyst. His recent work has appeared with Down and Out Books, Gutter Books, Rock and a Hard Place Press, and Fahrenheit Press.

Christopher Bond: I Wanna Be Well

Christopher Bond has spent most of his adult life moving between Hawaii and the Midwest, traveling and going to concerts everywhere in between.

Clark Boyd: I Wanna Live

Clark Boyd lives and works in the Netherlands. His fiction has appeared in Fatal Flaw Magazine, Scare Street, Havok, Frost Zone Zine, and various horror anthologies. One of his stories has also been chosen for inclusion in this year's Bouchercon mystery and crime anthology. He's currently writing a book about windmills. Or cheese. Maybe both.

Mike Burr: Cretin Hop

R. Mike Burr is a teacher and writer currently located in the southern United States. His fiction has appeared in the Psycho Drive-In's Noirlahotep and American Carnage anthologies. He saw the Adios Amigos tour in Pittsburgh and vowed that he would never mosh again.

Philip Charter: It's Not My Place

Philip Charter is a British writer who teaches writing skills to non-native English speakers. His work has been featured in The Lit Quarterly, Fictive Dream, and many other publications. In 2021, he won the Loft Books Short Story Prize. He hates oranges, but likes orange cats.

Amanda Crum: 7/11

Amanda Crum is a writer and artist whose work has appeared in Barren Magazine, Shotgun Honey, and more. She's been nominated for the Pushcart Prize and the Best of the Net Award. Amanda lives and finds inspiration in the lush hills of Kentucky.

Wendy Davis: Sheena Is A Punk Rocker

Wendy Davis is an award-winning copywriter living in Nashville, TN. Her work has been featured at Mystery Tribune, Shotgun Honey, Welcome to Twin Peaks, Story and Grit, and 25 Years Later. Years ago, she played guitar and wrote songs for The Superlatives, a female punk band with heaps of attitude and some talent.

Christina Delia: I Don't Wanna Go Down To The Basement

Christina Delia is a horror writer from New Jersey, and an affiliate member of the Horror Writers Association (HWA). Her stories are included in the anthologies What Monsters Do For Love: Volume Three, Shadowy Natures, and most recently in Dark Dispatch and the LGBTQ+ dark fiction anthology *Unburied*. Christina has a story forthcoming in Planet Scumm issue #11 "*Snake Eyes*".

Derek Farrell: Suzy Is A Headbanger

Derek Farrell is the Author of the Danny Bird Mysteries as well as *What Goes Around* (Fahrenzine #4) and *'The Return' (Noir From The Bar)*. When he's not in New York, he's normally figuring out how he can get back there.

Vinnie Hansen: I Wanna Be Your Boyfriend

The day after high school graduation, Vinnie Hansen fled the howling winds of South Dakota and headed for the California coast. There the subversive clutches of college dragged her into the insanity of writing. A two-time Claymore Award finalist, she's the author of the Carol Sabala mystery series, the novel *Lostart Street*, and numerous short stories.

Tina Jackson: Baby I Love You

Tina Jackson is a UK writer and journalist, and the author of *The Beloved Children*, published by Fahrenheit Press in 2020. A highlight of her time as Arts Editor of The Big Issue was interviewing the legendary Ronnie Spector around the release of 1999's *She Talks To Rainbows* - produced by Joey Ramone.

Joshua L. James: Merry Christmas (I Don't Want To Fight Tonight)

Joshua L. James is an English teacher, journalist and writer of fiction. He spends his days thinking of and documenting creative ways to kill people. He never acts on it that you know of. Growing up, he spent most weekends doing the Cretin Hop. He lives in Arkansas with his beautiful wife and mischievous son.

Bret Nelson: My Brain Is Hanging Upside Down (Bonzo Goes To Bitburg)

When Bret Nelson isn't writing stories, he works on TV programs, movies, and stage shows. Plus video and tabletop games. And TOYS. Right now, he's working on things he can't talk about (that's what the contracts say).

Gregory Nicoll: Chainsaw

Gregory Nicoll is a professional author and journalist whose work has been honored both in *The Year's Best Horror Stories* and *The Year's Best Music Writing*. He proudly points out that his tale in this book is a rare example where his talents in both fields were successfully synchronized. The Ramones are his favorite band of all time.

David Noonan: Do You Remember Rock 'n Roll Radio

David Noonan is a drummer, author, Myofascial Release therapist, tai chi practitioner, podcaster and Dungeon Master. He has recorded and toured nationally and internationally with The Cryptkeeper Five, Blitzkid, Argyle Goolsby & The Roving Midnight and The Independents. He lives in Bensalem, Pennsylvania with his girlfriend, and fellow therapist, Bonnie, and their two dogs – Peter and Swiper.

Hannah O'Doom: Danny Says

Hannah O'Doom is currently working toward her Masters of Library Science at the University of Kentucky at night while working as a project manager by day. When not writing stories about robots, cats, or magical coffees, she can be found playing roller derby with her team Roller Derby of Central Kentucky, drinking gin and tonics and reading odd books. Her work can be found at hannahodoom.com

Jon Park: Too Tough To Die

Jon Park lives in Gateshead. His flash fiction has appeared in Yellow Mama.

Thomas Pluck: S.L.U.G.

Thomas Pluck has slung hash, worked on the docks, trained in martial arts in Japan, and even swept the Guggenheim museum (but not as part of a clever heist). He is the author of *Blade of Dishonor* and the Jay Desmarteaux crime thrillers, including the Anthony-nominated *Bad Boy Boogie*. and the upcoming *The Boy From County Hell*.

Kelly Robinson: Pinhead

Kelly Robinson is a two-time Bram Stoker Award finalist for her work in horror non-fiction and was awarded Writer of the Year in the annual Rondo Hatton Classic Horror Awards. A newcomer to fiction, her first short story "Mrs. Betty Briggs and the Angel Food Cake From Hell" was recently published in *Slashertorte: An Anthology of Cake Horror*.

James Ryan: Here Today, Gone Tomorrow

James Ryan wrote the novel *Red Jenny and the Pirates of Buffalo*, a compilation of stories from the website Rooftop Sessions entitled *Alt Together Now*, and the monograph *The Pirates of New York*. His work has also appeared in Rebeat Magazine, where he authored the weekly column "Fantasia Obscura," Pyramid Online, Dragon, The Urbanite, The Dream Zone and Rational Magic.

Lex Vranick: Rockaway Beach

Lex Vranick is a poet and dark fiction writer from Long Island, New York. She currently lives in Florida with her dog and an over-abundance of houseplants. Lex holds a B.A. from Excelsior College and is a J.D. candidate at Florida State University. Her work has been published by Eerie River Publishing, Kissing Dynamite, and Cagibi, among others.

Joseph S. Walker: Main Man

Joseph S. Walker lives in Indiana and teaches college literature. His fiction has appeared in Alfred Hitchcock's Mystery Magazine, Ellery Queen's Mystery Magazine, and a number of other magazines and anthologies. He has been a finalist for the Edgar Award and the Derringer Award, and has won the Bill Crider Prize for Short Fiction and the Al Blanchard Award.

ACKNOWLEDGEMENTS

First off thanks must go to Anthony Neil Smith and Matthew Gomez who first raised the idea of publishing an anthology of fiction inspired by the music of the Ramones. Despite heavy schedules they also gave up their time to help with the judging/ranking of the many hundreds of submissions we received so double-thanks to both of them.

Thanks also to Fiona Davis who stepped in at the last minute to help with the judging.

Huge thanks to Brenda Perlin who wrote the preface for this volume and has been unstinting in her support of the project in private and in public every step of the way.

And finally thanks to every single person who sent us a story. We were blown away by the response to this anthology from writers all around the world. We had no idea what sort of response we'd get when we issued our call for submissions and we were knocked flat by the hundreds of stories you shared with us. There are literally too many of you to list here but you know who you are and we will be forever grateful for your support.

Deer Shoots Man by Tyler Knight

It's a much over-used phrase, but this book by Tyler Knight really is one of the most extraordinary debuts we've ever published.

Set in a near future Los Angeles, jobbing cage fighter and man about town, DeShawn Trustfall finds himself in a high-octane chase to track down the genetic code that could cure a disease that threatens the lives of hundreds of thousands of people, including himself and his son.

Set against a background of a global pandemic, a corrupt government pushing a cure for its own self-interest, genetically altered CRISPR babies and civil unrest in the streets you could be forgiven for thinking the author Tyler Knight is part writer, part Nostradamus.

The writing in this book is razor sharp and the flights of tech/cyber creative inventiveness are right up there with the very best authors in the genre and as if all that wasn't enough Tyler Knight writes noir like he was born to it…

King Of The Crows by Russell Day

"Ocean's 11 meets 28 Days Later…"

2028, eight years after a pandemic swept across Europe, the virus has been defeated and normal life has resumed.
   Memories of The Lockdown have already become clouded by myths, rumour and conspiracy. Books have been written, movies have been released and the names Robertson, Miller & Maccallan have slipped into legend.
   Together they hauled The Crows, a ragged group of virus survivors, across the ruins of London. Kept them alive, kept them safe, kept them moving.
   But not all myths are true and not all heroes are heroes.
   Questions are starting to be asked about what really happened during those days when society crumbled and the capital city became a killing ground. Finally the truth will be revealed.
   King Of The Crows is a truly genre-busting novel in terms of both content and structure. The story is told over the span of 8 years from 2020-2028 using flashbacks and extracts from survivor accounts, screenplays, academic studies, online chat-rooms and police reports.

The Beloved Children by Tina Jackson

Three young women; Chrysanthemum, Rose & Orage are thrown together on the stage of Fankes' Theatre during the closing days of the Second World War performing as The Three Graces.
   It's there they come under the spell of wardrobe mistresses Dolores and Janna – a chance encounter that will guide and change all of their fates forever.
   Set in the dying days of vaudeville theatre and laced with mysticism, fortune tellers, ghosts, and evocative descriptions of the closing days of the War - The Beloved Children will literally make you laugh out loud and perhaps even shed the odd tear.
   The Beloved Children is wise, funny, heart-breaking, joyous, poignant, and entirely, entirely enthralling.

Know Me From Smoke by Matt Phillips

Stella Radney, long-time lounge singer, still has a bullet lodged in her hip from the night when a rain of gunshots killed her husband.

    That was twenty years ago and it's a surprise when the unsolved murder is reopened after the district attorney discovers new evidence. Royal Atkins is a convicted killer who just got out of prison on a legal technicality. At first, he's thinking he'll play it straight. Doesn't take long before that plan turns to smoke—was it ever really an option?

    When Stella and Royal meet one night, they're drawn to each other. But Royal has a secret. How long before Stella discovers that the man she's falling for isn't who he seems? A noir of gripping suspense and violence, *Know Me from Smoke* is a journey into the shadowy terrain of murder, lost love, and the heart's lust for vengeance.

Souljourner by Paul Steven Stone

"We are not human beings on a spiritual journey, we are spiritual beings on a human journey." – and that my friends sets the stage perfectly for all that follows.

The novel, if it is indeed a novel (the narrator insists it is in fact a warning letter from your soul's previous incarnation and aimed directly at you dear reader).

One of the central premises of the novel/letter is that our souls make their eternal journey towards enlightenment in the company of a single unchanging 'karmic pod' of companion souls who take on different roles in each of our incarnations.

In one life a soul may appear as your mother, in the next your best friend, in the next your sworn enemy, in the next your lover and so on for eternity. The identities of the souls in your 'karmic pod' are hidden from you in life – this letter/novel seeks to wise you up to who's who in your karmic pod to help you avoid making the same mistakes that landed the narrator, David Rockwood Worthington in prison serving a life sentence for murder.

Slow Bear by Anthony Neil Smith

This is noir at its deepest, at its most savage, at its most vital, from an acknowledged modern master of the genre.

"Anthony Neil Smith mixes dark humor, menace, mayhem and a washed-out, one-armed hero in a noirish tale that never stops to take a breath." - Linwood Barclay, author of *No Time for Goodbye* and *Too Close to Home*

"*Slow Bear* is everything I love about dark fiction and don't see nearly enough of. Anthony Neil Smith writes uncompromisingly dark fiction without sacrificing the humanity or entertainment value of his characters. If you always wondered what Jim Rockford would be if he went full dark, *Slow Bear* is the book for you." Bryon Quertermous

"*Slow Bear* is many things: a bull in a china shop; a raging lion; a stubborn mule; a wise old bird. a drunken old skunk; and a murderous hyena. What's more, he's the kind of noir anti-hero who'll have you rooting for him all the way, which is good because, the way things are going, he certainly needs someone on his side. Another stunning creation by Anthony Neil Smith." - Nigel Bird

All these titles and 100s more available from

www.Fahrenheit-Press.com

IF YOU BUY THE PAPERBACK VERSION OF ANY OF OUR BOOKS DIRECT FROM US WE'LL ALWAYS GIVE YOU THE EBOOK DOWNLOAD FOR FREE

"It's NOIR if we say it's NOIR…"

www.ingramcontent.com/pod-product-compliance
Lightning Source LLC
Chambersburg PA
CBHW082104280426
43661CB00089B/848